D0998545

THE YALE EDITION OF THE
WORKS OF SAMUEL JOHNSON
VOLUME IX

A Journey to the Western Islands of Scotland

SAMUEL JOHNSON

A Journey to the Western
Islands of Scotland

EDITED BY MARY LASCELLES

NEW HAVEN AND LONDON : YALE UNIVERSITY PRESS

1971

Copyright © 1971 by Yale University.
All rights reserved. This book may not be
reproduced, in whole or in part, in any form
(except by reviewers for the public press),
without written permission from the publishers.
Library of Congress catalog card number: 57–11918
International standard book number: 0–300–01251–9
Set in Baskerville type,
and printed in the United States of America by
Connecticut Printers, Inc., Hartford, Connecticut.
Distributed in Great Britain, Europe, and Africa by
Yale University Press, Ltd., London; in Canada by
McGill-Queen's University Press, Montreal; in Mexico
by Centro Interamericano de Libros Académicos,
Mexico City; in Australasia by Australia and New
Zealand Book Co., Pty., Ltd., Artarmon, New South
Wales; in India by UBS Publishers' Distributors Pvt.,
Ltd., Delhi; in Japan by John Weatherhill, Inc.,
Tokyo.

EDITORIAL COMMITTEE

HERMAN W. LIEBERT, *Chairman*

JOHN H. MIDDENDORF, *General Editor*

ROBERT F. METZDORF, *Secretary*

W. J. BATE	M. J. C. HODGART
BERTRAND H. BRONSON	ARTHUR A. HOUGHTON, JR.
JAMES L. CLIFFORD	MRS. DONALD F. HYDE
DONALD J. GREENE	WILLIAM R. KEAST
ROBERT HALSBAND	MARY LASCELLES
ALLEN T. HAZEN	L. F. POWELL
FREDERICK W. HILLES	W. K. WIMSATT

84051

PREFACE

The starting-point for any editor of Johnson's *Journey* must be
R. W. Chapman's editions: that of 1924 for the notes, that of
1930 for the text. In some few instances, where the present
editor considered that to paraphrase a particular note would be
merely officious, it has been quoted *verbatim*[1] over the initials
R.W.C.; but in many more the note has both prompted and
furthered investigation. The *Journey* is an exceptionally al-
lusive book. If Johnson himself had annotated it on the scale
favoured by some of his contemporaries, the text would occupy
a smaller share of many pages than the notes. One whole cate-
gory of its references is the province of Dr. L. F. Powell who,
in annotating Boswell's *Tour,* has assembled so particular and
exact a body of information about the persons mentioned by
both travellers that it has often seemed best to refer the reader
to the proper passage in his edition of the *Life,* of which the
Tour occupies the fifth volume. A few items of information,
unrelated to Boswell's narrative, bear his initials; but these direct communications to the editor afford no measure of the
debt owed him. He has been consulted throughout; and his
counsel has consisted of something much more important than
answers to questions: he has shown what questions must be
asked.

I am indebted to Dr. J. D. Fleeman and Professor J. P.
Hardy for generous help, especially in the difficult later stages
of the work, and to Professor J. H. Middendorf for his patience
and care throughout its vicissitudes. The following members

1. With the permission of the Clarendon Press.

of the editorial committee have read the proofs with helpful
attention: Professors Bertrand H. Bronson of the University
of California at Berkeley, Donald J. Greene of the University
of Southern California, Allen T. Hazen of Columbia University, and Frederick W. Hilles of Yale University. To the kindness of Mr. R. G. Cant, of the University of St. Andrews, I
owe the knowledge of John Oliphant's drawings, and to that
of Mr. D. MacArthur, Librarian of the University Library, the
opportunity of reproducing them. Mrs. Hollis, a graduate of
St. Andrews, has given expert help in the composition of my index, and Mrs. M. Elizabeth MacAndrew in its preparation for
the press; I am particularly grateful to Miss Claire Lamont for
her valuable assistance during its final revision.

M. L.

It is with regret that the Editorial Committee here records the
death, in April 1969, of E. L. McAdam, Jr., one of its original,
most devoted members, and the editor of two volumes in this
series: Volume I, *Diaries, Prayers, and Annals,* with Donald
and Mary Hyde; and Volume VI, *Poems,* with George Milne.

CONTENTS

ILLUSTRATIONS

INTRODUCTION

Johnson's *Journey to the Western Islands of Scotland* enjoys certain advantages of position, not all of which could have been foreseen by its author. A fortunate chain of circumstances allows us to regard the story, the characters, the setting, as it were stereoscopically: in the round. Of the hundred days which Johnson and Boswell spent in one another's company north of the Border—for both of them a spell of heightened consciousness and exceptional happiness—we have at least four principal accounts, besides a good deal of marginal comment. We should have five, but the book of Remarks which Johnson kept is lost. For comparison with his published narrative, however, there are the letters which he sent to Mrs. Thrale almost weekly. He asked her to preserve them, and, since she did more than this (making a fair copy, probably for his use, and surrendering this to the printer when she published their correspondence), the originals survive almost intact, here and there relieving his retrospective account with the more vivid colours of immediate impression. There is, moreover, the version of Boswell's journal published as *A Tour to the Hebrides with Samuel Johnson, LL.D.*, together with the *Journal* itself.[1] Boswell's narration of the same episode, in his *Life of Johnson*, though necessarily brief, is so independently framed that it may be called a fourth account; and something may be claimed

1. To the annotation of the *Tour* (*Life*, v, ed. Hill-Powell, revised Powell, 1965) I am deeply indebted; also to the edition of the *Journal* by F. A. Pottle and C. H. Bennett (revised 1963). For particulars of persons and places mentioned by Johnson it has frequently seemed best to give no more than a reference to the relevant note by Dr. Powell.

for his *Remarks*,[2] correcting and supplementing the particulars of Johnson's narrative. The diary of a later traveller, the Rev. James Bailey of Otley in Yorkshire,[3] who was inspired by Johnson's book to follow his route in 1787, may add a little to our understanding of the tale. Boswell's narrative gift, his command of particulars, lends it continuity. Johnson's capacity for reflection and generalization gives it richness of texture.

His curiosity had been engaged by the Hebrides—so he told Boswell in the first year of their friendship—when, as a boy, he was given Martin Martin's *Description of the Western Islands of Scotland* by his father. Boswell had fostered the project of a visit in his company; successfully, in so far as Johnson's mind reverted to it from time to time in the following ten years.[4] The deliberate imprecision of his opening sentence takes his own original impulse and Boswell's practical encouragement into the reckoning, and perhaps leaves room for a third factor. An observation in a letter to Boswell after the event—"Pennant has much in his notions that I do not like; but still I think him a very intelligent traveller"[5]—may intimate that Pennant[6] had had his part in prompting Johnson to see and judge for himself. Notions with which he disagreed were always grist to his mill.

The narrative framework of the *Journey* can be indicated in a few lines. The first four and the last ten of its hundred days were spent in Edinburgh: the earlier spell gave Boswell the opportunity to exhibit his friend; the latter allowed Johnson to consolidate his ideas. The interim, during which these ideas had been gathered, was occupied by a journey, interspersed

2. A copy, consisting of eleven folio pages in the hand of Boswell's clerk, John Lawrie, is in the Hyde Collection, where I enjoyed the privilege of reading it. A transcript (not quite accurate) is printed in the *Catalogue of the Johnsonian Collection of R. B. Adam* (1921), and a photographic reproduction appears in *The R. B. Adam Library Relating to Dr. Samuel Johnson and his Era* (1929–30), Vol. II.

3. This manuscript (MS. 3294-5 in the National Library of Scotland) was brought to my notice by Dr. J. D. Fleeman. It consists of two octavo volumes (812 pages) closely written, entitled: *A Journey in Scotland with Sketches of Some Picturesque Ruins in that interesting Country.* I concur with Dr. Fleeman in believing that Bailey had not read Boswell's *Tour.*

4. See *Letters* 250 and 274.

5. *Letters* 575.

6. *A Tour in Scotland MDCCLXIX* (Chester, 1771) and *A Tour in Scotland and Voyage to the Hebrides MDCCLXXII* (Chester, 1774). The second part of this latter *Tour* was not published until 1776.

with visits, when and where hospitality and the weather detained the travellers. They traversed in its course regions of Scotland remarkably various: making their way northwards up the east coast to the Moray Firth; westwards by the shore of Loch Ness and Fort Augustus to Glenelg; visiting Skye (twice), Raasay, Col (unintentionally), Mull, Ulva, Inchkenneth, Iona; and making an irregular circuit of the south-west, to include Auchinleck.

Johnson's sympathies, and antipathies, were closely engaged by what he learned in the Highlands, and (even more notably) in the Isles. He exposed his full powers of apprehension to the impact of what had happened, was happening, and was likely to follow. That is why the book holds a peculiar place in his writings. It is like the rest in the deliberate counterpoise of evidence,[7] the structure of the argument. It is unlike, in the intensity of concern as to the outcome, and also in the fact of his own presence, however unobtrusively conveyed. The ideas burn, as in the heart of a fire, and are communicated in a manner he uses nowhere else.

The experience and the argument may be regarded in several different contexts, of which I see these as the most notable: the context of a given moment in Scottish history; the context of a particular phase in Johnson's life (new friendships formed and antagonisms encountered); the context of a distinct literary tradition (that of the itineraries and topographies in which the eighteenth-century sense of place was finding expression).

Johnson's relations with all but one of his hosts were, and remained, cordial[8]; but, by an irony of circumstance, his book (particularly when re-read in the light of Boswell's less discreet record) came to be regarded as a betrayal of hospitality. At this distance of time it should be possible to see the affair in perspective, and reduce misconception to manageable proportions. These were the hearts of controversy into which he was drawn—some through a long-standing interest in Scottish his

7. So delicate is the equipoise that readers, from that day to this, have drawn opposite inferences from them. Even now, when former controversy is abated, there are differences so great as those between Jeffrey Hart, "Johnson's *A Journey to the Western Islands*: History as Art," in *Essays in Criticism*, Vol. x, No. 1, January 1960, and Donald J. Greene, "Johnsonian Critics," ibid., No. 4, October.
8. This is frequently confirmed by Bailey.

tory, some by the result of fresh discovery: the antiquity of Scottish civilization; the Stuart tragedy, reaching back to the enigma of the Casket Letters; the decay of the Highlands, with its accompanying threat of depopulation; and superstitions, especially as to the second sight. There are strands here which it is impossible to hold apart; in attempting to disentangle any one, we must bear in mind its possible relation with almost every other: Highland poverty with the '45 and the Stuart cause; the Tudor-Stuart conflict with the Reformation; and the Reformation in Scotland with the destruction of memorials to Scottish learning and letters.

Though Johnson did not go to Scotland without some critical preconceptions, it is clear that he went intending to be interested, and therefore pleased. He was interested, even beyond expectation; and the pleasure he obtained was by no means limited to the satisfaction of his initial curiosity. Ten years later he summed up the experience: "I got an acquisition of more ideas by it than by any thing that I remember. I saw quite a different system of life."[9] He did not, it is true, acquiesce in all the ideas presented to him; but there is more than one side to this case. On the one hand his scepticism as to that "Celtic empire, which," according to Sir John Dalrymple,[1] "once stretched from the Pillars of Hercules to Archangel," was not unwarranted. Thomas Innes of the Scots College in Paris, alienated from his countrymen by another intellectual discipline than theirs, declared of them: "The more they were ignorant of what passed before their own time, the more they were inclined to run up their antiquities to incredible heights; nay, some even before the creation of the world."[2] On the other hand it could fairly be argued that, in a country which had fostered and advanced antiquarian studies, Johnson's reliance on the written word as sole witness must necessarily be censured as reactionary. There were men better informed than he on Scottish antiquities who could make his argument as to what an object ought to have been look ridiculous by their

9. *Life*, IV.199.
1. *Memoirs of Great Britain and Ireland* (Vol. I, 1771), p. 47.
2. *A Critical Essay on the Ancient Inhabitants of the Northern Parts of Britain, or Scotland* (1729), I.iii.

demonstration of what it was. He was here following his customary course, holding himself free, in default of literary evidence, to rely on that sense of the probable which he had cultivated so effectually. Such a practice gave more offence—perhaps with less justification—when he submitted oral tradition to this favourite criterion. Lord Mansfield, discussing the *Journey* with Boswell on its first appearance, praised Johnson's good humour in these terms: "He speaks ill of nobody but Ossian."[3] The exception was to prove of some consequence. Johnson seems to have waded into the Ossianic controversy without taking soundings. Since "Ossian" was in his judgement quite unenjoyable, he did not indict Macpherson alone of conspiratorial behaviour but found all who professed enjoyment guilty of a conspiracy against candour and good sense. On antiquities Pennant might be more knowledgeable; on ancient tradition, more tactful; yet there is no question as to which of these two travellers felt more deeply the plight of a people on whom the past had left its scars. Nor could Pennant compare with Johnson in his grasp of the whole pattern of a former way of life, its causes and effects.

There had been more than one attempt to sound those deep waters that were vexed by the meeting of past and present in eighteenth-century Scotland. "Our Geographers," Defoe wrote in 1727, "seem to be almost as much at a loss in the Description of this North Part of *Scotland*, as the *Romans* were to conquer it; and they are oblig'd to fill it up with Hills and Mountains, as they do the inner parts of *Africa*, with Lyons and Elephants, for want of knowing what else to place there."[4] His admission presently acquired fresh significance, and from 1745 onwards successive travellers reported on the state of the Highlands—not all the reports being intended for publication. Among the authors of published tours none was better equipped than Pennant to obtain information and command attention. Naturalist as well as antiquary, and capable of a ready if shallow response to the moods of those he met in social intercourse, he confidently expected a welcome for himself and

---

3. *Private Papers of James Boswell*, ed. G. Scott and F. A. Pottle, privately printed (1928–34), X.149.
4. *Tour thro the Whole Island of Great Britain* (Vol. III, 1727), p. 200.

his books, and was not disappointed. Johnson, however, on learning at Coirechatachan that "a curious specimen of Highland antiquity" had been presented to Pennant, objected: "Sir, it was more than he deserved: the dog is a Whig."[5] What he meant by the terms Whig and Tory, especially in his latter years, is open to question; what he meant by calling Pennant a Whig in this particular context is evident from the two *Tours* which he had read before completing his own book.[6] Here, for example, is one of Pennant's references to Culloden: "Let a veil be flung over a few excesses consequential of a day productive of so much benefit to the united kingdoms"[7]; here, his view of the consequences of pacification: "The halcyon days are near at hand: oppression will beget depopulation; and depopulation will give us a dear-bought tranquillity."[8] To advance so Swiftian a proposition without ironical intention (there is no trace of irony in Pennant's writings), while preserving confidence in his own humanity and a character for benevolence, argues some defect of sensibility, alike in Pennant and his adherents. As a reformer, hot for certainty, he noted the rents and patches in the cloak flung over Highland poverty with relentless zeal. He censured the faulty economy of the Isles, and peremptorily demanded authoritative intervention. He was all for increasing the usefulness of the poor by bringing them into employment at an earlier age than hitherto, and for preventing them from following their own devices. He would have fishing forbidden to crofters, husbandry to fishermen—this, in a region where no man's holding of fertile land can be very large. Even as pure theory, his notions are ill concerted: two passages in praise of the management of the Breadalbane estates allege, one "the abolition of the feudal tenures, or vassalage," the other, the stipulation that every tenant shall practise some craft serviceable to his landlord.[9] Such writing surely perpetuated in Johnson's mind an association between circum-

5. *Life*, v.157.
6. For the mutual interest of Johnson and Pennant, and Johnson's familiarity with Pennant's Hebridean travels, see p. 128 n. 2 below.
7. *Tour* (1771), p. 136.
8. *Tour and Voyage* (1774), p. 212. The oppression is that of the chiefs; Johnson did not minimize this, but sought another remedy than depopulation.
9. *Tour* (1771), pp. 87, 82-3.

stances he could not forget—"Our ramble in the islands hangs
upon my imagination," he told Boswell in 1777[1]—and some
failure of sympathy on the part of those who "are strangers to
the language and the manners, to the advantages and wants of
the people, whose life they would model, and whose evils they
would remedy."[2] Yet it was Pennant who came to be regarded
as the sympathetic visitor, Johnson as the surly and censorious.

Johnson was daunted by the general aspect of Highland
landscape.[3] Moreover, he paid little attention to those eccen-
tricities of nature with which Pennant diverted his readers. He
had, respecting natural phenomena, more in common than
either would have cared to admit with Horace Walpole, who
wrote (after reading Pennant's *Tour and Voyage*): "Mr. Banks
. . . found whole islands that bear nothing but columns, as other
places do grass and barley."[4] He would have taken more notice
of grass and barley, in a country so barren that one-third of each
year's harvest must be kept for seed. The high-road of life was
his fairest prospect. Pretending to apologize for some "diminutive observations," he maintained that "The true state of every
nation is the state of common life."[5] This was no new preoccupation. What he particularly sought, however, when he turned
his back on Fort Augustus, was "the manners of a people" seen
in an uncommon light, and from a peculiar vantage-point. He
was reckoning on a fold in the web of time: the opportunity to
observe living people still tracing a pattern of life elsewhere
extinct, one which he had hitherto apprehended only through
the historical imagination. If travel in the region described by
Martin answered to his expectation, he would take advantage
of this wrinkle in time, and get what he vainly asked of historians: "contemporary evidence" of "common life"[6] as it was
once lived throughout Britain. He was obliged to admit that
his hopes were ill founded: Martin had written when "the

1. *Letters* 528. Boswell had reported to him some recent misfortunes of their
friends.
2. *Journey*, p. 88 below. He is here speaking specifically of the Lowland
Scots.
3. Bailey, evidently familiar with hills, and apparently endowed with good
sight, saw it differently. He was, besides, lucky with the weather.
4. *Letters*, ed. Toynbee, IX.2.
5. *Journey*, p. 22 below.
6. *Life*, V.403 and III.333.

mountains were yet unpenetrated"[7]; that era was closed, and whatever he had failed to tell could no longer be told.

What Johnson found, however, was to prove more engrossing than what he sought: a people in the throes of change, threatened with hasty innovation, and surrounded with evidence of the havoc which former innovation had wrought. He may fairly be accused of reading this evidence in terms of its impact on his own sensibility, and therefore too simply; but it should be remembered that the *Journey* was, among other things, the record of a personal experience, and certain impressions, formed early in its course, were likely to prove ineffaceable. Although it was not until he had left behind the last considerable military post on his itinerary and penetrated the Highlands that Johnson resolved on telling this story, his theme had been given him a fortnight earlier, at St. Andrews: a city dominated, even in its present prosperity, by the gaunt splendour of its ruins, and to more than one eighteenth-century traveller an image of desolation. The outcome of Johnson's experience here was twofold. In the first place he learnt to see the initial cause of ecclesiastical ruins in "the tumult and violence of Knox's reformation."[8] Another and more significant consequence was his realization that destruction, however begun, might be a continuous process, within the power if not the will of every generation to arrest, and that apathy and self-interest could be more insidious enemies than revolution.

Fear of these destructive forces was to pervade Johnson's thought on the condition of the Highlands, particularly when it was directed to emigration. This theme is woven into his narrative with deliberate art. It is introduced as a subject of talk with the travellers' host at Anoch: "From him we first heard of the general dissatisfaction, which is now driving the Highlanders into the other hemisphere; and when I asked him whether they would stay at home, if they were well treated, he answered with indignation, that no man willingly left his native country."[9] We know from the *Tour* that Johnson had already discussed emigration with Boswell; but he chose to make it impinge

7. *Journey*, p. 65 below.
8. *Journey*, p. 5 below.
9. *Journey*, p. 38 below. (See note 8 on p. 35, respecting Johnson's informant.)

upon his readers' consciousness at the point where it had come to him direct from someone concerned. Thereafter it recurs insistently. Here, he will lay it aside, only to resume it in a fresh context; here, turn it to expose another aspect; and here content himself with a mere allusion, sufficient to keep it within view. It comes back upon the ear like a refrain, whether he listens to a song of farewell, or sees an emigrant ship waiting in the harbour of Portree.

In order to understand the burden of this refrain, we may frame some questions such as these, and look for Johnson's answers—or the means he provides for arriving at an answer. Was the structure of Highland society so far at fault that it ought to undergo big and immediate change? Why were the present effects of change so disquieting? Must this peculiar social structure be censured for failure to adapt itself, or should the blame rest with those who were forcing the pace, requiring that adaptation should be both swift and radical? In his farewell survey of Skye, Johnson sets himself squarely to assess the concomitant good and ill of this unfamiliar way of life. The marked inequality of station he accepts. That it should, until lately, have remained a fixed condition he attributes to the absence of any kind of commerce, and the peculiar system of land tenure. He is troubled, however, by the freedom from accountability of the remoter chiefs. "The laird has all those in his power that live upon his farms. Kings can, for the most part, only exalt or degrade. The laird at pleasure can feed or starve, can give bread, or withhold it. This inherent power was yet strengthened by the kindness of consanguinity, and the reverence of patriarchal authority. The laird was the father of the clan, and his tenants commonly bore his name. And to these principles of original command was added, for many ages, an exclusive right of legal jurisdiction."[1] The change of tense is plainly deliberate, designed to suggest that economic dependence is no longer softened by that patriarchal relationship which formerly mitigated some of the hardships of an even more stringent subordination of weak to strong. That he was aware of these hardships is plain from the tales of former violence which he recounts as he heard them: tales of armed strength prevailing,

1. *Journey*, pp. 85–86 below.

unless restrained by kinship, or—that last refuge of the weak in a lawless society—the traditional sanctity of the pledged word. He defends the position of the tacksman—held in the Highlands by virtue of kindred and tradition—maintaining that, like the tradesman in a mercantile society, he gives resilience to the economy.[2] And he watches, always with foreboding, the fumbling hand of reform at work. The pacification of the Highlands has been accompanied with petty restrictions, ruffling the surface of daily life. It is, moreover, open to question whether the power that disarmed them is as yet sufficient to protect them.

Were these the evils merely of a transitional phase? Or were the reformers justified in crying out against this anomaly within the United Kingdom, and urging that the obsolete economy of this one part of it should be brought into line with the rest? There is an odd failure even among sympathetic observers (Johnson always excepted) to foresee that what they reckon admirable may not survive the changes they recommend. Thus Martin appears to notice no discrepancy between his praise of St. Kilda as an Arcadian community, in which the use of money is unknown, and his demand that the Islands shall be integrated with the commercial system of the whole nation.[3] At the outset of the *Journey* Johnson had looked hopefully in that direction. "They are now acquainted with money," he says of the Highlanders, "and the possibility of gain will by degrees make them industrious."[4] Doubt presently grew upon him. With the change from a natural to a money economy,[5] and the weakening of former ties, the owner of the land was letting it, not to the traditional claimant but to the highest bidder, who acknowledged no obligation but to pay. "The commodiousness of money," Johnson concedes, "is indeed great; but there are some advantages which money cannot buy,

2. *Journey*, pp. 86–89 below. Johnson admits that this is not the Lowland view, and even that stalwart Johnsonian, Bailey, calls the tacksmen "those worse than locusts in these famished countries" (II.364).

3. *Voyage to St. Kilda* (1698), p. 132; *Description of the Western Islands of Scotland* (1703), pp. 336–49.

4. *Journey*, p. 58 below.

5. For the premises of Johnson's economic thought, see John H. Middendorf, "Johnson on Wealth and Commerce," in *Johnson, Boswell and their Circle* (1965).

and which therefore no wise man will by the love of money be tempted to forego."[6] All in one way or another were caught up in the consequences of economic change. "The chiefs, divested of their prerogatives, necessarily turned their thoughts to the improvement of their revenues, and expect more rent, as they have less homage."[7] (Again, the tense changes significantly within the sentence.) Having already received some financial compensation for lost privileges, they see wealth as the alternative to power—perhaps the more desirable, certainly the more attainable good, under the new dispensation. So they become mere traffickers in land. "Thus the estate perhaps is improved, but the clan is broken." Johnson himself acknowledges a doubt whether this change has not gone so far that nothing is left but to push it to its logical conclusion—"whether the general good does not require that the landlords be, for a time, restrained in their demands, and kept quiet by pensions proportionate to their loss."[8] This is a remedy to be used only if no other way can be found to staunch the flow of emigration.

It will be asked: Why should the tenants *not* emigrate if they can thereby better their lot? Johnson does not idealize their condition: their former contentment with it he discounts as "a muddy mixture of pride and ignorance"; and improvement is hardly to be expected from measures which are turning "patriarchal rulers" into "rapacious landlords."[9] Two of the reformers' principal demands had been the written lease and the rent paid in money—not, as heretofore, in goods and service. The advantages of this latter innovation Johnson came to question, on the score that it might well increase absenteeism among landlords.[1] He was doubtless wrong in supposing that an obsolete way of discharging the obligation of tenant to landlord could be perpetuated; right in believing that the obligation of landlord to tenant can never be discharged in absence. Surely he was right also in his general assumption of sudden and ill-advised economic change as a factor in the manifestly

6. *Journey*, p. 86 below.
7. *Journey*, p. 94 below.
8. *Journey*, p. 97 below.
9. *Journey*, p. 89 below.
 1. Absenteeism is the wasting disease of such regions: even where the landlord has disappeared, a large part of the land in a crofting community may be held by men with no more than a contingent purpose of living on it.

worsening relationship between these two parties? He had a shrewd eye for the perplexities of a community passing rapidly from a natural to a money economy. Even on the little Isle of Col, where he found the mutual obligations of landlord and tenant fulfilled, "the rents have, till within seven years, been paid in kind, but the tenants finding that cattle and corn varied in their price, desired for the future to give their landlord money; which, not having yet arrived at the philosophy of commerce, they consider as being every year of the same value."[2] He recognized that more was involved in this enforced assimilation of a primitive to a progressive society than economic change: "In the beginning of the present century . . . every man [in the Highlands] was a soldier." The qualities peculiar to a soldier are such as no nation can afford to neglect; but he can be "a very troublesome and pernicious animal in time of peace."[3] It is now demanded of the Highlanders that they shall change their historic character; and, so long as this demand is palliated only by the raising of Highland regiments, their retort will be emigration. "To hinder insurrection, by driving away the people, and to govern peaceably, by having no subjects, is an expedient that argues no great profundity of politicks."[4] The causes of emigration, then, are not creditable to the ruling power. Must the outcome be condoned merely on the score that (as Johnson himself admits, in respect of disarmament) "in political regulations, good cannot be complete, it can only be predominant"?[5] He could not foresee the future course of Highland history; but he saw enough to make him afraid. Fear is proportionate to hope; and hope, to the value set on that which is to be won, or lost. Johnson set a high value on some elements in the traditional life of the Isles, because his brief experience of sharing it had communicated to him a sense of happiness he had not known elsewhere. Boswell was right in applying Gray's words, "the sunshine of the breast," to the mood of those days. True, it was a mood shot with sadness; but sadness did not annul nor cancel happiness for Johnson: he went in life-long dread, not of pain but of apathy. Thus

2. *Journey*, p. 129 below.
3. *Journey*, pp. 91, 92 below.
4. *Journey*, p. 97 below.
5. *Journey*, p. 90 below.

it was in terms of happiness that he came to assess the problem of emigration: "It may be thought that they are happier by the change; but they are not happy as a nation, for they are a nation no longer."[6] On this reckoning, it was necessary that the balance of material gain and loss should be tilted in favour of remaining at home.

These, it will be objected, are merely the opinions of an English onlooker; an old man besides, and incapable of seeing beyond his own angry reaction to the American war. Yet there is a remarkably close counterpart to them in the letter which Walter Scott wrote to Lord Dalkeith on the comparable depopulation of the Border. For him, emigration signified "farms where the old people remember twenty *smoking chimneys* & where there are now not two."[7] He traced the resemblance, showing that, whereas the causes of decline in the two regions were the same, in the Highlands they had operated with deadly speed and effect; on the border slowly, because the rewards of greed were less apparent. This was little more than thirty years after Johnson had formulated his fears.

"No scheme of policy has, in any country, yet brought the rich and poor on equal terms into courts of judicature. Perhaps experience, improving on experience, may in time effect it."[8] But this passage is set over against another which weighs traditional ascendancy with that given by wealth, and finds wealth heavy in the scales. Johnson had recognized early in his travels that violence was not the sole enemy; he was to find that the plain iniquity of self-interest might still not be the worst. As he proceeds, we can discern between the lines of his text that figure without which an argument must crumble: the figure of a representative adversary. He is a disturber of the peace, but not by rebellion; Johnson had been a rebel when young and continued to maintain that rebellion was natural to man, and 'unnatural rebellion' a political fiction. Rather is the adversary a man who defends with alacrity liberties which are not in danger, and imperils just claims by his haste to formulate them; who will handle what he could not

6. *Journey*, p. 131 below.
7. *Letters*, ed. Grierson (Vol. 1, 1932), p. 333.
8. *Journey*, p. 93 below.

have made and cannot, if he mars it, mend: the very fabric of human relationships. From the general tenor of his talk, I think that Johnson might have called such a man a Whig. If, as Boswell reports, he smiled when using the term of Pennant,[9] it was not so much at his own vehemence as at the inadequacy of political jargon.

Where then shall Hope and Fear their objects find?

Scott saw grounds for hope only in the pride of some landlords and the compassion of others. Johnson looked beyond compassion for the intellectual capacity and energy which might make good will effectual. Courtesy forbids him to assess his hosts—though not to single out endeavour for praise. His comparison between "Young Col" going to work on an English farm and Peter the Great in the ship-yards of Deptford is no mere shallow merriment. Hope is a tender plant, and he often fences it with pleasantry. In the same vein, he allows a deep preoccupation to break surface when, impressed by Braidwood's pupils, he asks: "After having seen the deaf taught arithmetick, who would be afraid to cultivate the Hebrides?"[1]

Was this ability to cultivate the Hebrides evident among the islanders? Alone with Boswell, Johnson allowed himself to criticize them and assert that Maclean of Corneck was "the most distinct man that he had met with in these isles; he did not shut his eyes, or put his fingers in his ears, which he seemed to think was a good deal the mode with most of the people whom we have seen of late."[2] He had, it is clear, no illusions about the serenity that delighted him: it was threatened, and not only from without. Apart from the ministers, most of the men whom he met had been out in the '45, and had afterwards carried their swords or their skills abroad. They were recently returned, to enjoy a St. Martin's summer, and could hardly be expected to see very far along a road they would not themselves travel.[3] It is in this context that he reverts to his own favourite project, reafforestation, and admits: "He that calculates the growth of trees, has the unwelcome re-

9. *Life*, III.274.
1. *Journey*, p. 164 below.
2. *Life*, V.294.
3. Twelve years later Bailey, visiting the same families, found himself entertained by the sons and successors of Johnson's hosts.

membrance of the shortness of life driven hard upon him."[4]
It so happened that, of the younger men from whom he hoped
much, neither was able to fulfil his promise: 'Young Col' was
dead before the *Journey* came out, and Norman Macleod, who
had inherited Dunvegan loaded with debt, and of whom Johnson said, "If he gets the better of all this, he'll be a hero,"[5] disappointed him: finding another sort of heroism more feasible, he
served with distinction in India, but the estate remained em-
barrassed.[6]

These alternations of hope and fear give the *Journey* an advantage even over its nearest counterpart among Johnson's
works, *Rasselas*; for a moral apologue is not free to develop
this element in narrative art quite so far as it is developed in
the course of Johnson's own quest. Here, the face of things
changes as he and the reader draw near them. The menace
of the Highland landscape is banished by Highland hospitality.
Husbandry, on the other hand, wears a more forbidding aspect
the closer it is examined. Whereas the purpose of both books
requires that reflection should be integrated with narrative,
general with particular, in the *Journey* alone subject and form
alike invite some personal reference: the particulars are part
of the author's own unfolding experience. Thus, passages of
reflective analysis appear as pauses in a process of discovery,
occasions for taking stock of facts which we have been allowed to watch him gathering, opportunities for entertaining
and assessing newly acquired ideas. In the words of Robert
Orme to Boswell: there were in the *Journey* "great thoughts
which had been rolled and rolled in Johnson's mind, as in
the sea."[7]

---

4. *Journey*, p. 139 below. The passage of which this forms part contrasts significantly with his earlier optimism about planting.
5. *Life*, v.176, 526ff.
6. *Life*, ii.428 and v.526–28.
7. *Boswell's Private Papers*, x.148.

THE TEXT

If we set aside, as the observation of an isolated phenomenon, the attention paid to two cancels,[1] the textual study of Johnson's *Journey* may be said to have begun when R. W. Chapman carried with him on active service a tall copy of the first edition, lacking its *Errata* leaf, and, in July 1918, relieved the tedium of the Macedonian campaign by conjectural emendation of this volume and of the three earliest editions of Boswell's *Tour*. By 20 March 1919, when his essay on "The Textual Criticism of English Classics" appeared as a leading article in the *Times Literary Supplement*, he had obtained confirmation of his conjectures as to the *Journey* from the recovered leaf. His reference to this elicited from Mr. S. C. (afterwards Sir Sydney) Roberts a letter to the *Literary Supplement* (3 April 1919), establishing the existence of two distinct lists of errata, a longer and a shorter, and suggesting that "the book was reprinted in 1775." On 24 April Chapman replied: he had now seen the copy with the reduced errata list and affirmed that it was "a new impression, reset throughout"; the edition of 1785 could no longer be called the *second*. Thereafter the course of the enquiry was to be devious, and sometimes retrograde; as when Chapman, confronted by discrepancies for which the available evidence did not account, propounded (in 1932) a theory of three (authorized) editions all bearing the date 1775 on their title-pages.[2] This supposition was given currency in the *Supplement* to *Courtney* and in the *Cambridge Bibliography of English Literature*.

1. See pp. xxx–xxxi, [xxxiv]–xxxvi below.
2. "Johnson's *Journey*, 1775," *Review of English Studies*, VIII (July 1932).

In 1948 Mr. Herman Liebert advanced the hypothesis of a made-up copy in preference to that of a third edition in the year of publication.[3] In his edition of Johnson's *Letters* (1952), R. W. Chapman summarily referred to "the two editions commonly called two issues"[4]—thus laying the ghost of a third, but leaving the cause of its appearance to be explained. Mr. Liebert's contention still held good: "The construction of a hypothesis satisfying the new facts will require more searching investigation than has yet been undertaken, including careful collation of dozens, if not hundreds of copies."[5] Work on this scale was presently carried out by Professor W. B. Todd,[6] who was thereby enabled to propound an explanation agreeable to the known facts, and to the hitherto imperfectly known bibliographical evidence which he commanded and now marshalled in full.

To summarize so extensive and intricate an operation would be impossible; but a narrative account of what may be supposed to have occurred can now be constructed, in reliance on Professor Todd's diagnosis of the following symptoms[7] and his application of the diagnosis to those facts already ascertainable. The irregularities which he enumerates include: disturbed signatures; discrepancy between copies in which certain sheets have been corrected in part (not wholly) by reference to some (not all) of the errata, and copies without these corrections; diversity among copies in respect of certain other passages.

The sequence of events with which the bibliographical phenomena must be reconciled is ascertainable principally from Johnson's letters. On 20 June 1774 the first sheets of the *Journey* were put to press. Printing proceeded (B to G) until 4 July, when Johnson left for Wales. On his return (30 September), succeeding sheets (H to Q) were briskly completed, and on 20

3. "This Harmless Drudge," *The New Colophon*, Vol. I, Part ii (New York, 1948), pp. 175–83.
4. II.12., n. 4.
5. Liebert, p. 180.
6. "The printing of Johnson's *Journey* (1775)," *Studies in Bibliography*, VI (Charlottesville, Virginia, 1953), 247–54.
7. By *symptoms* I mean printing irregularities which require explanation. There are others, noticed by W. B. Todd, which (while they may contribute something towards this explanation) would not have made it necessary to seek one.

October he was expecting the book to appear within a month. A period of delay—almost stagnation—followed, and the last proofs were not corrected until 25 November. Five days later, Johnson asked for a cancel (D8), and a half-sheet designed for Title, Errata and Cancels was presently put in hand, to be completed (on Professor Todd's reckoning) not earlier than 12 December. The special copies prepared for the King[8] and Mrs. Thrale[9] were ready by 17 December; but, since the Christmas holiday was approaching, publication was deferred until 18 January 1775.[1]

Professor Todd's study of the bibliographical evidence yields the following account of the progress of the book through the press and explains the fluctuations in pace. At some time before the final proofs were returned, Strahan decided to double the number of copies (2,000) on which he had reckoned. He therefore arranged to print twice as many of the sheets "in hand or in prospect" as he had intended, and to set up afresh those that had been completed, in order to produce another 2,000 of them. Here was steady work for the printer, if Johnson should dally with the remaining proofs. This decision was probably reached and implemented on 7 November. On the evidence of type, press figures and headlines, Professor Todd reaches the conclusion that sheets B to Y8^r—with the exception of S—had already been printed and the type distributed; Y8^v, Z and Aa were intact, S, Bb and the half-sheet which was eventually to contain Title, Errata and Cancels remained to be set up. The evidence for excepting S from the series of completed sheets is bibliographical, but, since S contains the attack on Macpherson's veracity which provoked him to demand a withdrawal and apology, some hesitation on Strahan's part might be expected.

8. I concur with Dr. Powell in assuming that Horace Walpole was mistaken when he wrote to Lady Ossory (19, 21 January 1775): "The King sent for the book in MS . . ." (*Walpole's Correspondence*, ed. W. S. Lewis, XXXII.225). There is no trace of so remarkable a circumstance in the writings of Johnson or Boswell, and it is unlikely that the manuscript, if it could be reassembled, would be legible by any eye but a printer's.

9. See *Letters* 365.2 (17 December 1774).

1. On 14 January 1775, Johnson requested Strahan to send him "three dozen of the Journey in boards" (Charles Ryskamp, "A Letter and a Portrait of Dr. Johnson," *Princeton University Library Chronicle*, XXIV [Autumn 1962], 32.) The letter is at Princeton.

Professor Todd dates the printing of this sheet 7–12 November. He shows, moreover, that the other sheets which had to be set up afresh were not taken in chronological order. From the failure to correct the first six errata in the reset sheets he infers that the Errata list was not received until the sheets containing them were in the press, and reckons that these—H, N, L, M—were printed (in this order) between 14 and 31 December; whereas the four sheets of which the errata were corrected—P, T, Q, O— went through the press (in this order) between 2 and 10 January. He concludes that the first edition, which can now be designated 1775a, was completed on 12 December 1774; and the second (1775b) on 16 January 1775.

To this narrative two particulars may be added: at some point Johnson required a second cancel $(U4)^2$; and, after learning of the death of Donald Maclean (Young Col), he inserted a valedictory passage on p. 339 (Z2^r, of which the corrected proof could still be recalled for alteration).[3]

Such a pattern of events might seem to confer superior authority on 1775b, since, on this showing, Johnson could have made, or approved, corrections on pp. 1–256 and 273–335. The area of possibility appears large, but the outcome is small. Besides achieving the correction of five out of the eleven errata, and introducing four stylistic improvements (all in sheet C) which must be attributed to Johnson, 1775b offers only two significant variants,[4] neither of them clearly preferable to the text of 1775a, and retains eleven indubitable errors, besides some doubtful readings. It adds, moreover, some misprints.

For the present edition, therefore, 1775a is accepted as the authoritative text,[5] and, while 1775b is consulted where it affords substantive variants, each of these is considered on its merits. The edition of 1785 has no intrinsic authority: not

2. This, Dr. Fleeman tells me, must have been very late in the train of events, since neither the copy given to Mrs. Thrale nor that which Johnson gave to Dr. William Hunter on 29 December 1774 (see *Letters* 369.1) has undergone cancellation of U4. See pp. xxxiv–xxxvi below.

3. Johnson's enquiry (27 October 1774) was crossed by Boswell's confirmation of the report of Maclean's death. See *Life*, II.287–88 and p. 145 below. Z2^r, according to Todd's chronology, was printed between 29 October and 5 November.

4. See p. 126 n. 9 and p. 138 n. w. below.

5. The presentation is modified in conformity with the practice of the present edition.

only was it posthumous, it followed the death of Johnson's printer, William Strahan, and whoever was responsible for the printing made no endeavour to correct errors known to both Johnson and Boswell[6]; a solitary reference to Johnson's acknowledgement of a fault is evidently prompted by Boswell's *Tour* and, admittedly an afterthought, stops short of amendment.[7] This edition contains, however, a few printing-house corrections,[8] similar in character and value to those in the 1787 *Works*. Both have therefore been consulted. Of R. W. Chapman's conjectural emendations those only have been retained which, in the present editor's estimation, indubitably represent what Johnson must have written.[9] Others, which seek to recover what Johnson must surely have intended to write, are noted. So are some errors which, deviating from the account given in letters to Mrs. Thrale and conforming to a pattern of misreading common with Johnson's hand, may be supposed misprints. Divergence between letters and *Journey* will not alone suffice to shift responsibility for error to the printer: Johnson sometimes forgot. "Ignorance cannot be certainly inferred from inaccuracy. Knowledge is not always present."[1]

In conformity with the general policy of the Yale Edition, the spelling, punctuation and hyphenation of the copy-text (1775a) have been preserved, except for a very few silent corrections of slight errors (e.g., *betwen* for *between*). Unusual and even inconsistent spellings are kept if they were acceptable in Johnson's time. Johnson's spelling of place-names, here retained, often differs from the accepted modern spelling, which may be found in the Index (see headnote, p. 169). Capitals have been modernized. Italic type is used generally in the copy-text for proper names, for words defined, for Gaelic words, and for quotations. In this edition italics have been re-

6. See Mary Lascelles, "Notions and Facts: Johnson and Boswell on their Travels," in *Johnson, Boswell and their Circle* (1965).

7. See p. 59 n. 2, and Appendix II below.

8. Thus, while 1775b is followed in respect of the two variants noted above, the misprints *least* for *last* (p. 47 1. 7) and *many* for *man* (p. 95 1. 9 below) are correctly printed, as in 1775a.

9. See, e.g., p. 66 n. 5 below.

1. Johnson's *Shakespeare*, IV.431 (Yale ed. VIII.551). Knowledge was not present when he departed from his former, correct, account of the administration of Aberdeen (*Journey*, p. 13 n. 2 below). For this reason some very seductive conjectures have been denied admittance to the text.

tained for the Gaelic and altered to roman for proper nouns, words defined, and quotations (for which quotation marks have been silently inserted).

In the textual notes the following sigla are used to identify the editions of the *Journey*:

1775a, 1st ed.	*75a*
1775b, 2d ed.	*75b*
1785	*85*
1787 *Works*	*87*
R. W. Chapman's emendations	RWC

CANCELS

It has long been common knowledge that two leaves of the *Journey* were, independently, cancelled.

Of D8 (pp. 47–48) the final paragraph ("Let us not ... imperfect constitution") originally read:

> Let us not however make too much haste to despise our neighbours. There is now, as I have heard, a body of men, not less decent or virtuous than the Scottish council, longing to melt the lead of an English cathedral. What they shall melt, it were just that they should swallow.[2]

Johnson's reason for cancelling this passage, which anyone in Lichfield would recognize as an implicit reference to the Dean and Chapter, is given in a letter to Strahan:

> ... The Dean did me a kindness about forty years ago. He is now very old, and I am not young. Reproach can do him no good, and in myself I know not whether it is zeal or wantonness.[3]

He offered to bear the cost and "write something to fill up the vacuum"—hence the generalized reproof which concludes p. 48 in the published text. Copies of 1775a bear traces of alteration: a stub and a wrong fount page number.

Of U4 (pp. 295–96) the concluding lines on p. 295 were modified (from "a cave which contains memorials of an old transaction" to "the cave in which a former generation of the

2. See illustration facing page 24.
3. *Letters* 364 (30 November 1774).

Islanders were smothered by Macleod"), in order to prepare for a radical rewriting of the first paragraph on p. 296. This originally read:

> The inhabitants once laid hold on a boat manned by Macleod, and tying the crew hand and foot, pushed them off into the ocean. Which way they escaped is not told. Macleod was informed how his vassals had been treated, and demanded the offenders, whom the inhabitants refused to deliver. Nothing now remained but force. The people of Egg had a very capacious cavern, to which they all retreated, and where they imagined themselves safe; but Macleod used the usual method of forcing subterraneous fortresses, and kept a fire at the mouth till they were all destroyed.[4]

The cancellation of a tendentious passage on D8 was known within ten days of the book's appearance, and Johnson's enemies became eager to obtain copies of the original leaf. On 28 January 1775 Francis Grose wrote to Thomas Pennant that Johnson's friends had "persuaded him to cancel a piece of abuse against the Chapter of some one of our Cathedrals," and continued: "Hooper got the Book for me in sheets, & I preserved the cancelled leaves."[5] A correspondent wrote to the *Middlesex Journal* for 20 February 1775,[6] signing himself "W.H.," and alleging that he and a friend found their copies at variance in respect of this passage. Which of them, he asked ironically, was to be accepted as authentic?

The provenance and present whereabouts of copies, and transcripts, of the uncancelled text of D8 are discussed by Dr. Fleeman.[7]

Archdeacon Wrangham appears to have been the first to record both cancels:

4. See illustration between pages 127 and 128.

5. See J. D. Fleeman, "Johnson's *Journey* (1775), and its Cancels," *Papers of the Bibliographical Society of America*, Vol. LVIII, 3d quarter, 1964.

6. This letter was published by Miss Helen McGuffie of Bethany College, West Virginia, in her Columbia University dissertation, "Samuel Johnson and the Hostile Press" (1961). I owe the reference to Professor Allen T. Hazen. See Appendix I.

7. Fleeman, pp. 233–38.

In a copy sold at Dr. Lort's sale for 15s. were preserved the cancelled parts of p. 84. (sic) relative to Lichfield Cathedral, and of p. 296. respecting the Cave of Egg and the transaction at that place . . .[8]

Professor Hazen was able to reconstruct, from an offset in a copy of the *Journey* possessed by Yale University Library, enough of the original state of p. 296 both to confirm Wrangham's intimation of its content and to show that Johnson rewrote it because he found that he was repeating himself: he had told the story of the massacre on p. 154.[9] Mr. Fleeman's discovery of the U4 *cancellandum* in the copies presented to Mrs. Thrale and Dr. Hunter completes the tale.[1]

8. [Francis Wrangham], *The English Portion of the Library of the Ven. Francis Wrangham* . . . (Malton, 1826; unpublished).

9. A. T. Hazen, "The Cancels in Johnson's *Journey*, 1775," *Review of English Studies*, xvii (April 1941), 201–03.

1. For Mrs. Thrale's copy, see the article cited in n. 5, p. xxxv, above. Dr. Hunter's has since been found by Dr. Fleeman in Glasgow University Library (Bo–3.25).

SHORT TITLES

Bailey—James Bailey, MS. diary: *A Journey in Scotland with Sketches of Some Picturesque Ruins in that interesting Country*, in the National Library of Scotland, MS. 3294,5.

Carruthers—*The Journal of a Tour to the Hebrides*, ed. Robert Carruthers, 1852, being Volume v of the edition of Boswell's *Life of Johnson* published by the National Illustrated Library, 1851.

Chapman—Johnson's *Journey to the Western Islands of Scotland* and Boswell's *Journal of a Tour to the Hebrides*, ed. R. W. Chapman, 1924 (except where explicit reference is made to the 1930 reprint).

Courtney—William P. Courtney and D. Nichol Smith, *Bibliography of Samuel Johnson*, 1915 (Oxford Historical and Literary Studies, iv).

Dictionary—Johnson's Dictionary, 4th ed., 1773.

Dwelly—Edward Dwelly, *The Illustrated Gaelic-English Dictionary*, 1949.

Journal—Boswell's *Journal of a Tour to the Hebrides, edited from the Original Manuscript* by F. A. Pottle and C. H. Bennett, 1962.

Letters—*The Letters of Samuel Johnson*, ed. R. W. Chapman, 3 vols. 1952; referred to by number.

Life—Boswell's *Life of Johnson*, ed. G. B. Hill, revised and enlarged by L. F. Powell, 6 vols. 1934–50; Vols. v and vi (2d ed.), 1964.

Lives—Lives of the English Poets, ed. G. B. Hill, 3 vols. 1905.

Martin—Martin Martin, *A Description of the Western Islands of Scotland*, 1703.

Remarks—Boswell's *Remarks. On the Journey to the Western Islands of Scotland* (MS. in Hyde Collection).

A JOURNEY TO THE WESTERN ISLANDS
OF SCOTLAND

I had desired to visit the Hebrides, or Western Islands of Scotland, so long, that I scarcely remember how the wish was originally excited;[1] and was in the autumn of the year 1773 induced to undertake the journey, by finding in Mr. Boswell a companion, whose acuteness would help my inquiry, and whose gaiety of conversation and civility of manners are sufficient to counteract the inconveniencies of travel, in countries less hospitable than we have passed.

On the eighteenth of August we left Edinburgh, a city too well known to admit description, and directed our course northward, along the eastern coast of Scotland, accompanied the first day by another gentleman,[2] who could stay with us only long enough to shew us how much we lost at separation.

As we crossed the Frith of Forth, our curiosity was attracted by Inch Keith, a small island, which neither of my companions had ever visited, though, lying within their view, it had all their lives solicited their notice. Here, by climbing with some difficulty over shattered crags, we made the first experiment of unfrequented coasts. Inch Keith is nothing more than a rock covered with a thin layer of earth, not wholly bare of grass, and very fertile of thistles. A small herd of cows grazes annually upon it in the summer. It seems never to have afforded to man or beast a permanent habitation.

We found only the ruins of a small fort, not so injured by time but that it might be easily restored to its former state. It seems never to have been intended as a place of strength, nor was built to endure a siege, but merely to afford cover to a few soldiers, who perhaps had the charge of a battery, or were sta-

---

1. Boswell comments: "but he told me, in summer, 1763, that his father put Martin's Account into his hands when he was very young, and that he was much pleased with it" (*Life*, v.13). See also *ibid.*, 1.450. Martin Martin, *A* *Description of the Western Islands of Scotland* (1703).
2. William Nairne, afterwards Lord Dunsinnan. See *Life*, v.53–54 and 475–76.

tioned to give signals of approaching danger. There is therefore no provision of water within the walls, though the spring is so near, that it might have been easily enclosed. One of the stones had this inscription: "Maria Reg. 1564."[3] It has probably been neglected from the time that the whole island had the same king.

We left this little island with our thoughts employed awhile on the different appearance that it would have made, if it had been placed at the same distance from London, with the same facility of approach; with what emulation of price a few rocky acres would have been purchased, and with what expensive industry they would have been cultivated and adorned.

When we landed, we found our chaise ready, and passed through Kinghorn, Kirkaldy, and Cowpar, places not unlike the small or straggling market-towns in those parts of England where commerce and manufactures have not yet produced opulence.

Though we were yet in the most populous part of Scotland, and at so small a distance from the capital, we met few passengers.

The roads are neither rough nor dirty; and it affords a southern stranger a new kind of pleasure to travel so commodiously without the interruption of toll-gates. Where the bottom is rocky, as it seems commonly to be in Scotland, a smooth way is made indeed with great labour, but it never wants repairs; and in those parts where adventitious materials are necessary, the ground once consolidated is rarely broken; for the inland commerce is not great, nor are heavy commodities often transported otherwise than by water. The carriages in common use are small carts, drawn each by one little horse; and a man seems to derive some degree of dignity and importance from the reputation of possessing a two-horse cart.

ST. ANDREWS

At an hour somewhat late we came to St. Andrews, a city once archiepiscopal; where that university still subsists in

3. For Johnson's championship of Mary Stuart in Edinburgh, see *Life*, v.40. For his long-standing interest in her cause, see Mary Lascelles, "Johnson's Last Allusion to Mary Queen of Scots," *RES*, new series, VIII (February 1957), 32–37.

Ruins of the Cathedral at St. Andrews. From John Oliphant's *St. Andrews Delineated*, a manuscript volume in the possession of the University Library of St. Andrews, containing 18 drawings in pen and ink, and bearing the date 1767. By kind permission of the University of St. Andrews.

which philosophy was formerly taught by Buchanan,[4] whose
name has as fair a claim to immortality as can be conferred by
modern latinity, and perhaps a fairer than the instability of
vernacular languages admits.

We found, that by the interposition of some invisible
friend,[5] lodgings had been provided for us at the house of one
of the professors,[6] whose easy civility quickly made us forget
that we were strangers; and in the whole time of our stay we
were gratified by every mode of kindness, and entertained with
all the elegance of lettered hospitality.

In the morning we rose to perambulate a city, which only
history shews to have once flourished,[7] and surveyed the ruins
of ancient magnificence, of which even the ruins cannot long
be visible, unless some care be taken to preserve them; and
where is the pleasure of preserving such mournful memorials?
They have been till very lately so much neglected, that every
man carried away the stones who fancied that he wanted them.

The cathedral, of which the foundations may be still traced,[8]
and a small part of the wall is standing, appears to have been a
spacious and majestick building, not unsuitable to the primacy
of the kingdom. Of the architecture, the poor remains can
hardly exhibit, even to an artist, a sufficient specimen. It was
demolished, as is well known, in the tumult and violence of
Knox's reformation.[9]

---

4. George Buchanan (1506–82), humanist, historian, controversialist, opponent of Mary Stuart. Johnson, at his death, possessed *Buchanani Opera Omnia* (Edinburgh, 1715) and *Buchanani Poemata*, 8vo. (*Sale Catalogue*, 15).

5. Robert Arbuthnot. See *Life*, v.29.

6. Robert Watson, at that time Professor of Logic, Rhetoric and Metaphysics at the United College. See *Life*, v.481.

7. To Pennant, the sight of St. Andrews suggested successively the effects of pestilence, bombardment, earthquake (*A Tour in Scotland. 1772. Part II*, 1776, p. 189).

8. In Johnson's day, and for some while afterwards, they were merely *traceable* under accumulated rubble.

In 1807, the top of the "great altar" was "about four feet below the general surface of the rubbish" (James Grierson, *Delineations of St. Andrews*, Edinburgh, 1807, p. 122).

9. Modern historians attribute the general disrepair of Scottish ecclesiastical architecture to causes already operative before the Reformation—war, lawlessness, scarcity, and misappropriation of revenues. Johnson is not, however, responsible for this explanation of the peculiar desolation of St. Andrews: it had long been legendary. Thomas Innes, for example, reverts to it again and again as an example of the "destruction of historical, and of other ancient monuments, at the Scottish reformation" (*A Critical Essay on the Ancient Inhabitants of*

Not far from the cathedral, on the margin of the water, stands a fragment of the castle, in which the archbishop anciently resided. It was never very large, and was built with more attention to security than pleasure. Cardinal Beatoun[1] is said to have had workmen employed in improving its fortifications at the time when he was murdered by the ruffians of reformation, in the manner of which Knox has given what he himself calls a merry narrative.[2]

The change of religion in Scotland, eager and vehement as it was, raised an epidemical enthusiasm, compounded of sullen scrupulousness and warlike ferocity, which, in a people whom idleness resigned to their own thoughts, and who, conversing only with each other, suffered no dilution of their zeal from the gradual influx of new opinions, was long transmitted in its full strength from the old to the young, but by trade and intercourse with England, is now visibly abating, and giving way too fast to that[a] laxity of practice and indifference of opinion, in which men, not sufficiently instructed to find the middle point, too easily shelter themselves from rigour and constraint.

The city of St. Andrews, when it had lost its archiepiscopal preeminence, gradually decayed: One of its streets is now lost;[3] and in those that remain, there is the silence and solitude of inactive indigence and gloomy depopulation.

The university, within a few years, consisted of three colleges, but is now reduced to two;[4] the college of St. Leonard be-

a. that *85, RWC*]   their *75a, b*

---

the *Northern Parts of Britain, or Scotland*, 1729, II.561–86). Pennant's political sympathies do not hinder his acceptance of the legend: "The cathedral was the labor of a hundred and sixty years . . . yet in June 1559, John Knox effected its demolition in a single day" (*A Tour in Scotland. 1772. Part II*, 1776, p. 189).

1. David Beaton or Bethune (1494–1546), Cardinal and Archbishop of St. Andrews and Papal Legate. He opposed the Scottish Reformation, condemned George Wishart to be burned, and was assassinated by John and Norman Leslie.

2. John Knox, *History of the Reformation in Scotland*, ed. William Croft Dickinson (1949), I.79. The passage was notorious.

3. Swallow Street. See W. Douglass, *Some Historical Remarks on the City of St. Andrews in North-Britain* (1728), p. 7.

4. The original three were St. Salvator's, St. Leonard's, and St. Mary's. In 1747 the revenues of the first two were found insufficient, and the buildings of St. Leonard's ruinous beyond repair. St. Salvator's and St. Leonard's were therefore united.

The Chapel of St. Leonard's College, St. Andrews. From John Oliphant's *St. Andrews Delineated*. By kind permission of the University of St. Andrews.

ing lately dissolved by the sale of its buildings and the appropriation of its revenues to the professors of the two others. The chapel of the alienated college is yet standing, a fabrick not inelegant of external structure; but I was always, by some civil excuse, hindred from entering it. A decent attempt,[5] as I was since told, has been made to convert it into a kind of greenhouse, by planting its area with shrubs. This new method of gardening is unsuccessful; the plants do not hitherto prosper. To what use it will next be put I have no pleasure in conjecturing. It is something that its present state is at least not ostentatiously displayed. Where there is yet shame, there may in time be virtue.

The dissolution of St. Leonard's college was doubtless necessary; but of that necessity there is reason to complain. It is surely not without just reproach, that a nation, of which the commerce is hourly extending, and the wealth encreasing, denies any participation of its prosperity to its literary societies; and while its merchants or its nobles are raising palaces, suffers its universities to moulder into dust.

Of the two colleges yet standing, one is by the institution of its founder appropriated to divinity.[6] It is said to be capable of containing fifty students; but more than one must occupy a chamber. The library,[7] which is of late erection, is not very spacious, but elegant and luminous.

The doctor,[8] by whom it was shewn, hoped to irritate or subdue my English vanity by telling me, that we had no such repository of books in England.

Saint Andrews seems to be a place eminently adapted to study and education, being situated in a populous, yet a cheap country,[9] and exposing the minds and manners of young men neither to the levity and dissoluteness of a capital city, nor to

5. Although *decent* appears in the early editions, RWC thought it an unlikely reading and emended it to *recent* in 1924, but restored *decent* in 1930. The site and ruins had been sold so recently as 1772, but *decent* is in keeping with the irony of Johnson's comparison between "the sleepy laziness of men that erected churches" and "the fervid activity of those who

suffer them to fall" (p. 65).

6. St. Mary's College.

7. "Not the Library of St. Mary's College, but the upper room of the University Library" (*Life*, v.480).

8. James Murison, Principal of St. Mary's College from 1747 to 1779. See *Life*, v.480–81.

9. "Fife and Angus; *country* does not mean Scotland." RWC

the gross luxury of a town of commerce, places naturally un-propitious to learning; in one the desire of knowledge easily gives way to the love of pleasure, and in the other, is in danger of yielding to the love of money.

The students however are represented as at this time not exceeding a hundred. Perhaps it may be some obstruction to their increase that there is no episcopal chapel in the place. I saw no reason for imputing their paucity to the present professors; nor can the expence of an academical education be very reasonably objected. A student of the highest class may keep his annual session, or as the English call it, his term, which lasts seven months, for about fifteen pounds, and one of lower rank for less than ten; in which board, lodging, and instruction are all included.

The chief magistrate resident in the university, answering to our vice-chancellor, and to the *rector magnificus* on the continent, had commonly the title of Lord Rector; but being addressed only as "Mr. Rector" in an inauguratory speech by the present chancellor,[1] he has fallen from his former dignity of style. Lordship was very liberally annexed by our ancestors to any station or character of dignity: They said, the "Lord General," and "Lord Ambassador"; so we still say, "my Lord," to the judge upon the circuit, and yet retain in our Liturgy[2] "the Lords of the Council."

In walking among the ruins of religious buildings,[3] we came to two vaults over which had formerly stood the house of the sub-prior. One of the vaults was inhabited by an old woman, who claimed the right of abode there, as the widow of a man whose ancestors had possessed the same gloomy mansion for no less than four generations. The right, however it began, was considered as established by legal prescription,[4] and the old woman lives undisturbed. She thinks however that she has a claim to something more than sufferance; for as her husband's name was Bruce, she is allied to royalty, and told Mr. Boswell that when there were persons of quality in the place, she was distinguished by some notice; that indeed she is now

1. Thomas Hay, Earl of Kinnoul.
2. In the Litany.
3. Besides the great Augustinian priory, there were the monasteries of
Black and Grey Friars.
4. *prescription*: "custom continued until it has the force of law" (*Dictionary*).

neglected, but she spins a thread, has the company of her cat, and is troublesome to nobody.

Having now seen whatever this ancient city offered to our curiosity, we left it with good wishes, having reason to be highly pleased with the attention that was paid us. But whoever surveys the world must see many things that give him pain. The kindness of the professors did not contribute to abate the uneasy remembrance of an university declining,[5] a college alienated, and a church profaned and hastening to the ground.

St. Andrews indeed has formerly suffered more atrocious ravages and more extensive destruction, but recent evils affect with greater force. We were reconciled to the sight of archiepiscopal ruins. The distance of a calamity from the present time seems to preclude the mind from contact or sympathy. Events long past are barely known; they are not considered. We read with as little emotion the violence of Knox and his followers, as the irruptions of Alaric and the Goths. Had the university been destroyed two centuries ago, we should not have regretted it; but to see it pining in decay and struggling for life, fills the mind with mournful images and ineffectual wishes.

ABERBROTHICK

As we knew sorrow and wishes to be vain, it was now our business to mind our way. The roads of Scotland afford little diversion to the traveller, who seldom sees himself either encountered or overtaken, and who has nothing to contemplate but grounds that have no visible boundaries, or are separated by walls of loose stone. From the bank of the Tweed to St. Andrews I had never seen a single tree, which I did not believe to have grown up far within the present century. Now and then about a gentleman's house stands a small plantation, which in Scotch is called a *policy*, but of these there are few, and those few all very young. The variety of sun and shade is here utterly unknown. There is no tree for either shelter or timber. The oak and the thorn is equally a stranger, and the whole country

---

5. For the plight of the university in the eighteenth century, see R. G. Cant, *The University of St. Andrews:*   *A Short History* (Edinburgh, 1946), especially pp. 75–98.

is extended in uniform nakedness, except that in the road between Kirkaldy and Cowpar, I passed for a few yards between two hedges. A tree might be a show in Scotland as a horse in Venice. At St. Andrews Mr. Boswell found only one, and recommended it to my notice; I told him that it was rough and low, or looked as if I thought so. This, said he, is nothing to another a few miles off. I was still less delighted to hear that another tree was not to be seen nearer. Nay, said a gentleman that stood by, I know but of this and that tree in the country.

The Lowlands of Scotland had once undoubtedly an equal portion of woods with other countries. Forests are every where gradually diminished, as architecture and cultivation prevail by the increase of people and the introduction of arts. But I believe few regions have been denuded like this, where many centuries must have passed in waste without the least thought of future supply. Davies observes in his account of Ireland,[6] that no Irishman had ever planted an orchard. For that negligence some excuse might be drawn from an unsettled state of life, and the instability of property; but in Scotland possession has long been secure, and inheritance regular, yet it may be doubted whether before the Union any man[b] between Edinburgh and England had ever set a tree.[7]

Of this improvidence no other account can be given than that it probably began in times of tumult, and continued because it had begun. Established custom is not easily broken, till some great event shakes the whole system of things, and life seems to recommence upon new principles. That before the Union the Scots had little trade and little money, is no valid apology; for plantation is the least expensive of all methods of improvement. To drop a seed into the ground can cost nothing, and the trouble is not great of protecting the young plant, till it is out of danger; though it must be allowed to have some

b. man 75b] Lowlander 75a

---

6. "Sir John Davies (1569–1626), Attorney-General for Ireland, whose *Discoverie of the true Causes why Ireland was never entirely Subdued . . . untill the Beginning of his Majesties happie Raigne* (1612) is frequently cited in Johnson's Dictionary." RWC

7. Boswell remonstrated against this passage in his *Remarks* but attempted to explain it in his *Tour*. See *Life*, v.69–70.

difficulty in places like these, where they have neither wood for palisades, nor thorns for hedges.

Our way was over the Firth of Tay, where, though the water was not wide, we paid four shillings for ferrying the chaise. In Scotland the necessaries of life are easily procured, but superfluities and elegancies are of the same price at least as in England, and therefore may be considered as much dearer.

We stopped a while at Dundee, where I remember nothing remarkable, and mounting our chaise again, came about the close of the day to Aberbrothick.

The monastery of Aberbrothick is of great renown in the history of Scotland. Its ruins afford ample testimony of its ancient magnificence: Its extent might, I suppose, easily be found by following the walls among the grass and weeds, and its height is known by some parts yet standing. The arch of one of the gates is entire, and of another only so far dilapidated as to diversify the appearance. A square apartment of great loftiness is yet standing; its use I could not conjecture, as its elevation was very disproportionate to its area. Two corner towers, particularly attracted our attention. Mr. Boswell, whose inquisitiveness is seconded by great activity, scrambled in at a high window, but found the stairs within broken, and could not reach the top. Of the other tower we were told that the inhabitants sometimes climbed it, but we did not immediately discern the entrance, and as the night was gathering upon us, thought proper to desist. Men skilled in architecture might do what we did not attempt: They might probably form an exact ground-plot of this venerable edifice. They may from some parts yet standing conjecture its general form, and perhaps by comparing it with other buildings of the same kind and the same age, attain an idea very near to truth. I should scarcely have regretted my journey, had it afforded nothing more than the sight of Aberbrothick.

MONTROSE

Leaving these fragments of magnificence, we travelled on to Montrose, which we surveyed in the morning, and found it well built, airy, and clean. The townhouse is a handsome fabrick with a portico. We then went to view the English chapel, and found a small church, clean to a degree unknown in any other part of Scotland, with commodious galleries, and what was yet less expected, with an organ.[8]

At our inn we did not find a reception such as we thought proportionate to the commercial opulence of the place; but Mr. Boswell desired me to observe that the innkeeper was an Englishman, and I then defended him as well as I could.

When I had proceeded thus far, I had opportunities of observing what I had never heard, that there are many beggars in Scotland. In Edinburgh the proportion is, I think, not less than in London, and in the smaller places it is far greater than in English towns of the same extent. It must, however, be allowed that they are not importunate, nor clamorous. They solicit silently, or very modestly, and therefore though their behaviour may strike with more force the heart of a stranger, they are certainly in danger of missing the attention of their countrymen. Novelty has always some power, an unaccustomed mode of begging excites an unaccustomed degree of pity. But the force of novelty is by its own nature soon at an end; the efficacy of outcry and perseverance is permanent and certain.

The road from Montrose exhibited a continuation of the same appearances. The country is still naked, the hedges are of stone, and the fields so generally plowed that it is hard to imagine where grass is found for the horses that till them. The harvest, which was almost ripe, appeared very plentiful.

Early in the afternoon Mr. Boswell observed that we were at no great distance from the house of Lord Monboddo.[9] The magnetism of his conversation easily drew us out of our way, and the entertainment which we received would have been a sufficient recompence for a much greater deviation.

The roads beyond Edinburgh, as they are less frequented, must be expected to grow gradually rougher; but they were hitherto by no means incommodious. We travelled on with the

---

8. English chapel: one in which the English liturgy was used. See p. 17, n. 4. For the rarity of organs in Scottish churches, see *Journal*, p. 457. For the Montrose chapel and incumbent, see

Life, v.488.

9. James Burnett, Lord Monboddo (1714–99), author of *The Origin and Progress of Language* (1773) and other works.

gentle pace of a Scotch driver, who having no rivals in expedition, neither gives himself nor his horses unnecessary trouble. We did not affect the impatience we did not feel, but were satisfied with the company of each other as well riding in the chaise, as sitting at an inn. The night and the day are equally solitary and equally safe; for where there are so few travellers, why should there be robbers.

ABERDEEN

We came somewhat late to Aberdeen, and found the inn so full, that we had some difficulty in obtaining admission, till Mr. Boswell made himself known: His name overpowered all objection, and we found a very good house and civil treatment.

I received the next day a very kind letter from Sir Alexander Gordon,[1] whom I had formerly known in London, and after a cessation of all intercourse for near twenty years met[c] here professor of physic in the King's College. Such unexpected renewals of acquaintance may be numbered among the most pleasing incidents of life.

The knowledge of one professor soon procured me the notice of the rest, and I did not want any token of regard, being conducted wherever there was any thing which I desired to see, and entertained at once with the novelty of the place, and the kindness of communication.

To write of the cities of our own island with the solemnity of geographical description, as if we had been cast upon a newly discovered coast, has the appearance of very frivolous ostentation; yet as Scotland is little known to the greater part of those who may read these observations, it is not superfluous to relate, that under the name of Aberdeen are comprised two towns standing about a mile distant from each other, but governed, I think, by the same magistrates.[2]

c. met 75b] found 75a

1. Johnson's earlier acquaintance with Gordon has not been traced, but, as he admitted to Mrs. Thrale, they had "not seen nor perhaps thought on one another for many years" (*Letters* 321). For Gordon's career, see *Life*, v.493–94.

2. Boswell, in his *Remarks*, pointed out what Johnson himself had known when he wrote to Mrs. Thrale that "the two cities have their separate Magistrates" (*Letters* 321).

Old Aberdeen is the ancient episcopal city, in which are still to be seen the remains of the cathedral. It has the appearance of a town in decay, having been situated[d] in times when commerce was yet unstudied, with very little attention to the commodities of the harbour.

New Aberdeen has all the bustle of prosperous trade, and all the shew of increasing opulence. It is built by the waterside. The houses are large and lofty, and the streets spacious and clean. They build almost wholly with the granite used in the new pavement of the streets of London, which is well known not to want hardness, yet they shape it easily. It is beautiful and must be very lasting.

What particular parts of commerce are chiefly exercised by the merchants of Aberdeen, I have not inquired. The manufacture which forces itself upon a stranger's eye is that of knit-stockings, on which the women of the lower class are visibly employed.

In each of these towns there is a college, or in stricter language, an university; for in both there are professors of the same parts of learning, and the colleges hold their sessions and confer degrees separately, with total independence of one on the other.

In Old Aberdeen stands the King's College, of which the first president was Hector Boece, or Boethius,[3] who may be justly reverenced as[e] one of the revivers of elegant learning. When he studied at Paris, he was acquainted with Erasmus, who afterwards gave him a public testimony of his esteem, by inscribing to him a catalogue of his works.[4] The stile of Boethius, though,

d. having been situated 75b] being built 75a   e. as 1787, RWC] omitted
75a, b; 85

---

3. Hector Boece or Boethius (1465?–1536), first principal of Aberdeen University. His *Scotorum Historiae* (1526) contains *Scotorum regni descriptio*, of which a translation was included in Holinshed's *Chronicles*, so becoming familiar to English readers. Boswell records finding a copy of the Latin at Coirechatachan (*Life*, v.158).
    4. The letter from Erasmus to Boece and the catalogue with its flattering inscription—"Eruditissimo   Boeotio"

(sic)—are found in *Magni Erasmi Roterodami, Vita Accedunt Epistolae Illustres* (Leyden, 1642), pp. 132–44, and in Desiderii Erasmi Roterodami, *Opera Omnia* (10 vols. Leyden, 1703), where they are set out with some splendour (Vol. I. fol. *** *** 3). They are twice mentioned in John Jortin, *Life of Erasmus* (1758–60), which Johnson knew (see II.132 and 447).

perhaps, not always rigorously pure, is formed with great diligence upon ancient models, and wholly uninfected with monastic barbarity. His history is written with elegance and vigour, but his fabulousness and credulity are justly blamed. His fabulousness, if he was the author of the fictions, is a fault for which no apology can be made; but his credulity may be excused in an age, when all men were credulous. Learning was then rising on the world; but ages so long accustomed to darkness, were too much dazzled with its light to see any thing distinctly. The first race of scholars, in the fifteenth century, and some time after, were, for the most part, learning to speak, rather than to think, and were therefore more studious of elegance than of truth. The contemporaries of Boethius thought it sufficient to know what the ancients had delivered. The examination of tenets and of facts was reserved for another generation.

Boethius, as president of the university, enjoyed a revenue of forty Scottish marks, about two pounds four shillings and sixpence of sterling money. In the present age of trade and taxes, it is difficult even for the imagination so to raise the value of money, or so to diminish the demands of life, as to suppose four and forty shillings a year, an honourable stipend; yet it was probably equal, not only to the needs, but to the rank of Boethius. The wealth of England was undoubtedly to that of Scotland more than five to one, and it is known that Henry the Eighth, among whose faults avarice was never reckoned, granted to Roger Ascham, as a reward of his learning, a pension of ten pounds a year.[5]

The other, called the Marischal College, is in the new town. The hall is large and well lighted. One of its ornaments is the picture of Arthur Johnston,[6] who was principal of the college, and who holds among the Latin poets of Scotland the next place to the elegant Buchanan.

In the library I was shewn some curiosities; a Hebrew manu-

---

5. Roger Ascham (1515–68), author and teacher. For Johnson's account of Ascham's pension and surmise as to its actual value, see his *Life* (1761), in *Works* (1825), VI.511.

6. Arthur Johnston (1587–1641), writer of Latin verse and rector of King's College, Aberdeen. Johnson had tried to buy his poems in Aberdeen (*Life*, v.95) and was to write on 18 February 1777, asking Boswell to obtain for him *Johnstoni Poemata* (Middelburg, 1642). See *Letters* 507.

script of exquisite penmanship, and a Latin translation of Aristotle's *Politicks* by Leonardus Aretinus,[7] written in the Roman character with nicety and beauty, which, as the art of printing has made them no longer necessary, are not now to be found. This was one of the latest performances of the transcribers, for Aretinus died but about twenty years before typography was invented. This version has been printed, and may be found in libraries, but is little read; for the same books have been since translated both by Victorius[8] and Lambinus,[9] who lived in an age more cultivated, but perhaps owed in part to Aretinus that they were able to excel him. Much is due to those who first broke the way to knowledge, and left only to their successors the task of smoothing it.

In both these colleges the methods of instruction are nearly the same; the lectures differing only by the accidental difference of diligence, or ability in the professors. The students wear scarlet gowns and the professors black, which is, I believe, the academical dress in all the Scottish universities, except that of Edinburgh, where the scholars are not distinguished by any particular habit. In the King's College there is kept a public table, but the scholars of the Marischal College are boarded in the town. The expence of living is here, according to the information that I could obtain, somewhat more than at St. Andrews.

The course of education is extended to four years, at the end of which those who take a degree, who are not many, become masters of arts, and whoever is a master may, if he pleases, immediately commence[f] doctor. The title of doctor, however, was for a considerable time bestowed only on physicians. The advocates are examined and approved by their own body; the ministers were not ambitious of titles, or were afraid of being censured for ambition; and the doctorate in every faculty was

f. commence 75*b*]   become a 75*a*

7. Leonardo Bruni Aretino (1369–1444), author of a history of Florence and lives of Dante and Petrarch. For the "Hebrew manuscript of exquisite penmanship," see C. Roth, "The Aberdeen Codex of the Hebrew Bible," *Aberdeen University Studies*, No. 138

(1958).

8. Pietro Vettori, the elder (1499–1585), editor of Aristotle and other classical authors.

9. Denis Lambin (1520–72), translator into Latin of Aristotle's *Ethics* (1558) and *Politics* (1567).

commonly given or sold into other countries. The ministers are now reconciled to distinction, and as it must always happen that some will excel others, have thought graduation a proper testimony of uncommon abilities or acquisitions.

The indiscriminate collation of degrees[1] has justly taken away that respect which they originally claimed as stamps, by which the literary value of men so distinguished was authoritatively denoted. That academical honours, or any others should be conferred with exact proportion to merit, is more than human judgment or human integrity have given reason to expect. Perhaps degrees in universities cannot be better adjusted by any general rule than by the length of time passed in the public profession of learning. An English or Irish doctorate cannot be obtained by a very young man, and it is reasonable to suppose, what is likewise by experience commonly found true, that he who is by age qualified to be a doctor, has in so much time gained learning sufficient not to disgrace the title, or wit sufficient not to desire it.

The Scotch universities hold but one term or session in the year. That of St. Andrews continues eight months,[2] that of Aberdeen only five, from the first of November to the first of April.

In Aberdeen there is an English chapel,[3] in which the congregation was numerous and splendid. The form of public worship used by the Church of England is in Scotland legally practised in licensed chapels served by clergymen of English or Irish ordination, and by tacit connivance quietly permitted in separate congregations supplied with ministers by the successors of the bishops who were deprived at the Revolution.[4]

---

1. *collation*: "the act of conferring or bestowing" (*Dictionary*).

2. An error for *seven*, which Johnson had given correctly on p. 8, and in writing to Mrs. Thrale (*Letters* 321).

3. Edward Burt mentions this as a church "where there is an organ, the only one I know of [*sc.* in Scotland], and the service is chanted as in our cathedrals" (*Letters from a Gentleman in the North of Scotland*, 1754, I.259). For an account of this building, and of Episcopalians in Aberdeen, see *Jour-*

nal, p. 458.

4. Johnson's discreet reference to a division within the episcopalian communion in Scotland recalls the outcome of the oaths prescribed in 1693: a separation between Jacobite and non-Jacobite Scottish episcopalians. See J. H. S. Burleigh, *A Church History of Scotland* (1960), p. 265. On the one hand was the Scottish Episcopal Church, owning allegiance not only to an exiled dynasty but also to a proscribed episcopate—repugnant alike to

We came to Aberdeen on Saturday August 21. On Monday we were invited into the town-hall, where I had the freedom of the city given me by the Lord Provost. The honour conferred had all the decorations that politeness could add, and what I am afraid I should not have had to say of any city south of the Tweed, I found no petty officer bowing for a fee.

The parchment containing the record of admission is, with the seal appending, fastened to a riband and worn for one day by the new citizen in his hat.

By a lady who saw us at the chapel, the Earl of Errol[5] was informed of our arrival, and we had the honour of an invitation to his seat, called Slanes Castle, as I am told, improperly, from the castle of that name, which once stood at a place not far distant.[6]

The road beyond Aberdeen grew more stony, and continued equally naked of all vegetable decoration. We travelled over a tract of ground near the sea, which, not long ago, suffered a very uncommon, and unexpected calamity. The sand of the shore was raised by a tempest in such quantities, and carried to such a distance, that an estate was overwhelmed and lost. Such and so hopeless was the barrenness superinduced, that the owner, when he was required to pay the usual tax, desired rather to resign the ground.

SLANES CASTLE. THE BULLER OF BUCHAN

We came in the afternoon to Slanes Castle, built upon the margin of the sea, so that the walls of one of the towers seem

---

the civil government (though the law was no longer rigorously enforced) and to the Presbyterian Church; on the other, independent congregations, to whom the law allowed the ministration of clergymen of English or Irish ordination, in "qualified" chapels, and the use of the English liturgy.

5. James Boyd, 15th earl. Boswell relates how the travellers prolonged their visit to await his return. Beattie wrote to Mrs. Montagu: "I remember Dr. Samuel Johnson was positive, that

he resembled Homer's Sarpedon" (Sir William Forbes, *An Account of the Life and Writings of James Beattie*, Edinburgh, 1806, II.351).

The lady at the chapel was Lady Diana Middleton. See *Letters* 322.

6. Johnson scruples to apply the title of castle to a mere great house. Thus, he distinguishes between the house of Dunvegan and its "skeleton of a castle," and at Inveraray refers to the Duke's "seat," which Boswell calls the castle.

only a continuation of a perpendicular rock, the foot of which is beaten by the waves. To walk round the house seemed impracticable. From the windows the eye wanders over the sea that separates Scotland from Norway, and when the winds beat with violence must enjoy all the terrifick grandeur of the tempestuous ocean. I would not for my amusement wish for a storm; but as storms, whether wished or not, will sometimes happen, I may say, without violation of humanity, that I should willingly look out upon them from Slanes Castle.

When we were about to take our leave, our departure was prohibited by the countess till we should have seen two places upon the coast, which she rightly considered as worthy of curiosity, Dun Buy, and the Buller of Buchan, to which Mr. Boyd[7] very kindly conducted us.

Dun Buy, which in Erse is said to signify the "Yellow Rock," is a double protuberance of stone, open to the main sea on one side, and parted from the land by a very narrow channel on the other. It has its name and its colour from the dung of innumerable sea-fowls, which in the spring chuse this place as convenient for incubation, and have their eggs and their young taken in great abundance. One of the birds that frequent this rock has, as we were told, its body not larger than a duck's, and yet lays eggs as large as those of a goose. This bird is by the inhabitants named a "coot." That which is called "coot" in England, is here a "cooter."

Upon these rocks there was nothing that could long detain attention, and we soon turned our eyes to the Buller, or Bouilloir of Buchan, which no man can see with indifference, who has either sense of danger or delight in rarity. It is a rock perpendicularly tubulated, united on one side with a high shore, and on the other rising steep to a great height, above the main sea. The top is open, from which may be seen a dark gulf of water which flows into the cavity, through a breach made in the lower part of the inclosing rock. It has the appearance of a vast well bordered with a wall. The edge of the Buller is not wide, and to those that walk round, appears very narrow. He that ventures to look downward sees, that if his foot should slip, he must fall from his dreadful elevation upon stones on one side,

---

7. The Hon. Charles Boyd, brother of the Earl of Errol.

or into the water on the other. We however went round, and were glad when the circuit was completed.

When we came down to the sea, we saw some boats, and rowers, and resolved to explore the Buller at the bottom. We entered the arch, which the water had made, and found ourselves in a place, which, though we could not think ourselves in danger, we could scarcely survey without some recoil of the mind. The bason in which we floated was nearly circular, perhaps thirty yards in diameter. We were inclosed by a natural wall, rising steep on every side to a height which produced the idea of insurmountable confinement. The interception of all lateral light caused a dismal gloom. Round us was a perpendicular rock, above us the distant sky, and below an unknown profundity of water. If I had any malice against a walking spirit, instead of laying him in the Red-sea, I would condemn him to reside in the Buller of Buchan.[8]

But terrour without danger is only one of the sports of fancy, a voluntary agitation of the mind that is permitted no longer than it pleases. We were soon at leisure to examine the place with minute inspection, and found many cavities which, as the watermen told us, went backward to a depth[9] which they had never explored. Their extent we had not time to try; they are said to serve different purposes. Ladies come hither sometimes in the summer with collations, and smugglers make them storehouses for clandestine merchandise. It is hardly to be

---

8. Johnson's reference to the laying of a spirit in the Red Sea may be a recollection of Addison's censure of popular superstitions in *Spectator* 12 (14 March 1711). Among the walking spirits of whom he has heard women talking are some who have "been conjured into the Red-Sea, for disturbing people's rest." Addison developed this pleasantry in *The Drummer, or, the Haunted House* (1716), when he made the Butler promise that the (supposed) Conjurer, confronted with the (supposed) Ghost, would "lay him . . . in the Red-Sea—and then he's laid for ever" (II.i). But compare Dennis's reference to a spectre laid in the Red Sea, in his *Reflections Critical and Satyrical upon a late Rhapsody, call'd, an Essay upon Criticism* (1711) (See *The Critical Works of John Dennis*, ed. E. N. Hooker, Baltimore, 1939–43, 1.416). The origin of these pleasantries was probably the Order of Exorcism in the *Rituale Romanum* (1619): in the final exorcism, the evil spirit is exhorted to "yield to God, who by his servant Moses drowned thee and thy malice in Pharoah and in his army in the abyss" (See Rossell Hope Robbins, *Encyclopaedia of Witchcraft and Demonology*, New York, 1959).

9. "Is going *backward* to a *depth* right? Does not a depth mean downwards?" (Boswell, *Remarks*). Johnson evidently uses *depth* here, as on p. 146, to signify extent of penetration.

doubted but the pirates of ancient times often used them as
magazines of arms, or repositories of plunder.

To the little vessels used by the northern rowers,[1] the Buller
may have served as a shelter from storms, and perhaps as a retreat from enemies; the entrance might have been stopped, or
guarded with little difficulty, and though the vessels that were
stationed within would have been battered with stones
showered on them from above, yet the crews would have lain
safe in the caverns.

Next morning we continued our journey, pleased with our
reception at Slanes Castle, of which we had now leisure to recount the grandeur and the elegance; for our way afforded us
few topics of conversation. The ground was neither uncultivated nor unfruitful; but it was still all arable. Of flocks or
herds there was no appearance. I had now travelled two hundred miles in Scotland and seen only one tree not younger than
myself.

BAMFF

We dined this day at the house of Mr. Frazer of Streichton,[2]
who shewed us in his grounds some stones yet standing of a
druidical circle, and what I began to think more worthy of
notice, some forest trees of full growth.

At night we came to Bamff, where I remember nothing that
particularly claimed my attention. The ancient towns of Scotland have generally an appearance unusual to Englishmen.
The houses, whether great or small, are for the most part built
of stones. Their ends are now and then next the streets, and the
entrance into them is very often by a flight of steps, which
reaches up to the second story, the[g] floor which is level with the
ground being entered only by stairs descending within the
house.

The art of joining squares of glass with lead is little used in
Scotland, and in some places is totally forgotten. The frames of

g. story, the *RWC*]   story. The *75a, b; 85*; story; the *87*

1. Although the early editions give
rowers, RWC emended in 1930 to *rovers*.
This is intrinsically more probable;
but *rowers* is not impossible.
2. Alexander Fraser of Strichen. See
Life, v.500–01.

their windows are all of wood. They are more frugal of their glass than the English, and will often, in houses not otherwise mean, compose a square of two pieces, not joining like cracked glass, but with one edge laid perhaps half an inch over the other. Their windows do not move upon hinges, but are pushed up and drawn down in grooves, yet they are seldom accommodated with weights and pullies. He that would have his window open must hold it with his hand, unless what may be sometimes found among good contrivers, there be a nail which he may stick into a hole, to keep it from falling.

What cannot be done without some uncommon trouble or particular expedient, will not often be done at all. The incommodiousness of the Scotch windows keeps them very closely shut. The necessity of ventilating human habitations has not yet been found by our northern neighbours; and even in houses well built and elegantly furnished, a stranger may be sometimes forgiven, if he allows himself to wish for fresher air.

These diminutive observations seem to take away something from the dignity of writing, and therefore are never communicated but with hesitation, and a little fear of abasement and contempt. But it must be remembered, that life consists not of a series of illustrious actions, or elegant enjoyments; the greater part of our time passes in compliance with necessities, in the performance of daily duties, in the removal of small inconveniencies, in the procurement of petty pleasures; and we are well or ill at ease, as the main stream of life glides on smoothly, or is ruffled by small obstacles and frequent interruption. The true state of every nation is the state of common life. The manners of a people are not to be found in the schools of learning, or the palaces of greatness, where the national character is obscured or obliterated by travel or instruction, by philosophy or vanity; nor is public happiness to be estimated by the assemblies of the gay, or the banquets of the rich. The great mass of nations is neither rich nor gay: they whose aggregate constitutes the people, are found in the streets, and the villages, in the shops and farms; and from them collectively considered, must the measure of general prosperity be taken. As they approach to delicacy a nation is refined, as their conveniencies are multiplied, a nation, at least a commercial nation, must be denominated wealthy.

ELGIN

Finding nothing to detain us at Bamff, we set out in the morning, and having breakfasted at Cullen, about noon came to Elgin, where in the inn, that we supposed the best, a dinner was set before us, which we could not eat. This was the first time, and except one, the last, that I found any reason to complain of a Scotish table; and such disappointments, I suppose, must be expected in every country, where there is no great frequency of travellers.

The ruins of the cathedral of Elgin afforded us another proof of the waste of reformation. There is enough yet remaining to shew, that it was once magnificent. Its whole plot is easily traced. On the north side of the choir, the chapter-house, which is roofed with an arch of stone, remains entire; and on the south side, another mass of building, which we could not enter, is preserved by the care of the family of Gordon; but the body of the church is a mass of fragments.

A paper was here put into our hands, which deduced from sufficient authorities the history of this venerable ruin. The church of Elgin had, in the intestine tumults of the barbarous ages, been laid waste by the irruption of a highland chief, whom the bishop had offended; but it was gradually restored to the state, of which the traces may be now discerned, and was at last not destroyed by the tumultuous violence of Knox, but more shamefully suffered to dilapidate by deliberate robbery and frigid indifference. There is still extant, in the books of the council, an order, of which I cannot remember the date, but which was doubtless issued after the Reformation, directing that the lead, which covers the two cathedrals of Elgin and Aberdeen,[3] shall be taken away, and converted into money for the support of the army. A Scotch army was in those times very

---

3. The Order of the Privy Council of Scotland "Anent the Leid of Elgin and Abirdene" was given under the Regent Moray, 14 February 1567[8]. (See *Register of the Privy Council of Scotland*, Vol. I, ed. J. H. Burton, Edinburgh, 1877, pp. 608–09). Dr. T. I. Rae, of the National Library of Scotland, tells me that the original document was absent from Edinburgh in 1773. Johnson had probably in mind, therefore, Robert Keith's *History of the Affairs of Church and State in Scotland from the beginning of the Reformation in the Reign of King James V. to the Retreat of Queen Mary into England, Anno 1568* (Edinburgh, 1734), p. 468.

cheaply kept; yet the lead of two churches must have born so small a proportion to any military expence, that it is hard not to believe the reason alleged to be merely popular, and the money intended for some private purse. The order however was obeyed; the two churches were stripped, and the lead was shipped to be sold in Holland. I hope every reader will rejoice that this cargo of sacrilege was lost at sea.[4]

Let us not however make too much haste to despise our neighbours. Our own cathedrals are mouldering by unregarded dilapidation. It seems to be part of the despicable philosophy of the time to despise monuments of sacred magnificence, and we are in danger of doing that deliberately, which the Scots did not do but in the unsettled state of an imperfect constitution.[5]

Those who had once uncovered the cathedrals never wished to cover them again; and being thus made useless, they were first neglected, and perhaps, as the stone was wanted, afterwards demolished.

Elgin seems a place of little trade, and thinly inhabited. The episcopal cities of Scotland, I believe, generally fell with their churches, though some of them have since recovered by a situation convenient for commerce. Thus Glasgow, though it has no longer an archbishop, has risen beyond its original state by the opulence of its traders; and Aberdeen, though its ancient stock had decayed, flourishes by a new shoot in another place.

In the chief street of Elgin, the houses jut over the lowest story, like the old buildings of timber in London, but with greater prominence; so that there is sometimes a walk for a

---

4. Several of Johnson's contemporaries found this sentence ludicrous. Horace Walpole misquotes it as an instance of his ponderous style: "He hopes nobody but is glad that a boatful of sacrilege, a diverting sin! was shipwrecked" (to Lady Ossory, 19 January 1775, *Correspondence*, ed. W. S. Lewis, New Haven, XXXII.225). Gibbon alludes to it as an instance of bigotry: "The vessel which transported the relics of the Capitol was the only one of the whole fleet that suffered shipwreck. If a bigoted sophist, a Pagan bigot, had mentioned the accident, he

might have rejoiced that this cargo of sacrilege was lost in the sea" (*Decline and Fall*, ed. Bury (1898), IV.6. n. 12; noticed by T. E. Swanzy, letter to *TLS*, 12 July 1934). A letter to the *Middlesex Journal*, discovered by Miss Helen McGuffie, ridicules this passage, besides betraying knowledge of the cancel that follows. See Appendix I.

5. This general censure was substituted by Johnson for a particular, and far more severe, indictment. See illustration and the discussion of cancels, pp. xxxiv–xxxvi.

away, and converted into money for the
fupport of the army. A Scotch army was
in thofe times very cheaply kept ; yet the
lead of two churches muft have born fo
fmall a proportion to any military expence,
that it is hard not to believe the reafon
alleged to be merely popular, and the
money intended for fome private purfe.
The order however was obeyed ; the two
churches were ftripped, and the lead was
fhipped to be fold in Holland. I hope
every reader will rejoice that this cargo of
facrilege was loft at fea.

Let us not however make too much hafte
to defpife our neighbours. There is now,
as I have heard, a body of men, not lefs
decent or virtuous than the Scotifh council,
longing to melt the lead of an Englifh cathedral. What they fhall melt, it were
juft that they fhould fwallow.

*This Leaf was cancelled by
the Author & is rectioned curious on
account of this last Paragraph.
Lichfield is the Cathedral alluded to.*   Thofe

The cancelled text of leaf D8. By kind permission of Mrs. Donald F. Hyde.

considerable length under a cloister, or portico, which is now indeed frequently broken, because the new houses have another form, but seems to have been uniformly continued in the old city.

FORES. CALDER. FORT GEORGE

We went forwards the same day to Fores, the town to which Macbeth was travelling, when he met the weird sisters in his way. This to an Englishman is classic ground. Our imaginations were heated, and our thoughts recalled to their old amusements.

We had now a prelude to the Highlands. We began to leave fertility and culture behind us, and saw for a great length of road nothing but heath; yet at Fochabars, a seat belonging to the Duke of Gordon, there is an orchard, which in Scotland I had never seen before, with some timber trees, and a plantation of oaks.

At Fores we found good accommodation, but nothing worthy of particular remark, and next morning entered upon the road, on which Macbeth heard the fatal prediction; but we travelled on not interrupted by promises of kingdoms, and came to Nairn, a royal burgh, which, if once it flourished, is now in a state of miserable decay; but I know not whether its chief annual magistrate has not still the title of Lord Provost.

At Nairn we may fix the verge of the Highlands; for here I first saw peat fires, and first heard the Erse language.[6] We had no motive to stay longer than to breakfast, and went forward to the house of Mr. Macaulay, the minister who published an ac-

---

6. Johnson's adversaries were prone to regard his use of *Erse*, or *Earse*, for the Gaelic of Scotland as a deliberate affront. In the eighteenth century, however, this usage was by no means confined to English or Lowland writers. Martin confuses the issue by calling the language of the Western Isles *Irish* (*Description*, p. 336); but John Campbell (among others) says of the Highlanders, "Their language is called Earse" (*A Full and Particular Descrip-* tion of the Highlands of Scotland, 1752, p. 8). M'Nicol's charge that it "is only a barbarous term introduced by strangers" is therefore groundless; see Donald M'Nicol, *Remarks on Dr. Samuel Johnson's Journey to the Hebrides* (1779), p. 260. For Johnson's distinction between *Earse* and *Irish*, see pp. 117–18. It might here be noted that either Johnson or his printer vacillated, using *Erse* in the first part of the *Journey*, *Earse* in the second.

count of St. Kilda,[7] and by his direction visited Calder Castle, from which Macbeth drew his second title. It has been formerly a place of strength. The draw-bridge is still to be seen, but the moat is now dry. The tower is very ancient: Its walls are of great thickness, arched on the top with stone, and surrounded with battlements.[8] The rest of the house is later, though far from modern.

We were favoured by a gentleman,[9] who lives in the castle, with a letter to one of the officers[1] at Fort George, which being the most regular fortification in the island, well deserves the notice of a traveller, who has never travelled before. We went thither next day, found a very kind reception, were led round the works by a gentleman, who explained the use of every part, and entertained by Sir Eyre Coote, the governour,[2] with such elegance of conversation as left us no attention to the delicacies of his table.

Of Fort George I shall not attempt to give any account. I cannot delineate it scientifically, and a loose and popular description is of use only when the imagination is to be amused. There was every where an appearance of the utmost neatness and regularity. But my suffrage is of little value, because this and Fort Augustus are the only garrisons that I ever saw.

We did not regret the time spent at the fort, though in consequence of our delay we came somewhat late to Inverness, the town which may properly be called the capital of the Highlands. Hither the inhabitants of the inland parts come to be supplied with what they cannot make for themselves: Hither

---

7. Kenneth Macaulay, *The History of St. Kilda* (1764). Boswell records the growth of doubt in Johnson's mind as to the authorship of a work which he had known before this meeting; see *Life*, v.119. Dr. Powell, however, has examined the evidence conclusively and shown that, while the book as published was the joint work of Macaulay and his friend John Macpherson, minister of Sleat, the more interesting and valuable part, the topographical account on which Johnson complimented Macaulay, was indeed his. See L. F. Powell, "The History of St. Kilda," *RES*, XVI (January 1940),

44–53.

8. RWC suggested that this should read: surmounted with battlements; but compare p. 154, ll. 28–29: "encompassed by battlements."

9. Valentine White, factor of the Cawdor estate. See *Life*, v.122 and 509.

1. George Ferne, Master of the Stores. See *Life*, v.123.

2. "Sir Eyre Coote is not *Governour* of Ft. George. He commanded, because his Regt. then lay there" (Boswell, *Remarks*). Sir Eyre Coote (1726–83) is memorable chiefly for his service in India.

the young nymphs of the mountains and valleys are sent for education, and as far as my observation has reached, are not sent in vain.

INVERNESS

Inverness was the last place which had a regular communication by high roads with the southern counties. All the ways beyond it have, I believe, been made by the soldiers in this century. At Inverness therefore Cromwell, when he subdued Scotland, stationed a garrison, as at the boundary of the Highlands. The soldiers seem to have incorporated afterwards with the inhabitants, and to have peopled the place with an English race; for the language of this town has been long considered as peculiarly elegant.[3]

Here is a castle, called the castle of Macbeth,[4] the walls of which are yet standing. It was no very capacious edifice, but stands upon a rock so high and steep, that I think it was once not accessible, but by the help of ladders, or a bridge. Over against it, on another hill, was a fort built by Cromwell, now totally demolished; for no faction of Scotland loved the name of Cromwell, or had any desire to continue his memory.

Yet what the Romans did to other nations, was in a great degree done by Cromwell to the Scots; he civilized them by conquests, and introduced by useful violence the arts of peace. I was told at Aberdeen that the people learned from Cromwell's soldiers to make shoes and to plant kail.[5]

---

3. Johnson may have been prepared to expect this command of English idiom among the people of Inverness by Defoe, who attributes it to the settlement of Cromwell's soldiers in the neighbourhood. See *Tour thro' the whole Island of Great Britain*, 1762, IV.225. (For the probability that this was the edition known to Johnson, see p. 29 n. 8 below.) The argument is weakened by Johnson's subsequent observation: "Those Highlanders that can speak English, commonly speak it well ..." (p. 36).

4. Boswell and Johnson confused the Castle of Inverness, of which the ruins remained, with Macbeth's castle, which had been razed to the ground. See *Life*, V.511.

5. "One of the professors told us, as we were mentioning a fort built by Cromwel, that the country owed much of its present industry to Cromwel's soldiers. They taught us said he, to raise cabbage, and make shoes" (*Letters* 321). Defoe had credited Cromwell's soldiers with good husbandry (*Tour*, 1762, IV.225).

How they lived without kail, it is not easy to guess: They cultivate hardly any other plant for common tables, and when they had not kail they probably had nothing. The numbers that go barefoot are still sufficient to shew that shoes may be spared: They are not yet considered as necessaries of life; for tall boys, not otherwise meanly dressed, run without them in the streets; and in the islands the[h] sons of gentlemen pass several of their first years with naked feet.

I know not whether it be not peculiar to the Scots to have attained the liberal, without the manual arts, to have excelled in ornamental knowledge, and to have wanted not only the elegancies, but the conveniencies of common life. Literature soon after its revival found its way to Scotland, and from the middle of the sixteenth century, almost to the middle of the seventeenth, the politer studies were very diligently pursued. The Latin poetry of *Deliciae Poëtarum Scotorum*[6] would have done honour to any nation, at least till the publication of May's *Supplement*[7] the English had very little to oppose.

Yet men thus ingenious and inquisitive were content to live in total ignorance of the trades by which human wants are supplied, and to supply them by the grossest means. Till the Union made them acquainted with English manners, the culture of their lands was unskillful, and their domestick life unformed; their tables were coarse as the feasts of Eskimeaux, and their houses filthy as the cottages of Hottentots.

Since they have known that their condition was capable of improvement, their progress in useful knowledge has been rapid and uniform. What remains to be done they will quickly do, and then wonder, like me, why that which was so necessary and so easy was so long delayed. But they must be for ever content to owe to the English that elegance and culture, which, if they had been vigilant and active, perhaps the English might have owed to them.

h. the streets; and in the islands the *87; RWC*] the streets and in the islands; the *75a, b; 85*

---

6. *Delitiae Poetarum Scotorum hujus aevi Illustrium* (Amsterdam, 1637), collected by Arthur Johnston.
7. Thomas May, the translator of Lucan, continued his narrative in Latin to the death of Julius Caesar:

Supplementum Lucani Libri Septem (Leyden, 1640). For Johnson's high opinion of May's Latin verse, see his "Life of Cowley," *Lives,* 1.13 (par. 34); cf. *Idler* 69.

Here the appearance of life began to alter. I had seen a few women with plaids at Aberdeen; but at Inverness the Highland manners are common. There is I think a kirk, in which only the Erse language is used.[8] There is likewise an English chapel,[9] but meanly built, where on Sunday we saw a very decent congregation.

We were now to bid farewel to the luxury of travelling, and to enter a country upon which perhaps no wheel has ever rolled. We could indeed have used our post-chaise one day longer, along the military road to Fort Augustus, but we could have hired no horses beyond Inverness, and we were not so sparing of ourselves, as to lead them, merely that we might have one day longer the indulgence of a carriage.

At Inverness therefore we procured three horses for ourselves and a servant,[1] and one more for our baggage, which was no very heavy load. We found in the course of our journey the convenience of having disencumbered ourselves, by laying aside whatever we could spare; for it is not to be imagined without experience, how in climbing crags, and treading bogs, and winding through narrow and obstructed passages, a little bulk will hinder, and a little weight will burthen; or how often a man that has pleased himself at home with his own resolution, will, in the hour of darkness and fatigue, be content to leave behind him every thing but himself.

LOUGH NESS

We took two Highlanders to run beside us, partly to shew us the way, and partly to take back from the sea-side the horses, of which they were the owners. One of them was a man of great liveliness and activity, of whom his companion said, that he would tire any horse in Inverness. Both of them were civil and ready-handed. Civility seems part of the national character of Highlanders. Every chieftain is a monarch, and politeness, the

---

8. St. Mary's, in Church Street. Johnson's "There is I think a kirk ..." may reflect his familiarity with the 1762 edition of Defoe's *Tour* and his failure to verify the expectation he had formed from it. According to the 1762 continuator: "Near the extreme part of the town, towards the north, are two churches, one for the English, the other for the Irish Tongue" (IV.228).

9. A room in a house; one of the places of worship used by the Episcopalians in Inverness. (See *Journal*, pp. 461–62.)

1. Boswell's servant, Joseph Ritter.

natural product of royal government, is diffused from the laird through the whole clan. But they are not commonly dexterous: their narrowness of life confines them to a few operations, and they are accustomed to endure little wants more than to remove them. We mounted our steeds on the thirtieth[2] of August, and directed our guides to conduct us to Fort Augustus. It is built at the head of Lough Ness, of which Inverness stands at the outlet. The way between them has been cut by the soldiers, and the greater part of it runs along a rock, levelled with great labour and exactness, near the water-side.

Most of this day's journey was very pleasant. The day, though bright, was not hot; and the appearance of the country, if I had not seen the Peak, would have been wholly new. We went upon a surface so hard and level, that we had little care to hold the bridle, and were therefore at full leisure for contemplation. On the left were high and steep rocks shaded with birch, the hardy native of the North, and covered with fern or heath. On the right the limpid waters of Lough Ness were beating their bank, and waving their surface by a gentle agitation. Beyond them were rocks sometimes covered with verdure, and sometimes towering in horrid nakedness. Now and then we espied a little corn-field, which served to impress more strongly the general barrenness.

Lough Ness is about twenty-four miles long, and from one mile to two miles broad. It is remarkable that Boethius, in his description of Scotland, gives it twelve miles of breadth. When historians or geographers exhibit false accounts of places far distant, they may be forgiven, because they can tell but what they are told; and that their accounts exceed the truth may be justly supposed, because most men exaggerate to others, if not to themselves: but Boethius lived at no great distance; if he

2. thirtieth RWC (1930)] thirteenth 75a, b; 85; 87. "For thirteenth r. thirtieth" (Boswell, Remarks). Among early editions, that of 1800 alone reads thirtieth, and its general character favours the supposition that the variant may be not a correction but a misprint. That of 1792 alters the date arbitrarily to twenty-eighth, thereby laying a fresh trail of error. See Courtney, pp. 124 and 164–65. It is impossible that Johnson should have intended to write thirteenth, and unlikely that he wrote it. He had given "Aug. 30" as the date of departure from Inverness in Letters 323—one of those letters to Mrs. Thrale of which he made use in writing his narrative.

never saw the lake, he must have been very incurious, and if he had seen it, his veracity yielded to very slight temptations.

Lough Ness, though not twelve miles broad, is a very remarkable diffusion of water without islands. It fills a large hollow between two ridges of high rocks, being supplied partly by the torrents which fall into it on either side, and partly, as is supposed, by springs at the bottom. Its water is remarkably clear and pleasant, and is imagined by the natives to be medicinal. We were told, that it is in some places a hundred and forty fathom deep, a profundity scarcely credible, and which probably those that relate it have never sounded. Its fish are salmon, trout, and pike.

It was said at Fort Augustus, that Lough Ness is open in the hardest winters, though a lake not far from it is covered with ice. In discussing these exceptions from the course of nature, the first question is, whether the fact be justly stated. That which is strange is delightful, and a pleasing error is not willingly detected. Accuracy of narration is not very common, and there are few so rigidly philosophical, as not to represent as perpetual, what is only frequent, or as constant, what is really casual. If it be true that Lough Ness never freezes, it is either sheltered by its high banks from the cold blasts, and exposed only to those winds which have more power to agitate than congeal; or it is kept in perpetual motion by the rush of streams from the rocks that inclose it. Its profundity though it should be such as is represented can have little part in this exemption; for though deep wells are not frozen, because their water is secluded from the external air, yet where a wide surface is exposed to the full influence of a freezing atmosphere, I know not why the depth should keep it open. Natural philosophy is now one of the favourite studies of the Scottish nation, and Lough Ness well deserves to be diligently examined.

The road on which we travelled, and which was itself a source of entertainment, is made along the rock, in the direction of the lough, sometimes by breaking off protuberances, and sometimes by cutting the great mass of stone to a considerable depth. The fragments are piled in a loose wall on either side, with apertures left at very short spaces, to give a passage to the wintry currents. Part of it is bordered with low trees, from which our guides gathered nuts, and would have had the appearance of an English lane, except that an English lane is almost always dirty. It has been made with great labour, but has this advantage, that it cannot, without equal labour, be broken up.

Within our sight there were goats feeding or playing. The mountains have red deer, but they came not within view; and if what is said of their vigilance and subtlety be true, they have some claim to that palm of wisdom, which the eastern philosopher, whom Alexander interrogated, gave to those beasts which live furthest from men.[3]

Near the way, by the water side, we espied a cottage. This was the first Highland hut that I had seen; and as our business was with life and manners, we were willing to visit it. To enter a habitation without leave, seems to be not considered here as rudeness or intrusion. The old laws of hospitality still give this licence to a stranger.

A hut is constructed with loose stones, ranged for the most part with some tendency to circularity. It must be placed where the wind cannot act upon it with violence, because it has no cement; and where the water will run easily away, because it has no floor but the naked ground. The wall, which is commonly about six feet high, declines from the perpendicular a little inward. Such rafters as can be procured are then raised for a roof, and covered with heath, which makes a strong and warm thatch, kept from flying off by ropes of twisted heath, of which the ends, reaching from the center of the thatch to the top of the wall, are held firm by the weight of a large stone. No light is admitted but at the entrance, and through a hole in the thatch, which gives vent to the smoke. This hole is not directly over the fire, lest the rain should extinguish it; and the smoke therefore naturally fills the place before it escapes. Such is the general structure of the houses in which one of the nations of this opulent and powerful island has been hitherto content to live. Huts however are not more uniform than palaces; and this which we were inspecting was very far from one of the meanest, for it was divided into several apartments; and its inhabitants possessed such property as a pastoral poet might exalt into riches.

---

3. Plutarch's *Life of Alexander*: the answer of the third of the Wise Men of India.

When we entered, we found an old woman boiling goats-
flesh in a kettle. She spoke little English, but we had interpreters at hand; and she was willing enough to display her
whole system of economy. She has five children, of which none
are yet gone from her. The eldest, a boy of thirteen, and her
husband, who is eighty years old, were at work in the wood.
Her two next sons were gone to Inverness to buy "meal," by
which oatmeal is always meant. Meal she considered as expensive food, and told us, that in spring, when the goats gave milk,
the children could live without it. She is mistress of sixty goats,
and I saw many kids in an enclosure at the end of her house.
She had also some poultry. By the lake we saw a potatoe-garden,
and a small spot of ground on which stood four shucks,[4] containing each twelve sheaves of barley. She has all this from the
labour of their own hands, and for what is necessary to be
bought, her kids and her chickens are sent to market.

With the true pastoral hospitality, she asked us to sit down
and drink whisky. She is religious, and though the kirk is four
miles off, probably eight English miles, she goes thither every
Sunday. We gave her a shilling, and she begged snuff; for
snuff is the luxury of a Highland cottage.

Soon afterwards we came to the General's Hut, so called because it was the temporary abode of Wade,[5] while he superintended the works upon the road. It is now a house of entertainment for passengers, and we found it not ill stocked with
provisions.

FALL OF FIERS

Towards evening we crossed, by a bridge, the river which
makes the celebrated fall of Fiers. The country at the bridge
strikes the imagination with all the gloom and grandeur of
Siberian solitude. The way makes a flexure, and the mountains, covered with trees, rise at once on the left hand and in
the front. We desired our guides to shew us the fall, and dis-
mounting, clambered over very rugged crags, till I began to

---

4. Dialect form of *shock*; assigned
to Midland counties by Wright (*Dialect Dictionary*). This is one of the
country words Johnson allows himself
in the *Journey*, but not in the *Dictionary*.

5. George Wade (1673–1748), Field
Marshal, memorable as a builder of
roads, bridges and forts in the Highlands between 1726 and 1737—though
some of these forts were, as Johnson
recalled (p. 34), weakly held in the '45.

wish that our curiosity might have been gratified with less trouble and danger. We came at last to a place where we could overlook the river, and saw a channel torn, as it seems, through black piles of stone, by which the stream is obstructed and broken, till it comes to a very steep descent, of such dreadful depth, that we were naturally inclined to turn aside our eyes.

But we visited the place at an unseasonable time, and found it divested of its dignity and terror. Nature never gives every thing at once. A long continuance of dry weather, which made the rest of the way easy and delightful, deprived us of the pleasure expected from the fall of Fiers. The river having now no water but what the springs supply, showed us only a swift current, clear and shallow, fretting over the asperities of the rocky bottom, and we were left to exercise our thoughts, by endeavouring to conceive the effect of a thousand streams poured from the mountains into one channel, struggling for expansion in a narrow passage, exasperated by rocks rising in their way, and at last discharging all their violence of waters by a sudden fall through the horrid chasm.

The way now grew less easy, descending by an uneven declivity, but without either dirt or danger. We did not arrive at Fort Augustus till it was late. Mr. Boswell, who, between his father's merit and his own, is sure of reception wherever he comes, sent a servant before to beg admission and entertainment for that night. Mr. Trapaud,[6] the governor, treated us with that courtesy which is so closely connected with the military character. He came out to meet us beyond the gates, and apologized that, at so late an hour, the rules of a garrison suffered him to give us entrance only at the postern.

FORT AUGUSTUS

In the morning we viewed the fort, which is much less than that of St. George,[7] and is said to be commanded by the neighbouring hills. It was not long ago taken by the Highlanders. But its situation seems well chosen for pleasure, if not for

---

6. Alexander Trapaud, resident governor of Fort Augustus. See *Life*, v.512.

7. Boswell, in his *Remarks*, objects that "St." should be deleted, the fort having been named after George II. Johnson called it Fort George on p. 26. See also *Letters* 323. He may have written *Ft.* George.

strength; it stands at the head of the lake, and, by a sloop of sixty tuns, is supplied from Inverness with great convenience.

We were now to cross the Highlands towards the western coast, and to content ourselves with such accommodations, as a way so little frequented could afford. The journey was not formidable, for it was but of two days, very unequally divided, because the only house, where we could be entertained, was not further off than a third of the way. We soon came to a high hill, which we mounted by a military road, cut in traverses, so that as we went upon a higher stage, we saw the baggage following us below in a contrary direction. To make this way, the rock has been hewn to a level with labour that might have broken the perseverance of a Roman legion.

The country is totally denuded of its wood, but the stumps both of oaks and firs, which are still found, shew that it has been once a forest of large timber. I do not remember that we saw any animals, but we were told that, in the mountains, there are stags, roebucks, goats and rabbits.

We did not perceive that this tract was possessed by human beings, except that once we saw a corn field, in which a lady was walking with some gentlemen. Their house was certainly at no great distance, but so situated that we could not descry it.

Passing on through the dreariness of solitude, we found a party of soldiers from the fort, working on the road, under the superintendence of a serjeant. We told them how kindly we had been treated at the garrison, and as we were enjoying the benefit of their labours, begged leave to shew our gratitude by a small present.

ANOCH

Early in the afternoon we came to Anoch, a village in Glenmollison of three huts, one of which is distinguished by a chimney. Here we were to dine and lodge, and were conducted through the first room, that had the chimney, into another lighted by a small glass window. The landlord[8] attended us

8. ——— Macqueen, shrewdly characterized by Carruthers as a clever and prepossessing man whose inn, advantageously situated on the main drove road from the west, ensured his prosperity. He did not emigrate. See Carruthers, p. 102.

with great civility, and told us what he could give us to eat and drink. I found some books on a shelf, among which were a volume or more of Prideaux's *Connection*.[9]

This I mentioned as something unexpected, and perceived that I did not please him: I praised the propriety of his language, and was answered that I need not wonder, for he had learned it by grammar.[1]

By subsequent opportunities of observation, I found that my host's diction had nothing peculiar. Those Highlanders that can speak English, commonly speak it well, with few of the words, and little of the tone by which a Scotchman is distinguished. Their language seems to have been learned in the army or the navy, or by some communication with those who could give them good examples of accent and pronunciation. By their Lowland neighbours they would not willingly be taught; for they have long considered them as a mean and degenerate race. These prejudices are wearing fast away; but so much of them still remains, that when I asked a very learned minister[2] in the islands, which they considered as their most savage clans: "Those," said he, "that live next the Lowlands."

As we came hither early in the day, we had time sufficient to survey the place. The house was built like other huts of loose stones, but the part in which we dined and slept was lined with turf and wattled with twigs, which kept the earth from falling. Near it was a garden of turnips and a field of potatoes. It stands in a glen, or valley, pleasantly watered by a winding river. But this country, however it may delight the gazer or amuse the naturalist, is of no great advantage to its owners. Our landlord told us of a gentleman,[3] who possesses lands, eighteen Scotch miles in length, and three in breadth; a space containing at least a hundred square English miles. He has raised his rents, to the danger of depopulating his farms, and he sells his timber, and by exerting every art of augmentation, has obtained

---

9. Humphrey Prideaux (1648–1724), *The Old and New Testament Connected in the History of the Jews and Neighbouring Nations* (1716–18).

1. *Sc.* by Latin grammar.

2. Evidently Donald Macqueen. See p. 58 n. 8.

3. Peter Grant of Glenmoriston. See *Journal*, p. 104, n. 3. Carruthers vindicates the Laird's reputation from the charges brought by Macqueen and repeated by Boswell and Johnson (pp. 102–03).

an yearly revenue of four hundred pounds, which for a hundred square miles is three halfpence an acre.

Some time after dinner we were surprised by the entrance of a young woman, not inelegant either in mien or dress, who asked us whether we would have tea. We found that she was the daughter of our host, and desired her to make it. Her conversation, like her appearance, was gentle and pleasing. We knew that the girls of the Highlands are all gentlewomen, and treated her with great respect, which she received as customary and due, and was neither elated by it, nor confused, but repaid my civilities without embarassment, and told me how much I honoured her country by coming to survey it.

She had been at Inverness to gain the common female qualifications, and had, like her father, the English pronunciation. I presented her with a book,[4] which I happened to have about me, and should not be pleased to think that she forgets me.

In the evening the soldiers, whom we had passed on the road, came to spend at our inn the little money that we had given them. They had the true military impatience of coin in their pockets, and had marched at least six miles to find the first place where liquor could be bought. Having never been before in a place so wild and unfrequented, I was glad of their arrival, because I knew that we had made them friends, and to gain still more of their good will, we went to them, where they were carousing in the barn, and added something to our former gift. All that we gave was not much, but it detained them in the barn, either merry or quarrelling, the whole night, and in the morning they went back to their work, with great indignation at the bad qualities of whisky.

We had gained so much the favour of our host, that, when we left his house in the morning, he walked by us a great way, and entertained us with conversation both on his own condition, and that of the country. His life seemed to be merely pastoral, except that he differed from some of the ancient Nomades in having a settled dwelling. His wealth consists of one hundred sheep, as many goats, twelve milk-cows, and twenty-eight beeves ready for the drover.

---

4. Cocker's *Arithmetic* (1678). See *Letters* 323. "The book was long kept with care, but is now lost" (Carruthers, p. 104).

From him we first heard of the general dissatisfaction, which is now driving the Highlanders into the other hemisphere;[5] and when I asked him whether they would stay at home, if they were well treated, he answered with indignation, that no man willingly left his native country. Of the farm, which he himself occupied, the rent had, in twenty-five years, been advanced from five to twenty pounds, which he found himself so little able to pay, that he would be glad to try his fortune in some other place. Yet he owned the reasonableness of raising the Highland rents in a certain degree, and declared himself willing to pay ten pounds for the ground which he had formerly had for five.

Our host having amused us for a time, resigned us to our guides. The journey of this day was long, not that the distance was great, but that the way was difficult. We were now in the bosom of the Highlands, with full leisure to contemplate the appearance and properties of mountainous regions, such as have been, in many countries, the last shelters of national distress, and are every where the scenes of adventures, stratagems, surprises and escapes.

Mountainous countries are not passed but with difficulty, not merely from the labour of climbing; for to climb is not always necessary: but because that which is not mountain is commonly bog, through which the way must be picked with caution. Where there are hills, there is much rain, and the torrents pouring down into the intermediate spaces, seldom find so ready an outlet, as not to stagnate, till they have broken the texture of the ground.

Of the hills, which our journey offered to the view on either side, we did not take the height, nor did we see any that astonished us with their loftiness. Towards the summit of one, there was a white spot, which I should have called a naked rock, but the guides, who had better eyes, and were acquainted with the phaenomena of the country, declared it to be snow. It had already lasted to the end of August, and was likely to maintain its contest with the sun, till it should be reinforced by winter.

The height of mountains philosophically considered is properly computed from the surface of the next sea; but as it affects

---

5. But Boswell calls it "a common topick of discourse" while Johnson was with him in Edinburgh (*Life*, v.27). By "first heard" Johnson presumably intended "heard at first-hand."

the eye or imagination of the passenger, as it makes either a spectacle or an obstruction, it must be reckoned from the place where the rise begins to make a considerable angle with the plain. In extensive continents the land may, by gradual elevation, attain great height, without any other appearance than that of a plane gently inclined, and if a hill placed upon such raised ground be described, as having its altitude equal to the whole space above the sea, the representation will be fallacious.

These mountains may be properly enough measured from the inland base; for it is not much above the sea. As we advanced at evening towards the western coast, I did not observe the declivity to be greater than is necessary for the discharge of the inland waters.

We passed many rivers and rivulets, which commonly ran with a clear shallow stream over a hard pebbly bottom. These channels, which seem so much wider than the water that they convey would naturally require, are formed by the violence of wintry floods, produced by the accumulation of innumerable streams that fall in rainy weather from the hills, and bursting away with resistless impetuosity, make themselves a passage proportionate to their mass.

Such capricious and temporary waters cannot be expected to produce many fish. The rapidity of the wintry deluge sweeps them away, and the scantiness of the summer stream would hardly sustain them above the ground. This is the reason why in fording the northern rivers, no fishes are seen, as in England, wandering in the water.

Of the hills many may be called with Homer's Ida "abundant in springs," but few can deserve the epithet which he bestows upon Pelion by "waving their leaves."[5a] They exhibit very little variety; being almost wholly covered with dark heath, and even that seems to be checked in its growth. What is not heath is nakedness, a little diversified by now and then a stream rushing down the steep. An eye accustomed to flowery pastures and waving harvests is astonished and repelled by this wide extent of hopeless sterility. The appearance is that of matter incapable of form or usefulness, dismissed by nature from her care and disinherited of her favours, left in its original ele-

---

5a. Ida "abundant in springs," *Iliad* XXIII.117. Pelion "waving their leaves," *Ibid.* II.757.

mental state, or quickened only with one sullen power of useless vegetation.

It will very readily occur, that this uniformity of barrenness can afford very little amusement to the traveller; that it is easy to sit at home and conceive rocks and heath, and waterfalls; and that these journeys are useless labours, which neither impregnate the imagination, nor enlarge the understanding. It is true that of far the greater part of things, we must content ourselves with such knowledge as description may exhibit, or analogy supply; but it is true likewise, that these ideas are always incomplete, and that at least, till we have compared them with realities, we do not know them to be just. As we see more, we become possessed of more certainties, and consequently gain more principles of reasoning, and found a wider basis of analogy.

Regions mountainous and wild, thinly inhabited, and little cultivated, make a great part of the earth, and he that has never seen them, must live unacquainted with much of the face of nature, and with one of the great scenes of human existence.

As the day advanced towards noon, we entered a narrow valley not very flowery, but sufficiently verdant. Our guides told us, that the horses could not travel all day without rest or meat, and intreated us to stop here, because no grass would be found in any other place. The request was reasonable and the argument cogent. We therefore willingly dismounted and diverted ourselves as the place gave us opportunity.

I sat down on a bank, such as a writer of romance might have delighted to feign. I had indeed no trees to whisper over my head, but a clear rivulet streamed at my feet. The day was calm, the air soft, and all was rudeness, silence, and solitude. Before me, and on either side, were high hills, which by hindering the eye from ranging, forced the mind to find entertainment for itself. Whether I spent the hour well I know not; for here I first conceived the thought of this narration.[6]

We were in this place at ease and by choice, and had no evils to suffer or to fear; yet the imaginations excited by the view of

---

6. The spot where the travellers rested and Johnson formed his resolution has been indicated by Dr. Powell and more precisely established by Dr. J. D. Fleeman on "the old military road . . . just east of the small Loch Lundie, which is about half-way along the northern side of Loch Cluanie."

an unknown and untravelled wilderness are not such as arise
in the artificial solitude of parks and gardens, a flattering notion of self-sufficiency, a placid indulgence of voluntary delu-
sions, a secure expansion of the fancy, or a cool concentration
of the mental powers. The phantoms which haunt a desert are
want, and misery, and danger; the evils of dereliction rush
upon the thoughts; man is made unwillingly acquainted with
his own weakness, and meditation shews him only how little
he can sustain, and how little he can perform. There were
no traces of inhabitants, except perhaps a rude pile of clods
called a summer hut, in which a herdsman had rested in the
favourable seasons. Whoever had been in the place where I
then sat, unprovided with provisions and ignorant of the country, might, at least before the roads were made, have wandered
among the rocks, till he had perished with hardship, before he
could have found either food or shelter. Yet what are these
hillocks to the ridges of Taurus, or these spots of wildness to the
desarts of America?

It was not long before we were invited to mount, and continued our journey along the side of a lough, kept full by many
streams, which with more or less rapidity and noise, crossed the
road from the hills on the other hand. These currents, in their
diminished state, after several dry months, afford, to one who
has always lived in level countries, an unusual and delightful
spectacle; but in the rainy season, such as every winter may be
expected to bring, must precipitate an impetuous and tremendous flood. I suppose the way by which we went, is at that time
impassable.

GLENSHEALS

The lough at last ended in a river broad and shallow like the
rest, but that it may be passed when it is deeper, there is a

---

See his letter to *TLS*, 29 September
1961; and (for fuller circumstance) his
article in *The Scots Magazine*, November 1961. See also further suggestions
by the editors of Boswell's *Journal*, pp.
464–66.

Johnson told Mrs. Thrale: "I sat
down to take notes" (*Letters* 326), and
(later) "I keep a book of remarks"
(*Ibid.*, 329). This has not been found,
but Boswell's reference, in his *Remarks*, to "the grand Night-piece preserved" shows that it contained de-
scriptive passages of some fulness.

bridge over it. Beyond it is a valley called Glensheals, inhabited by the clan of Macrae. Here we found a village called Aukna-sheals, consisting of many huts, perhaps twenty, built all of "dry-stone," that is, stones piled up without mortar.

We had, by the direction of the officers at Fort Augustus, taken bread for ourselves, and tobacco for those Highlanders who might show us any kindness. We were now at a place where we could obtain milk, but must have wanted bread if we had not brought it. The people of this valley did not appear to know any English, and our guides now became doubly necessary as interpreters. A woman, whose hut was distinguished by greater spaciousness and better architecture, brought out some pails of milk. The villagers gathered about us in considerable numbers, I believe without any evil intention, but with a very savage wildness of aspect and manner. When our meal was over, Mr. Boswell sliced the bread, and divided it amongst them, as he supposed them never to have tasted a wheaten loaf before. He then gave them little pieces of twisted tobacco, and among the children we distributed a small handful of half-pence, which they received with great eagerness. Yet I have been since told, that the people of that valley are not indigent; and when we mentioned them afterwards as needy and pitiable, a Highland lady let us know, that we might spare our commiseration; for the dame whose milk we drank had probably more than a dozen milk-cows. She seemed unwilling to take any price, but being pressed to make a demand, at last named a shilling. Honesty is not greater where elegance is less. One of the by-standers, as we were told afterwards, advised her to ask more, but she said a shilling was enough. We gave her half a crown, and I hope got some credit by our behaviour; for the company said, if our interpreters did not flatter us, that they had not seen such a day since the old laird of Macleod passed through their country.

The Macraes, as we heard afterwards in the Hebrides, were originally an indigent and subordinate clan, and having no farms nor stock, were in great numbers servants to the Maclellans, who, in the war of Charles the First, took arms at the call of the heroic Montrose, and were, in one of his battles, almost all destroyed. The women that were left at home, being thus deprived of their husbands, like the Scythian ladies[7] of old, married their servants, and the Macraes became a considerable race.

THE HIGHLANDS

As we continued our journey, we were at leisure to extend our speculations, and to investigate the reason of those peculiarities by which such rugged regions as these before us are generally distinguished.

Mountainous countries commonly contain the original, at least the oldest race of inhabitants, for they are not easily conquered, because they must be entered by narrow ways, exposed to every power of mischief from those that occupy the heights; and every new ridge is a new fortress, where the defendants have again the same advantages. If the assailants either force the strait, or storm the summit, they gain only so much ground; their enemies are fled to take possession of the next rock, and the pursuers stand at gaze, knowing neither where the ways of escape wind among the steeps, nor where the bog has firmness to sustain them: besides that, mountaineers have an agility in climbing and descending distinct from strength or courage, and attainable only by use.

If the war be not soon concluded, the invaders are dislodged by hunger; for in those anxious and toilsome marches, provisions cannot easily be carried, and are never to be found. The wealth of mountains is cattle, which, while the men stand in the passes, the women drive away. Such lands at last cannot repay the expence of conquest, and therefore perhaps have not been so often invaded by the mere ambition of dominion; as by resentment of robberies and insults, or the desire of enjoying in security the more fruitful provinces.

As mountains are long before they are conquered, they are likewise long before they are civilized. Men are softened by

7. Herodotus, *History*, IV.ii. Johnson had used this episode metaphorically in *Rambler* 156: "Criticism . . . like the antient Scythians, by extend-ing her conquests over distant regions, . . . has left her throne vacant to her slaves." Cf. also *Taxation No Tyranny* (*Works*, VI.254).

intercourse mutually profitable, and instructed by comparing their own notions with those of others. Thus Caesar found the maritime parts of Britain made less barbarous by their commerce with the Gauls. Into a barren and rough tract no stranger is brought either by the hope of gain or of pleasure. The inhabitants having neither commodities for sale, nor money for purchase, seldom visit more polished places, or if they do visit them, seldom return.

It sometimes happens that by conquest, intermixture, or gradual refinement, the cultivated parts of a country change their language. The mountaineers then become a distinct nation, cut off by dissimilitude of speech from conversation with their neighbours. Thus in Biscay, the original Cantabrian, and in Dalecarlia,[8] the old Swedish still subsists. Thus Wales and the Highlands speak the tongue of the first inhabitants of Britain, while the other parts have received first the Saxon, and in some degree afterwards the French, and then formed a third language between them.

That the primitive manners are continued where the primitive language is spoken, no nation will desire me to suppose, for the manners of mountaineers are commonly savage, but they are rather produced by their situation than derived from their ancestors.

Such seems to be the disposition of man, that whatever makes a distinction produces rivalry. England, before other causes of enmity were found, was disturbed for some centuries by the contests of the northern and southern counties; so that at Oxford, the peace of study could for a long time be preserved only

---

8. Johnson's choice of the Cantabrians to illustrate his argument may be influenced by John Wallis, to whom he pays respectful, if not uncritical, tribute in his *Grammar of the English Tongue (Dictionary)*. Wallis, in his *Grammatica Linguae Anglicanae* (Oxford, 1653), asserts that the original language of Spain was Cantabrian, and suggests an analogy between that mountain tribe which long resisted Roman domination and the mountaineers of these islands (*Ad Lectorem Praefatio*, A 3ʳ, 4ʳ˒ ᵛ·). In citing the Dalecarlians (more apt as an example of independence than of mountain habitat), Johnson must surely have recalled his former interest in Henry Brooke's *Gustavus Vasa*, which he had defended in his ironical *Vindication of the Licensers of the Stage*. Performance being prohibited, Brooke's play was printed by subscription (1739), and Johnson's name appears in the list of subscribers. Brooke (whom Hawkins denounces as a Jacobite) makes the Dalecarlians serve his political allegory and represents them as mountaineers.

by chusing annually one of the Proctors from each side of the Trent. A tract intersected by many ridges of mountains, naturally divides its inhabitants into petty nations, which are made by a thousand causes enemies to each other. Each will exalt its own chiefs, each will boast the valour of its men, or the beauty of its women, and every claim of superiority irritates competition; injuries will sometimes be done, and be more injuriously defended; retaliation will sometimes be attempted, and the debt exacted with too much interest.

In the Highlands it was a law, that if a robber was sheltered from justice, any man of the same clan might be taken in his place. This was a kind of irregular justice, which, though necessary in savage times, could hardly fail to end in a feud, and a feud once kindled among an idle people with no variety of pursuits to divert their thoughts, burnt on for ages either sullenly glowing in secret mischief, or openly blazing into publick violence. Of the effects of this violent judicature, there are not wanting memorials. The cave is now to be seen to which one of the Campbells, who had injured the Macdonalds, retired with a body of his own clan. The Macdonalds required the offender, and being refused, made a fire at the mouth of the cave, by which he and his adherents were suffocated together.

Mountaineers are warlike, because by their feuds and competitions they consider themselves as surrounded with enemies, and are always prepared to repel incursions, or to make them. Like the Greeks in their unpolished state, described by Thucydides, the Highlanders, till lately, went always armed, and carried their weapons to visits, and to church.

Mountaineers are thievish, because they are poor, and having neither manufactures nor commerce, can grow richer only by robbery. They regularly plunder their neighbours, for their neighbours are commonly their enemies; and having lost that reverence for property, by which the order of civil life is preserved, soon consider all as enemies, whom they do not reckon as friends, and think themselves licensed to invade whatever they are not obliged to protect.

By a strict administration of the laws, since the laws have been introduced into the Highlands, this disposition to thievery is very much represt. Thirty years ago no herd had ever been conducted through the mountains, without paying tribute in the night, to some of the clans; but cattle are now driven, and passengers travel without danger, fear, or molestation.[9]

Among a warlike people, the quality of highest esteem is personal courage, and with the ostentatious display of courage are closely connected promptitude of offence and quickness of resentment. The Highlanders, before they were disarmed, were so addicted to quarrels, that the boys used to follow any publick procession or ceremony, however festive, or however solemn, in expectation of the battle, which was sure to happen before the company dispersed.

Mountainous regions are sometimes so remote from the seat of government, and so difficult of access, that they are very little under the influence of the sovereign, or within the reach of national justice. Law is nothing without power; and the sentence of a distant court could not be easily executed, nor perhaps very safely promulgated, among men ignorantly proud and habitually violent, unconnected with the general system, and accustomed to reverence only their own lords. It has therefore been necessary to erect many particular jurisdictions, and commit the punishment of crimes, and the decision of right to the proprietors of the country who could enforce their own decrees. It immediately appears that such judges will be often ignorant, and often partial; but in the immaturity of political establishments no better expedient could be found. As government advances towards perfection, provincial judicature is perhaps in every empire gradually abolished.

Those who had thus the dispensation of law, were by consequence themselves lawless. Their vassals had no shelter from outrages and oppressions; but were condemned to endure, without resistance, the caprices of wantonness, and the rage of cruelty.

In the Highlands, some great lords had an hereditary jurisdiction over counties; and some chieftains over their own lands; till the final conquest of the Highlands afforded an opportunity of crushing all the local courts, and of extending the general benefits of equal law to the low and the high, in the deepest recesses and obscurest corners.

While the chiefs had this resemblance of royalty, they had

---

9. RWC conjectured that Johnson wrote "without danger, or fear, of molestation."

little inclination to appeal, on any question, to superior judicatures. A claim of lands between two powerful lairds was decided like a contest for dominion between sovereign powers. They drew their forces into the field, and right attended on the strongest. This was, in ruder times, the common practice, which the kings of Scotland could seldom control.

Even so lately as in the last years of King William, a battle was fought at Mull Roy[i], on a plain a few miles to the south of Inverness, between the clans of Mackintosh and Macdonald of Keppoch. Col. Macdonald, the head of a small clan, refused to pay the dues demanded from him by Mackintosh, as his superior lord. They disdained the interposition of judges and laws, and calling each his followers to maintain the dignity of the clan, fought a formal battle, in which several considerable men fell on the side of Mackintosh, without a complete victory to either. This is said to have been the last open war made between the clans by their own authority.

The Highland lords made treaties, and formed alliances, of which some traces may still be found, and some consequences still remain as lasting evidences of petty regality. The terms of one of these confederacies were, that each should support the other in the right, or in the wrong, except against the king.

The inhabitants of mountains form distinct races, and are careful to preserve their genealogies. Men in a small district necessarily mingle blood by intermarriages, and combine at last into one family, with a common interest in the honour and disgrace of every individual. Then begins that union of affections, and co-operation of endeavours, that constitute a clan. They who consider themselves as ennobled by their family, will think highly of their progenitors, and they who through successive generations live always together in the same place, will preserve local stories and hereditary prejudices. Thus every Highlander can talk of his ancestors, and recount the outrages which they suffered from the wicked inhabitants of the next valley.

Such are the effects of habitation among mountains, and such were the qualities of the Highlanders, while their rocks secluded them from the rest of mankind, and kept them an unaltered and discriminated race. They are now losing their distinction, and hastening to mingle with the general community.

i. Mull Roy *Errata*] Mull Buy *75a, b*

GLENELG

We left Auknasheals and the Macraes in the afternoon, and in the evening came to Ratiken, a high hill on which a road is cut, but so steep and narrow, that it is very difficult. There is now a design of making another way round the bottom. Upon one of the precipices, my horse, weary with the steepness of the rise, staggered a little, and I called in haste to the Highlander to hold him. This was the only moment of my journey, in which I thought myself endangered.

Having surmounted the hill at last, we were told that at Glenelg, on the sea-side, we should come to a house of lime and slate and glass. This image of magnificence raised our expectation. At last we came to our inn weary and peevish, and began to inquire for meat and beds.

Of the provisions the negative catalogue was very copious. Here was no meat, no milk, no bread, no eggs, no wine. We did not express much satisfaction. Here however we were to stay. Whisky we might have, and I believe at last they caught a fowl and killed it. We had some bread, and with that we prepared ourselves to be contented, when we had a very eminent proof of Highland hospitality. Along some miles of the way, in the evening, a gentleman's servant had kept us company on foot with very little notice on our part. He left us near Glenelg, and we thought on him no more till he came to us again, in about two hours, with a present from his master of rum and sugar. The man had mentioned his company, and the gentleman, whose name, I think, is Gordon,[1] well knowing the penury of the place, had this attention to two men, whose names perhaps he had not heard, by whom his kindness was not likely to be ever repaid, and who could be recommended to him only by their necessities.

We were now to examine our lodging. Out of one of the beds, on which we were to repose, started up, at our entrance, a man black as a Cyclops from the forge. Other circumstances of no elegant recital concurred to disgust us. We had been frighted by a lady[2] at Edinburgh, with discouraging representations of Highland lodgings. Sleep, however, was necessary. Our High-

---

1. "In page 106, for *Gordon* read Murchison" (Boswell, letter to Johnson on receiving his copy of the *Jour-* *ney*. See *Life*, II.291).
2. Mrs. Boswell. See *Letters* 326.

landers had at last found some hay, with which the inn could not supply them. I directed them to bring a bundle into the room, and slept upon it in my riding coat. Mr. Boswell being more delicate, laid himself sheets with hay over and under him, and lay in linen like a gentleman.

SKY. ARMIDEL

In the morning, September the second,[3] we found ourselves on the edge of the sea. Having procured a boat, we dismissed our Highlanders, whom I would recommend to the service of any future travellers, and were ferried over to the Isle of Sky. We landed at Armidel, where we were met on the sands by Sir Alexander Macdonald,[4] who was at that time there with his lady, preparing to leave the island and reside at Edinburgh.

Armidel is a neat house, built where the Macdonalds had once a seat, which was burnt in the commotions that followed the Revolution. The walled orchard, which belonged to the former house, still remains. It is well shaded by tall ash trees, of a species, as Mr. Janes the fossilist[5] informed me, uncommonly valuable. This plantation is very properly mentioned by Dr. Campbell, in his new account of the state of Britain,[6] and deserves attention; because it proves that the present nakedness of the Hebrides is not wholly the fault of Nature.

As we sat at Sir Alexander's table, we were entertained, according to the ancient usage of the North, with the melody of the bagpipe. Every thing in those countries has its history. As the bagpiper was playing, an elderly gentleman informed us, that in some remote time, the Macdonalds of Glengary having been injured, or offended by the inhabitants of Culloden, and

---

3. second RWC] twentieth *75a, b; 85; 87.* Boswell inserted in the *Remarks,* in his own hand: "*for twentieth r. second.*" Here, as on p. 30 n. 2, the date in the printed text is at variance with that given in a letter to Mrs. Thrale (326). Johnson probably wrote "2d," which was misread by the printer as "20."

4. 9th Baronet of Sleat, afterwards 1st Baron Macdonald.

5. John Jeans, a mineralogist. See *Life,* v.517–18.

6. John Campbell, *A Political Survey of Britain* (1774). In support of the contention that trees might still thrive on Skye, he cites the report of a friend "who, in a late visit to this Isle, found at a place called Armadel a plantation of large thriving trees, containing a considerable quantity of valuable timber" (I.610. n.x).

resolving to have justice or vengeance, came to Culloden on a Sunday, where finding their enemies at worship, they shut them up in the church, which they set on fire; and this, said he, is the tune that the piper played while they were burning.

Narrations like this, however uncertain, deserve the notice of a traveller, because they are the only records of a nation that has no historians, and afford the most genuine representation of the life and character of the ancient Highlanders.

Under the denomination of "Highlander" are comprehended in Scotland all that now speak the Erse language, or retain the primitive manners, whether they live among the mountains or in the islands; and in that sense I use the name, when there is not some apparent reason for making a distinction.

In Sky I first observed the use of brogues, a kind of artless shoes, stitched with thongs so loosely, that though they defend the foot from stones, they do not exclude water. Brogues were formerly made of raw hides, with the hair[j] inwards, and such are perhaps still used in rude and remote parts; but they are said not to last above two days. Where life is somewhat improved, they are now made of leather tanned with oak bark, as in other places, or with the bark of birch, or roots of tormentil, a substance recommended in defect of bark, about forty years ago, to the Irish tanners, by one to whom the parliament of that kingdom voted a reward. The leather of Sky is not completely penetrated by vegetable matter, and therefore cannot be very durable.

My inquiries about brogues, gave me an early specimen of Highland information. One day I was told, that to make brogues was a domestick art, which every man practised for himself, and that a pair of brogues was the work of an hour. I supposed that the husband made brogues as the wife made an apron, till next day it was told me, that a brogue-maker was a trade, and that a pair would cost half a crown. It will easily occur that these representations may both be true, and that, in some places, men may buy them, and in others, make them for themselves; but I had both the accounts in the same house within two days.

j. hair *Errata*] skin 75a, b

Many of my subsequent inquiries upon more interesting topicks ended in the like uncertainty. He that travels in the Highlands may easily saturate his soul with intelligence, if he will acquiesce in the first account. The Highlander gives to every question an answer so prompt and peremptory, that skepticism itself is dared[7] into silence, and the mind sinks before the bold reporter in unresisting credulity; but, if a second question be ventured, it breaks the enchantment; for it is immediately discovered, that what was told so confidently was told at hazard, and that such fearlessness of assertion was either the sport of negligence, or the refuge of ignorance.

If individuals are thus at variance with themselves, it can be no wonder that the accounts of different men are contradictory. The traditions of an ignorant and savage people have been for ages negligently heard, and unskilfully related. Distant events must have been mingled together, and the actions of one man given to another. These, however, are deficiencies in story, for which no man is now to be censured. It were enough, if what there is yet opportunity of examining were accurately inspected, and justly represented; but such is the laxity of Highland conversation, that the inquirer is kept in continual suspense, and by a kind of intellectual retrogradation, knows less as he hears more.

In the islands the plaid is rarely worn. The law by which the Highlanders have been obliged to change the form of their dress,[8] has, in all the places that we have visited, been universally obeyed. I have seen only one gentleman completely clothed in the ancient habit, and by him it was worn only occasionally and wantonly. The common people do not think themselves under any legal necessity of having coats; for they say that the law

---

7. To *dare*: to intimidate and cause to cower; in common use from the thirteenth to the sixteenth century; confined to field sports by the seventeenth century; thereafter falling, with falconry, into disuse. A note in Johnson's *Shakespeare* (IV.446; i.e., *Henry V.*, IV.ii.36) affords the clearest illustration: "To dare the field is a phrase in falconry. Birds are dared when, by the falcon in the air, they are terrified

from rising, so that they will be sometimes taken by the hand."

8. The Disarming Act of 1746 proscribed the wearing of Highland dress. See D. C. Douglas, *English Historical Documents*, 1957, X.656. For the hardship entailed, see Colonel (afterwards General) David Stewart, *Sketches of . . . the Highlanders of Scotland with Details of the Military Service of the Highland Regiments* (1822), I.110–14.

against plaids was made by Lord Hardwicke,[1] and was in force only for his life: but the same poverty that made it then difficult for them to change their clothing, hinders them now from changing it again.

The fillibeg, or lower garment, is still very common, and the bonnet almost universal; but their attire is such as produces, in a sufficient degree, the effect intended by the law, of abolishing the dissimilitude of appearance between the Highlanders and the other inhabitants of Britain; and, if dress be supposed to have much influence, facilitates their coalition with their fellow-subjects.

What we have long used we naturally like, and therefore the Highlanders were unwilling to lay aside their plaid, which yet to an unprejudiced spectator must appear an incommodious and cumbersome dress; for hanging loose upon the body, it must flutter in a quick motion, or require one of the hands to keep it close. The Romans always laid aside the gown when they had any thing to do. It was a dress so unsuitable to war, that the same word which signified a gown signified peace. The chief use of a plaid seems to be this, that they could commodiously wrap themselves in it, when they were obliged to sleep without a better cover.

In our passage from Scotland to Sky, we were wet for the first time with a shower. This was the beginning of the Highland winter, after which we were told that a succession of three dry days was not to be expected for many months. The winter of the Hebrides consists of little more than rain and wind. As they are surrounded by an ocean never frozen, the blasts that come to them over the water are too much softened to have the power of congelation. The salt loughs, or inlets of the sea, which shoot very far into the island, never have any ice upon them, and the pools of fresh water will never bear the walker. The snow that sometimes falls, is soon dissolved by the air, or the rain.

This is not the description of a cruel climate, yet the dark months are here a time of great distress; because the summer can do little more than feed itself, and winter comes with its cold and its scarcity upon families very slenderly provided.

---

1. Philip Yorke, first earl (1690–1764).

CORIATACHAN IN SKY

The third or fourth day after our arrival at Armidel, brought us an invitation to the isle of Raasay, which lies east of Sky. It is incredible how soon the account of any event is propagated in these narrow countries by the love of talk, which much leisure produces, and the relief given to the mind in the penury of insular conversation by a new topick. The arrival of strangers at a place so rarely visited, excites rumour, and quickens curiosity. I know not whether we touched at any corner, where Fame had not already prepared us a reception.

To gain a commodious passage to Raasay, it was necessary to pass over a large part of Sky. We were furnished therefore with horses and a guide. In the Islands there are no roads, nor any marks by which a stranger may find his way. The horseman has always at his side a native of the place, who, by pursuing game, or tending cattle, or being often employed in messages or conduct, has learned where the ridge of the hill has breadth sufficient to allow a horse and his rider a passage, and where the moss or bog is hard enough to bear them. The bogs are avoided as toilsome at least, if not unsafe, and therefore the journey is made generally from precipice to precipice; from which if the eye ventures to look down, it sees below a gloomy cavity, whence the rush of water is sometimes heard.

But there seems to be in all this more alarm than danger. The Highlander walks carefully before, and the horse, accustomed to the ground, follows him with little deviation. Sometimes the hill is too steep for the horseman to keep his seat, and sometimes the moss is too tremulous to bear the double weight of horse and man. The rider then dismounts, and all shift as they can.

Journies made in this manner are rather tedious than long. A very few miles require several hours. From Armidel we came at night to Coriatachan, a house very pleasantly situated between two brooks, with one of the highest hills of the island behind it. It is the residence of Mr. Mackinnon,[2] by whom we were treated with very liberal hospitality, among a more numerous and elegant company than it could have been supposed easy to collect.

---

2. Lachlan Mackinnon of Coirechatachan. See *Life*, v.520.

The hill behind the house we did not climb. The weather was rough, and the height and steepness discouraged us. We were told that there is a cairne upon it. A cairne is a heap of stones thrown upon the grave of one eminent for dignity of birth, or splendour of atchievements. It is said that by digging, an urn is always found under these cairnes: they must therefore have been thus piled by a people whose custom was to burn the dead. To pile stones is, I believe, a northern custom, and to burn the body was the Roman practice; nor do I know when it was that these two acts of sepulture were united.

The weather was next day too violent for the continuation of our journey; but we had no reason to complain of the interruption. We saw in every place, what we chiefly desired to know, the manners of the people. We had company, and, if we had chosen retirement, we might have had books.

I never was in any house of the Islands, where I did not find books in more languages than one, if I staid long enough to want them, except one from which the family was removed. Literature is not neglected by the higher rank of the Hebridians.

It need not, I suppose, be mentioned, that in countries so little frequented as the Islands, there are no houses where travellers are entertained for money. He that wanders about these wilds, either procures recommendations to those whose habitations lie near his way, or, when night and weariness come upon him, takes the chance of general hospitality. If he finds only a cottage, he can expect little more than shelter; for the cottagers have little more for themselves: but if his good fortune brings him to the residence of a gentleman, he will be glad of a storm to prolong his stay. There is, however, one inn by the sea-side at Sconsor, in Sky, where the post-office is kept.

At the tables where a stranger is received, neither plenty nor delicacy is wanting. A tract of land so thinly inhabited, must have much wild-fowl; and I scarcely remember to have seen a dinner without them. The moorgame is every where to be had. That the sea abounds with fish, needs not be told, for it supplies a great part of Europe. The Isle of Sky has stags and roebucks, but no hares. They sell very numerous droves of oxen yearly to England, and therefore cannot be supposed to want beef at home. Sheep and goats are in great numbers, and they have the common domestick fowls.

But as here is nothing to be bought, every family must kill its own meat, and roast part of it somewhat sooner than Apicius[3] would prescribe. Every kind of flesh is undoubtedly excelled by the variety and emulation of English markets; but that which is not best may be yet very far[k] from bad, and he that shall complain of his fare in the Hebrides, has improved his delicacy more than his manhood.

Their fowls are not like those plumped for sale by the poulterers of London, but they are as good as other places commonly afford, except that the geese, by feeding in the sea, have universally a fishy rankness.

These geese seem to be of a middle race, between the wild and domestick kinds. They are so tame as to own a home, and so wild as sometimes to fly quite away.

Their native bread is made of oats, or barley. Of oatmeal they spread very thin cakes, coarse and hard, to which unaccustomed palates are not easily reconciled. The barley cakes are thicker and softer; I began to eat them without unwillingness; the blackness of their colour raises some dislike, but the taste is not disagreeable. In most houses there is wheat flower, with which we were sure to be treated, if we staid long enough to have it kneaded and baked. As neither yeast nor leaven are used among them, their bread of every kind is unfermented. They make only cakes, and never mould a loaf.

A man of the Hebrides, for of the women's diet I can give no account, as soon as he appears in the morning, swallows a glass of whisky; yet they are not a drunken race, at least I never was present at much intemperance; but no man is so abstemious as to refuse the morning dram, which they call a *skalk*.[4]

---

k. far *87; RWC* (in *1930*)]   free *75a, b; 85*

---

3. A proverbial epicure; he lived under Augustus and Tiberius and was said to have written on cookery.

4. *Sgailc*: morning bumper (Dwelly). Johnson must have depended on his own ear, or Boswell's, for the Gaelic words he mentions.

Alexander Macdonald's *Galick and English Vocabulary* (Edinburgh, 1741) may have passed through his hands while he was writing the *Journey* (see L. F. Powell, "Samuel Johnson: an Early 'Friend of the Bodleian'," *Bodleian Quarterly* 59, December 1928);

The word "whisky" signifies water, and is applied by way of eminence to "strong water," or distilled liquor. The spirit drunk in the North is drawn from barley. I never tasted it, except once for experiment at the inn in Inverary, when I thought it preferable to any English malt brandy. It was strong, but not pungent, and was free from the empyreumatick[5] taste or smell. What was the process I had no opportunity of inquiring, nor do I wish to improve the art of making poison pleasant.

Not long after the dram, may be expected the breakfast, a meal in which the Scots, whether of the lowlands or mountains, must be confessed to excel us. The tea and coffee are accompanied not only with butter, but with honey, conserves, and marmalades. If an epicure could remove by a wish, in quest of sensual gratifications, wherever he had supped he would breakfast in Scotland.

In the Islands however, they do what I found it not very easy to endure. They pollute the tea-table by plates piled with large slices of cheshire cheese, which mingles its less grateful odours with the fragrance of the tea.

Where many questions are to be asked, some will be omitted. I forgot to inquire how they were supplied with so much exotic luxury. Perhaps the French may bring them wine for wool, and the Dutch give them tea and coffee at the fishing season, in exchange for fresh provision. Their trade is unconstrained; they pay no customs, for there is no officer to demand them; whatever[6] therefore is made dear only by impost, is obtained here at an easy rate.

A dinner in the Western Islands differs very little from a dinner in England, except that in the place of tarts, there are always set different preparations of milk. This part of their diet will admit some improvement. Though they have milk, and eggs, and sugar, few of them know how to compound them in a

---

but, being published by the S.P.C.K. for use in "charity schools," it offers little help with these words. William Shaw's *Analysis of the Galic Language*, which he had seen shortly before publication, did not appear until 1778.

5. *empyreumatical*: "having the smell or taste of burnt substances" (*Dictionary*).

6. no customs, for . . . them; whatever RWC] no customs; for . . . them, whatever *75a*; no customs; for . . . them; whatever *75b, 85, 87*. The correction in *75b* is clearly required but does not go far enough.

custard. Their gardens afford them no great variety, but they have always some vegetables on the table. Potatoes at least are never wanting, which, though they have not known them long, are now one of the principal parts of their food. They are not of the mealy, but the viscous kind.

Their more elaborate cookery, or made dishes, an Englishman at the first taste is not likely to approve, but the culinary compositions of every country are often such as become grateful to other nations only by degrees; though I have read a French author, who, in the elation of his heart, says, that French cookery pleases all foreigners, but foreign cookery never satisfies a Frenchman.

Their suppers are, like their dinners, various and plentiful. The table is always covered with elegant linen. Their plates for common use are often of that kind of manufacture which is called cream coloured, or queen's ware. They use silver on all occasions where it is common in England, nor did I ever find the spoon of horn, but in one house.

The knives are not often either very bright, or very sharp. They are indeed instruments of which the Highlanders have not been long acquainted with the general use. They were not regularly laid on the table, before the prohibition of arms, and the change of dress. Thirty years ago the Highlander wore his knife as a companion to his dirk or dagger, and when the company sat down to meat, the men who had knives, cut the flesh into small pieces for the women, who with their fingers conveyed it to their mouths.

There was perhaps never any change of national manners so quick, so great, and so general, as that which has operated in the Highlands, by the last conquest, and the subsequent laws. We came thither too late to see what we expected, a people of peculiar appearance, and a system of antiquated life. The clans retain little now of their original character, their ferocity of temper is softened, their military ardour is extinguished, their dignity of independence is depressed, their contempt of government subdued, and their reverence for their chiefs abated. Of what they had before the late conquest of their country, there remain only their language and their poverty. Their language is attacked on every side. Schools are erected, in which English only is taught, and there were lately some who thought it reasonable to refuse them a version of the holy scriptures,[7] that they might have no monument of their mother-tongue.

That their poverty is gradually abated, cannot be mentioned among the unpleasing consequences of subjection. They are now acquainted with money, and the possibility of gain will by degrees make them industrious. Such is the effect of the late regulations, that a longer journey than to the Highlands must be taken by him whose curiosity pants for savage virtues and barbarous grandeur.

RAASAY

At the first intermission of the stormy weather we were informed, that the boat, which was to convey us to Raasay, attended us on the coast. We had from this time our intelligence facilitated, and our conversation enlarged, by the company of Mr. Macqueen,[8] minister of a parish in Sky, whose knowledge and politeness give him a title equally to kindness and respect, and who, from this time, never forsook us till we were preparing to leave Sky, and the adjacent places.

The boat was under the direction of Mr. Malcolm Macleod,[9] a gentleman of Raasay. The water was calm, and the rowers were vigorous; so that our passage was quick and pleasant. When we came near the island, we saw the laird's house, a neat modern fabrick, and found Mr. Macleod, the proprietor of the island, with many gentlemen, expecting us on the beach. We had, as at all other places, some difficulty in landing. The craggs were irregularly broken, and a false step would have been very mischievous.

It seemed that the rocks might, with no great labour, have been hewn almost into a regular flight of steps; and as there are no other landing places, I considered this rugged ascent as the consequence of a form of life inured to hardships, and therefore not studious of nice accommodations. But I know not whether,

---

7. See Johnson's remonstrance in his letter to William Drummond, 13 August 1766 (*Letters* 184).

8. Donald Macqueen, minister of Kilmuir in Skye. See *Life*, v.522.

9. Cousin to John Macleod, 9th chief of Raasay, the "proprietor of the island." See *Life*, v.523–24, for both men, especially for Malcolm Macleod's part in the '45.

Draft of the notice sent to the Edinburgh papers, apologizing for a mistake in the *Journey*, respecting the Macleod chieftainry. By kind permission of Yale University and the McGraw-Hill Book Co.

for many ages, it was not considered as a part of military policy, to keep the country not easily accessible. The rocks are natural fortifications, and an enemy climbing with difficulty, was easily destroyed by those who stood high above him.

Our reception exceeded our expectations. We found nothing but civility, elegance, and plenty. After the usual refreshments, and the usual conversation, the evening came upon us. The carpet was then rolled off the floor; the musician was called, and the whole company was invited to dance, nor did ever fairies trip with greater alacrity. The general air of festivity, which predominated in this place, so far remote from all those regions which the mind has been used to contemplate as the mansions of pleasure, struck the imagination with a delightful surprise, analogous to that which is felt at an unexpected emersion[1] from darkness into light.

When it was time to sup, the dance ceased, and six and thirty persons sat down to two tables in the same room. After supper the ladies sung Erse songs, to which I listened as an English audience to an Italian opera, delighted with the sound of words which I did not understand.

I inquired the subjects of the songs, and was told of one, that it was a love song, and of another, that it was a farewell composed by one of the Islanders that was going, in this epidemical fury of emigration, to seek his fortune in America. What sentiments would rise, on such an occasion, in the heart of one who had not been taught to lament by precedent, I should gladly have known; but the lady, by whom I sat, thought herself not equal to the work of translating.

Mr. Macleod is the proprietor of the islands of Raasay, Rona, and Fladda, and possesses an extensive district in Sky. The estate has not, during four hundred years, gained or lost a single acre. He acknowledges Macleod of Dunvegan as his chief,[2] though his ancestors have formerly disputed the pre-eminence.

---

1. *emersion*: "the time when a star, having been obscured by its too near approach to the sun, appears again" (*Dictionary*).

2. This statement, for which Johnson evidently relied on Boswell's report of his conversation with Macleod of Raasay (see *Journal*, p. 135, and Johnson's letter to Mrs. Thrale, *Letters* 327), gave serious offence to Macleod, who remonstrated to Boswell (see *Life*, v.410). Johnson wrote to apologize for having misapprehended the situation (see *Letters* 389). He promised to "omit or retract" the offending passage in "the next edition"; but,

One of the old Highland alliances has continued for two hundred years, and is still subsisting between Macleod of Raasay and Macdonald of Sky, in consequence of which, the survivor always inherits the arms of the deceased; a natural memorial of military friendship. At the death of the late Sir James Macdonald,[3] his sword was delivered to the present laird of Raasay.

The family of Raasay consists of the laird, the lady, three sons and ten daughters. For the sons there is a tutor in the house, and the lady is said to be very skilful and diligent in the education of her girls. More gentleness of manners, or a more pleasing appearance of domestick society, is not found in the most polished countries.

Raasay is the only inhabited island in Mr. Macleod's possession. Rona and Fladda afford only pasture for cattle, of which one hundred and sixty winter in Rona, under the superintendence of a solitary herdsman.

The length of Raasay is, by computation, fifteen miles, and the breadth two. These countries have never been measured, and the computation by miles is negligent and arbitrary. We observed in travelling, that the nominal and real distance of places had very little relation to each other. Raasay probably contains near a hundred square miles.[4] It affords not much ground, notwithstanding its extent, either for tillage, or pasture; for it is rough, rocky, and barren. The cattle often perish by falling from the precipices. It is like the other islands, I think, generally naked of shade, but it is naked by neglect; for the laird has an orchard, and very large forest trees grow about

---

since he could not tell when this would be, he had asked Boswell to "anticipate the correction" in the Edinburgh papers—a good office which Boswell performed, recording the particulars (see *Life*, v.412). An advertisement was framed (of which the original, preserved by Boswell, was found among the *Private Papers* in 1940) and was sent to the Edinburgh papers. A copy of it was prefixed to the 1785 edition of the *Journey*, but this has had little effect on editorial practice (see Courtney, pp. 123–25). Boswell,

assiduous as mediator, seems not to have acknowledged his share in the misunderstanding, and he removed traces of it from the *Tour* (see *Life*, v.167). For the Advertisement, see illustration and Appendix II.

3. 8th Baronet of Sleat, elder brother of Sir Alexander, Johnson's and Boswell's host at Armidale; died 1766.

4. "About 27 square miles" (E. S. de Beer, *Raasay To-day*, privately printed, 1961, p. 3).

his house. Like other hilly countries it has many rivulets. One of the brooks turns a corn-mill, and at least one produces trouts. In the streams or fresh lakes of the Islands, I have never heard of any other fish than trouts and eels. The trouts, which I have seen, are not large; the colour of their flesh is tinged as in England. Of their eels I can give no account, having never tasted them; for I believe they are not considered as wholesome food.

It is not very easy to fix the principles upon which mankind have agreed to eat some animals, and reject others; and as the principle is not evident, it is not uniform. That which is selected as delicate in one country, is by its neighbours abhorred as loathsome. The Neapolitans lately refused to eat potatoes in a famine. An Englishman is not easily persuaded to dine on snails with an Italian, on frogs with a Frenchman, or on horseflesh with a Tartar. The vulgar inhabitants of Sky, I know not whether of the other islands, have not only eels, but pork and bacon in abhorrence, and accordingly I never saw a hog in the Hebrides, except one at Dunvegan.

Raasay has wild fowl in abundance, but neither deer, hares, nor rabbits. Why it has them not, might be asked, but that of such questions there is no end. Why does any nation want what it might have? Why are not spices transplanted to America? Why does tea continue to be brought from China? Life improves but by slow degrees, and much in every place is yet to do. Attempts have been made to raise roebucks in Raasay, but without effect. The young ones it is extremely difficult to rear, and the old can very seldom be taken alive.

Hares and rabbits might be more easily obtained. That they have few or none of either in Sky, they impute to the ravage of the foxes, and have therefore set, for some years past, a price upon their heads, which, as the number was dimininished, has been gradually raised, from three shillings and sixpence to a guinea, a sum so great in this part of the world, that, in a short time, Sky may be as free from foxes, as England from wolves. The fund for these rewards is a tax of sixpence in the pound, imposed by the farmers on themselves, and said to be paid with great willingness.

The beasts of prey in the Islands are foxes, otters, and weasels. The foxes are bigger than those of England; but the otters exceed ours in a far greater proportion. I saw one at Armidel, of a size much beyond that which I supposed them ever to attain; and Mr. Maclean,[5] the heir of Col, a man of middle stature, informed me that he once shot an otter,[6] of which the tail reached the ground, when he held up the head to a level with his own. I expected the otter to have a foot particularly formed for the art of swimming; but upon examination, I did not find it differing much from that of a spaniel. As he preys in the sea, he does little visible mischief, and is killed only for his fur. White otters are sometimes seen.

In Raasay they might have hares and rabbits, for they have no foxes. Some depredations, such as were never made before, have caused a suspicion that a fox has been lately landed in the island by spite or wantonness. This imaginary stranger has never yet been seen, and therefore, perhaps, the mischief was done by some other animal. It is not likely that a creature so ungentle, whose head could have been sold in Sky for a guinea, should be kept alive only to gratify the malice of sending him to prey upon a neighbour: and the passage from Sky is wider than a fox would venture to swim, unless he were chased by dogs into the sea, and perhaps than his strength would enable him to cross. How beasts of prey came into any islands is not easy to guess. In cold countries they take advantage of hard winters, and travel over the ice: but this is a very scanty solution; for they are found where they have no discoverable means of coming.

The corn of this island is but little. I saw the harvest of a small field. The women reaped the corn, and the men bound up the sheaves. The strokes of the sickle were timed by the modulation of the harvest song, in which all their voices were united. They accompany in the Highlands every action, which can be done in equal time, with an appropriated strain, which has, they say, not much meaning; but its effects are regularity and cheerfulness. The ancient proceleusmatick[7] song, by which the

---

5. Donald Maclean of Coll. See *Life*, v.543–44.

6. The average length of the otter is only 2 ft. 6 in.; but, according to Martin, "The hunters say there is a big otter above the ordinary size with a white spot on its breast, and this they call the King of Otters, it is rarely seen

and very hard to be killed, seamen ascribe great vertues to the skin" (*Description*, p. 159).

7. *proceleusmatic*: Johnson here uses the epithet rather in its literal sense—animating, inspiriting—than with reference to Greek prosody.

rowers of gallies were animated, may be supposed to have been of this kind. There is now an "oar-song" used by the Hebridians.

The ground of Raasay seems fitter for cattle than for corn, and of black cattle I suppose the number is very great. The Laird himself keeps a herd of four hundred, one hundred of which are annually sold. Of an extensive domain, which he holds in his own hands, he considers the sale of cattle as repaying him the rent, and supports the plenty of a very liberal table with the remaining product.

Raasay is supposed to have been very long inhabited. On one side of it they show caves, into which the rude nations of the first ages retreated from the weather. These dreary vaults might have had other uses. There is still a cavity near the house called the "oar-cave," in which the seamen, after one of those[1] piratical expeditions, which in rougher times were very frequent, used, as tradition tells, to hide their oars. This hollow was near the sea, that nothing so necessary might be far to be fetched; and it was secret, that enemies, if they landed, could find nothing. Yet it is not very evident of what use it was to hide their oars from those, who, if they were masters of the coast, could take away their boats.

A proof much stronger of the distance at which the first possessors of this island lived from the present time, is afforded by the stone heads of arrows which are very frequently picked up. The people call them "elf-bolts," and believe that the fairies shoot them at the cattle. They nearly resemble those which Mr. Banks[8] has lately brought from the savage countries in the Pacifick Ocean, and must have been made by a nation to which the use of metals was unknown.

The number of this little community has never been counted by its ruler, nor have I obtained any positive account, consistent with the result of political computation. Not many years ago, the late laird led out one hundred men upon a military expedition.[1] The sixth part of a people is supposed capable of bearing

---

1. those *85; RWC*] these *75a, b*

---

8. Joseph (afterwards Sir Joseph) Banks (1743–1820), traveller and naturalist, accompanied Captain Cook in the *Endeavour* (1768–71); he was a member of the Club.

1. Johnson's references to the '45 are always delicately oblique. Cf. p. 126 n. 7.

arms: Raasay had therefore six hundred inhabitants. But because it is not likely, that every man able to serve in the field would follow the summons, or that the chief would leave his lands totally defenceless, or take away all the hands qualified for labour, let it be supposed, that half as many might be permitted to stay at home. The whole number will then be nine hundred, or nine to a square mile; a degree of populousness greater than those tracts of desolation can often show. They are content with their country, and faithful to their chiefs, and yet[2] uninfected with the fever of migration.

Near the house, at Raasay, is a chapel unroofed and ruinous, which has long been used only as a place of burial. About the churches, in the Islands, are small squares inclosed with stone, which belong to particular families, as repositories for the dead. At Raasay there is one, I think, for the proprietor, and one for some collateral house.

It is told by Martin,[3] that at the death of the Lady of the Island, it has been here the custom to erect a cross. This we found not to be true. The stones that stand about the chapel at a small distance, some of which perhaps have crosses cut upon them, are believed to have been not funeral monuments, but the ancient boundaries of the sanctuary or consecrated ground.[4]

Martin was a man not illiterate: he was an inhabitant of Sky, and therefore was within reach of intelligence, and with no great difficulty might have visited the places which he undertakes to describe; yet with all his opportunities, he has often suffered himself to be deceived. He lived in the last century, when the chiefs of the clans had lost little of their original in-

2. " 'They are content with their country & faithful to their chiefs (dele s) and yet uninfected with the fever of emigration' Is *yet* a good word here Should it not be *still* or some other expression. Content and faithful yet uninfected etc. no wonder they are uninfected when content & faithful. This may occur to a heedless reader from one sense of the word yet. (A remark by my wife) would *as yet* be clearer?" (Boswell, *Remarks*). Johnson elsewhere uses *yet* (meaning *hitherto*); but Mrs. Boswell's emendation removes a possible ambiguity, and Johnson may have written, or intended writing, *as yet*.

3. *Description*, p. 164. Martin's *Description of the Western Islands*, though less authoritative than his *Voyage to St. Kilda* (1698), remained the principal source of information on the Isles for a century. Johnson and Boswell took with them the copy belonging to the Advocates' Library. (See William Beattie and T. I. Rae, "Boswell and the Advocates' Library," in *Johnson, Boswell and their Circle*, 1965.)

4. Donald Macqueen's supposition. See *Life*, v.170.

fluence. The mountains were yet unpenetrated, no inlet was opened to foreign novelties, and the feudal institutions operated upon life with their full force. He might therefore have displayed a series of subordination and a form of government, which, in more luminous and improved regions, have been long forgotten, and have delighted his readers with many uncouth customs that are now disused, and wild opinions that prevail no longer. But he probably had not knowledge of the world sufficient to qualify him for judging what would deserve or gain the attention of mankind. The mode of life which was familiar to himself, he did not suppose unknown to others, nor imagined that he could give pleasure by telling that of which it was, in his little country, impossible to be ignorant.

What he has neglected cannot now be performed. In nations, where there is hardly the use of letters, what is once out of sight is lost for ever. They think but little, and of their few thoughts, none are wasted on the past, in which they are neither interested by fear nor hope. Their only registers are stated observances and practical representations. For this reason an age of ignorance is an age of ceremony. Pageants, and processions, and commemorations, gradually shrink away, as better methods come into use of recording events, and preserving rights.

It is not only in Raasay that the chapel is unroofed and useless; through the few islands which we visited, we neither saw nor heard of any house of prayer, except in Sky, that was not in ruins. The malignant influence of Calvinism has blasted ceremony and decency together; and if the remembrance of papal superstition is obliterated, the monuments of papal piety are likewise effaced.

It has been, for many years, popular to talk of the lazy devotion of the Romish clergy; over the sleepy laziness of men that erected churches, we may indulge our superiority with a new triumph, by comparing it with the fervid activity of those who suffer them to fall.

Of the destruction of churches, the decay of religion must in time be the consequence; for while the publick acts of the ministry are now performed in houses, a very small number can be present; and as the greater part of the Islanders make no use of books, all must necessarily live in total ignorance who want the opportunity of vocal instruction.

From these remains of ancient sanctity, which are every

where to be found, it has been conjectured, that, for the last two centuries, the inhabitants of the Islands[m] have decreased in number. This argument, which supposes that the churches have been suffered to fall, only because they were no longer necessary, would have some force, if the houses of worship still remaining were sufficient for the people. But since they have now no churches at all, these venerable fragments do not prove the people of former times to have been more numerous, but to have been more devout. If the inhabitants were doubled with their present principles, it appears not that any provision for publick worship would be made. Where the religion of a country enforces consecrated buildings, the number of those buildings may be supposed to afford some indication, however uncertain, of the populousness of the place; but where by a change of manners a nation is contented to live without them, their decay implies no diminution of inhabitants.

Some of these dilapidations are said to be found in islands now uninhabited; but I doubt whether we can thence infer that they were ever peopled. The religion of the middle age, is well known to have placed too much hope in lonely austerities. Voluntary solitude was the great act[5] of propitiation, by which crimes were effaced, and conscience was appeased; it is therefore not unlikely, that oratories were often built in places where retirement was sure to have no disturbance.

Raasay has little that can detain a traveller, except the Laird and his family; but their power wants no auxiliaries. Such a seat of hospitality, amidst the winds and waters, fills the imagination with a delightful contrariety of images. Without is the rough ocean and the rocky land, the beating billows and the howling storm: within is plenty and elegance, beauty and gaiety, the song and the dance. In Raasay, if I could have found an Ulysses, I had fancied a Phaeacia.[6]

m. Islands *Errata*]   Island *75a, b*

---

5. act RWC] art *75a, b; 85; 87.* RWC denied that Johnson could ever have called solitude an art (MS. note, correcting his own note of 1924) and cited the misreading of *art* for *act* in the Piozzi *Letters* (1788), in a letter of 7 July 1771, to show that the words might be interchangeable in Johnson's handwriting.

6. Johnson, by alluding to the welcome Ulysses found in Phaeacia, implicitly likens Macleod hospitality to that of King Alcinous, but explicitly forbears comparing himself with Ulysses. Boswell, apparently confused by the elaborate structure of this compliment, feared it might be taken amiss on Raasay (*Remarks*).

DUNVEGAN

At Raasay, by good fortune, Macleod,[7] so the chief of the clan is called, was paying a visit, and by him we were invited to his seat at Dunvegan.[8] Raasay has a stout boat, built in Norway, in which, with six oars, he conveyed us back to Sky. We landed at Port Re, so called, because James the Fifth of Scotland, who had curiosity to visit the Islands, came into it. The port is made by an inlet of the sea, deep and narrow, where a ship lay waiting to dispeople Sky, by carrying the natives away to America.

In coasting Sky, we passed by the cavern in which it was the custom, as Martin relates,[9] to catch birds in the night, by making a fire at the entrance. This practice is disused; for the birds, as is known often to happen, have changed their haunts.

Here we dined at a publick house, I believe the only inn[1] of the island, and having mounted our horses, travelled in the manner already described, till we came to Kingsborough, a place distinguished by that name, because the King lodged here when he landed at Port Re. We were entertained with the usual hospitality by Mr. Macdonald[2] and his lady, Flora Macdonald, a name that will be mentioned in history, and if courage and fidelity be virtues, mentioned with honour.[3] She is a woman of middle stature, soft features, gentle manners, and elegant presence.

In the morning we sent our horses round a promontory[4] to meet us, and spared ourselves part of the day's fatigue, by crossing an arm of the sea. We had at last some difficulty in coming

---

7. Norman Macleod, 20th Chief. Johnson admired his endeavours to relieve an encumbered estate. See *Letters* 329 and *Life*, v.176; and, for the outcome, *Life*, v.526–28.

8. "Ane starke strengthe, biggit upon ane craig" (Donald Monro, *A Description of the Western Isles of Scotland, called Hybrides, circa* 1549, Edinburgh, 1774).

9. *Description*, p. 151.

1. Boswell points out that Johnson has forgotten his own mention of Sconser (see p. 54), adding: "Might not some sharp rogues lay hold of this in a traveller so rigidly exact as you are?" (*Remarks*).

2. Allan Macdonald. See *Life*, v.529.

3. This tribute is inscribed on a cross erected over Flora Macdonald's grave at Kilmuir, Skye, and on her statue at Castle Hill, Inverness (LFP).

4. This expression is hard to reconcile with the route the horses must have taken, yet Boswell on a comparable occasion wrote: "We sent our horses round a point of land" (*Life*, v.257). The editors of the *Journal* suggest that *across two points of land* would better suit the terrain (p. 426). The horses, however, had still (on both occasions) to circumvent "an arm of the sea."

to Dunvegan; for our way led over an extensive moor, where every step was to be taken with caution, and we were often obliged to alight, because the ground could not be trusted. In travelling this watery flat, I perceived that it had a visible declivity, and might without much expence or difficulty be drained. But difficulty and expence are relative terms, which have different meanings in different places.

To Dunvegan we came, very willing to be at rest, and found our fatigue amply recompensed by our reception. Lady Macleod,[5] who had lived many years in England, was newly come hither with her son and four daughters, who knew all the arts of southern elegance, and all the modes of English economy. Here therefore we settled, and did not spoil the present hour with thoughts of departure.

Dunvegan is a rocky prominence, that juts out into a bay, on the west side of Sky. The house, which is the principal seat of Macleod, is partly old and partly modern; it is built upon the rock, and looks upon the water. It forms two sides of a small square: on the third side is the skeleton of a castle of unknown antiquity, supposed to have been a Norwegian fortress, when the Danes were masters of the Islands. It is so nearly entire, that it might have easily been made habitable, were there not an ominous tradition in the family, that the owner shall not long outlive the reparation. The grandfather of the present laird, in defiance of prediction, began the work, but desisted in a little time, and applied his money to worse uses.

As the inhabitants of the Hebrides lived, for many ages, in continual expectation of hostilities, the chief of every clan resided in a fortress. This house was accessible only from the water, till the last possessor opened an entrance by stairs upon the land.

They had formerly reason to be afraid, not only of declared wars and authorized invaders, or of roving pirates, which, in the northern seas, must have been very common; but of inroads and insults from rival clans, who, in the plenitude of feudal independence, asked no leave of their Sovereign to make war on one another. Sky has been ravaged by a feud between the two mighty powers of Macdonald and Macleod. Macdonald having

---

5. Mother of the Chief, Norman Macleod.

married a Macleod, upon some discontent dismissed her, perhaps because she had brought him no children. Before the reign of James the Fifth, a Highland laird made a trial of his wife for a certain time, and if she did not please him, he was then at liberty to send her away. This however must always have offended, and Macleod resenting the injury, whatever were its circumstances, declared, that the wedding had been solemnized without a bonfire, but that the separation should be better illuminated; and raising a little army, set fire to the territories of Macdonald, who returned the visit, and prevailed.

Another story may show the disorderly state of insular neighbourhood. The inhabitants of the Isle of Egg, meeting a boat manned by Macleods, tied the crew hand and foot, and set them a-drift. Macleod landed upon Egg, and demanded the offenders; but the inhabitants refusing to surrender them, retreated to a cavern, into which they thought their enemies unlikely to follow them. Macleod choked them with smoke, and left them lying dead by families as they stood.[6]

Here the violence of the weather confined us for some time, not at all to our discontent or inconvenience. We would indeed very willingly have visited the islands, which might be seen from the house scattered in the sea, and I was particularly desirous to have viewed Isay; but the storms did not permit us to launch a boat, and we were condemned to listen in idleness to the wind, except when we were better engaged by listening to the ladies.

We had here more wind than waves, and suffered the severity of a tempest, without enjoying its magnificence. The sea being broken by the multitude of islands, does not roar with so much noise, nor beat the storm[7] with such foamy violence, as I have

---

6. For the relation between this story and that on p. 127, see the discussion of cancels, pp. xxxiv–xxxv.

7. Despite the concurrence of early editions, RWC found *beat the storm* so questionable an expression that he emended to *beat the shore*; but Johnson elsewhere uses *beat* (as a transitive verb) meaning to *contend with*: he says, of the futility of attacks on Bentley, "It was attacking a man who would not beat them, because his beating them would make them live longer" (*Life*, v.174). The sea could be regarded as contending with the storm on an open beach, in contrast with the motion of its waves on a deeply indented shore. The letters contain many descriptions of this motion, as though Johnson were searching for the right word.

remarked on the coast of Sussex. Though, while I was in the Hebrides, the wind was extremely turbulent, I never saw very high billows.

The country about Dunvegan is rough and barren. There are no trees, except in the orchard, which is a low sheltered spot surrounded with a wall.

When this house was intended to sustain a siege, a well was made in the court, by boring the rock downwards, till water was found, which though so near to the sea, I have not heard mentioned as brackish, though it has some hardness, or other qualities, which make it less fit for use; and the family is now better supplied from a stream, which runs by the rock, from two pleasing water-falls.

Here we saw some traces of former manners, and heard some standing traditions. In the house is kept an ox's horn, hollowed so as to hold perhaps two quarts, which the heir of Macleod was expected to swallow at one draught, as a test of his manhood, before he was permitted to bear arms, or could claim a seat among the men. It is held that the return of the laird to Dunvegan, after any considerable absence, produces a plentiful capture of herrings; and that, if any woman crosses the water to the opposite island, the herrings will desert the coast. Boetius tells the same of some other place. This tradition is not uniform. Some hold that no woman may pass, and others that none may pass but a Macleod.

Among other guests, which the hospitality of Dunvegan brought to the table, a visit was paid by the laird and lady of a small island south of Sky, of which the proper name is Muack, which signifies swine. It is commonly called Muck, which the proprietor not liking, has endeavoured, without effect, to change to Monk. It is usual to call gentlemen in Scotland by the name of their possessions, as Raasay, Bernera, Loch Buy, a practice necessary in countries inhabited by clans, where all that live in the same territory have one name, and must be therefore discriminated by some addition. This gentleman, whose name, I think, is Maclean, should be regularly called Muck; but the appellation, which he thinks too coarse for his island, he would like still less for himself, and he is therefore addressed by the title of, Isle of Muck.

This little island, however it be named, is of considerable

value. It is two English miles long, and three quarters of a mile broad, and consequently contains only nine hundred and sixty English acres. It is chiefly arable. Half of this little dominion the Laird retains in his own hand, and on the other half, live one hundred and sixty persons, who pay their rent by exported corn. What rent they pay, we were not told, and could not decently inquire. The proportion of the people to the land is such, as the most fertile countries do not commonly maintain.

The Laird having all his people under his immediate view, seems to be very attentive to their happiness. The devastation of the small-pox, when it visits places where it comes seldom, is well known. He has disarmed it of its terrour at Muack, by inoculating eighty of his people. The expence was two shillings and sixpence a head. Many trades they cannot have among them, but upon occasion, he fetches a smith from the Isle of Egg, and has a tailor from the main land, six times a year. This island well deserved to be seen, but the Laird's absence left us no opportunity.

Every inhabited island has its appendant and subordinate islets. Muck, however small, has yet others smaller about it, one of which has only ground sufficient to afford pasture for three wethers.

At Dunvegan I had tasted lotus, and was in danger of forgetting that I was ever to depart, till Mr. Boswell sagely reproached me with my sluggishness and softness. I had no very forcible defence to make; and we agreed to pursue our journey. Macleod accompanied us to Ulinish, where we were entertained by the sheriff of the island.

ULINISH

Mr. Macqueen travelled with us, and directed our attention to all that was worthy of observation. With him we went to see an ancient building, called a *dun* or borough.[8] It was a circular inclosure, about forty-two feet in diameter, walled round with loose stones, perhaps to the height of nine feet. The walls are

---

8. *Dùn* (Gaelic) and borough (variant of burrow) have, among their meanings, one in common: hill stronghold.

very thick, diminishing a little towards the top, and though in these countries, stone is not brought far, must have been raised with much labour. Within the great circle were several smaller rounds of wall, which formed distinct apartments. Its date, and its use are unknown. Some suppose it the original seat of the chiefs of the Macleods. Mr. Macqueen thought it a Danish fort.

The entrance is covered with flat stones, and is narrow, because it was necessary that the stones which lie over it, should reach from one wall to the other; yet, strait as the passage is, they seem heavier than could have been placed where they now lie, by the naked strength of as many men as might stand about them. They were probably raised by putting long pieces of wood under them, to which the action of a long line of lifters might be applied. Savages, in all countries, have patience proportionate to their unskilfulness, and are content to attain their end by very tedious methods.

If it was ever roofed, it might once have been a dwelling, but as there is no provision for water, it could not have been a fortress. In Sky, as in every other place, there is an ambition of exalting whatever has survived memory, to some important use, and referring it to very remote ages. I am inclined to suspect, that in lawless times, when the inhabitants of every mountain stole the cattle of their neighbour, these inclosures were used to secure the herds and flocks in the night. When they were driven within the wall, they might be easily watched, and defended as long as could be needful; for the robbers durst not wait till the injured clan should find them in the morning.

The interior inclosures, if the whole building were once a house, were the chambers of the chief inhabitants. If it was a place of security for cattle, they were probably the shelters of the keepers.

From the *dun* we were conducted to another place of security, a cave carried a great way underground, which had been discovered by digging after a fox. These caves, of which many have been found, and many probably remain concealed, are formed, I believe, commonly by taking advantage of a hollow, where banks or rocks rise on either side. If no such place can be found, the ground must be cut away. The walls are made by piling stones against the earth, on either side. It is then roofed by larger stones laid across the cavern, which therefore cannot be wide. Over the roof, turfs were placed, and grass was suffered to grow; and the mouth was concealed by bushes, or some other cover.

These caves were represented to us as the cabins of the first rude inhabitants, of which, however, I am by no means persuaded. This was so low, that no man could stand upright in it. By their construction they are all so narrow, that two can never pass along them together, and being subterraneous, they must be always damp. They are not the work of an age much ruder than the present; for they are formed with as much art as the construction of a common hut requires. I imagine them to have been places only of occasional use, in which the Islander, upon a sudden alarm, hid his utensils, or his cloaths, and perhaps sometimes his wife and children.

This cave we entered, but could not proceed the whole length, and went away without knowing how far it was carried. For this omission we shall be blamed, as we perhaps have blamed other travellers;[9] but the day was rainy, and the ground was damp. We had with us neither spades nor pickaxes, and if love of ease surmounted our desire of knowledge, the offence has not the invidiousness of singularity.

Edifices, either standing or ruined, are the chief records of an illiterate nation. In some part of this journey, at no great distance from our way, stood a shattered fortress, of which the learned minister, to whose communication we are much indebted, gave us an account.

Those, said he, are the walls of a place of refuge, built in the time of James the Sixth, by Hugh Macdonald, who was next heir to the dignity and fortune of his chief. Hugh, being so near his wish, was impatient of delay; and had art and influence sufficient to engage several gentlemen in a plot against the laird's life. Something must be stipulated on both sides; for they would not dip their hands in blood merely for Hugh's advancement. The compact was formally written, signed by the conspirators, and placed in the hands of one Macleod.

It happened that Macleod had sold some cattle to a drover, who, not having ready money, gave him a bond for payment. The debt was discharged, and the bond redemanded; which

---

9. Johnson may well have recalled his own strictures in *Idler* 97.

Macleod, who could not read, intending to put into his hands, gave him the conspiracy. The drover, when he had read the paper, delivered it privately to Macdonald; who, being thus informed of his danger, called his friends together, and provided for his safety. He made a publick feast, and inviting Hugh Macdonald and his confederates, placed each of them at the table between two men of known fidelity. The compact of conspiracy was then shewn, and every man confronted with his own name. Macdonald acted with great moderation. He upbraided Hugh, both with disloyalty and ingratitude; but told the rest, that he considered them as men deluded and misinformed. Hugh was sworn to fidelity, and dismissed with his companions; but he was not generous enough to be reclaimed by lenity; and finding no longer any countenance among the gentlemen, endeavoured to execute the same design by meaner hands. In this practice he was detected, taken to Macdonald's castle, and imprisoned in the dungeon. When he was hungry, they let down a plentiful meal of salted meat; and when, after his repast, he called for drink, conveyed to him a covered cup, which, when he lifted the lid, he found empty. From that time they visited him no more, but left him to perish in solitude and darkness.

We were then told of a cavern by the sea-side, remarkable for the powerful reverberation of sounds. After dinner we took a boat, to explore this curious cavity. The boatmen, who seemed to be of a rank above that of common drudges, inquired who the strangers were, and being told we came one from Scotland, and the other from England, asked if the Englishman could recount a long genealogy. What answer was given them, the conversation being in Erse, I was not much inclined to examine.

They expected no good event of the voyage; for one of them declared that he heard the cry of an English ghost. This omen I was not told till after our return, and therefore cannot claim the dignity of despising it.

The sea was smooth. We never left the shore, and came without any disaster to the cavern, which we found rugged and misshapen, about one hundred and eighty feet long, thirty wide in the broadest part, and in the loftiest, as we guessed, about thirty high. It was now dry, but at high water the sea rises in it near six feet. Here I saw what I had never seen before, limpets and mussels in their natural state. But, as a new testimony to the veracity of common fame, here was no echo to be heard.

We then walked through a natural arch in the rock, which might have pleased us by its novelty, had the stones, which incumbered our feet, given us leisure to consider it. We were shown the gummy seed of the kelp, that fastens itself to a stone, from which it grows into a strong stalk.

In our return, we found a little boy upon the point of a rock, catching with his angle, a supper for the family. We rowed up to him, and borrowed his rod, with which Mr. Boswell caught a cuddy.

The cuddy is a fish of which I know not the philosophical name.[1] It is not much bigger than a gudgeon, but is of great use in these islands, as it affords the lower people both food, and oil for their lamps. Cuddies are so abundant, at some times of the year, that they are caught like white bait in the Thames, only by dipping a basket and drawing it back.

If it were always practicable to fish, these islands could never be in much danger from famine; but unhappily in the winter, when other provision fails, the seas are commonly too rough for nets, or boats.

TALISKER IN SKY

From Ulinish, our next stage was to Talisker, the house of Colonel Macleod,[2] an officer in the Dutch service, who, in this time of universal peace, has for several years been permitted to be absent from his regiment. Having been bred to physick, he is consequently a scholar, and his lady, by accompanying him in his different places of residence, is become skilful in several languages. Talisker is the place beyond all that I have seen, from which the gay and the jovial seem utterly excluded; and where the hermit might expect to grow old in meditation, without possibility of disturbance or interruption. It is situated very near the sea, but upon a coast where no vessel lands but when it is driven by a tempest on the rocks. Towards the land are lofty hills streaming with water-falls. The garden is sheltered by firs or pines, which grow there so prosperously, that some, which the present inhabitant planted, are very high and thick.

---

1. Cuddy (Gaelic *cudaig, cudainn*): a name for the young of the coal-fish   or saith (OED).

2. John Macleod. See *Life*, v.524.

At this place we very happily met Mr. Donald Maclean,[2a] a young gentleman, the eldest son of the Laird of Col, heir to a very great extent of land, and so desirous of improving his inheritance, that he spent a considerable time among the farmers of Hertfordshire, and Hampshire, to learn their practice. He worked with his own hands at the principal operations of agriculture, that he might not deceive himself by a false opinion of skill, which, if he should find it deficient at home, he had no means of completing. If the world has agreed to praise the travels and manual labours of the Czar of Muscovy,[3] let Col have his share of the like applause, in the proportion of his dominions to the empire of Russia.

This young gentleman was sporting in the mountains of Sky, and when he was weary with following his game, repaired for lodging to Talisker. At night he missed one of his dogs, and when he went to seek him in the morning, found two eagles feeding on his carcass.

Col, for he must be named by his possessions, hearing that our intention was to visit Iona, offered to conduct us to his chief, Sir Allan Maclean,[4] who lived in the isle of Inch Kenneth, and would readily find us a convenient passage. From this time was formed an acquaintance, which being begun by kindness, was accidentally continued by constraint; we derived much pleasure from it, and I hope have given him no reason to repent it.

The weather was now almost one continued storm, and we were to snatch some happy intermission to be conveyed to Mull, the third[n] island of the Hebrides, lying about a degree south of Sky, whence we might easily find our way to Inch Kenneth, where Sir Allan Maclean resided, and afterward to Iona.

For this purpose, the most commodious station that we could take was Armidel, which Sir Alexander Macdonald had now left to a gentleman,[5] who lived there as his factor or steward.

In our way to Armidel was Coriatachan, where we had al-

n. third *Errata*] second *75a, b*

2a. Boswell had been given a letter of introduction to him by Professor Macleod in Aberdeen. See *Life*, v.95.

3. Peter the Great.

4. 18th Chief of Duart and 6th Baronet of Brolas. See *Life*, v.556.

5. James Macdonald. See *Life*, v.275.

ready been, and to which therefore we were very willing to return. We staid however so long at Talisker, that a great part of our journey was performed in the gloom of the evening. In travelling even thus almost without light thro' naked solitude, when there is a guide whose conduct may be trusted, a mind not naturally too much disposed to fear, may preserve some degree of cheerfulness; but what must be the solicitude of him who should be wandering, among the craggs and hollows, benighted, ignorant, and alone?

The fictions of the Gothick romances were not so remote from credibility as they are now thought. In the full prevalence of the feudal institution, when violence desolated the world, and every baron lived in a fortress, forests and castles were regularly succeeded by each other, and the adventurer might very suddenly pass from the gloom of woods, or the ruggedness of moors, to seats of plenty, gaiety, and magnificence. Whatever is imaged in the wildest tale, if giants, dragons, and enchantment be excepted, would be felt by him, who, wandering in the mountains without a guide, or upon the sea without a pilot, should be carried amidst his terror and uncertainty, to the hospitality and elegance of Raasay or Dunvegan.[6]

To Coriatachan at last we came, and found ourselves welcomed as before. Here we staid two days, and made such inquiries as curiosity suggested. The house was filled with company, among whom Mr. Macpherson[7] and his sister distinguished themselves by their politeness and accomplishments. By him we were invited to Ostig, a house not far from Armidel, where we might easily hear of a boat, when the weather would suffer us to leave the island.

---

6. Compare pp. 155–56. "These castles afford another evidence . . . dungeon." This was a favourite argument of the literary antiquarians. Hurd, for example, uses it in defence of Spenser: *Letters on Chivalry and Romance* (1762), Letter XI. How, he asks, are the generality of readers to be persuaded "that the romantic manners are to be accounted *natural*, when not one in ten-thousand knows enough of the barbarous ages, in which they arose, to believe they ever really existed?" (For a wide range of illustrations of this theme, see Arthur Johnston, *Enchanted Ground: A Study of Mediaeval Romance in the Eighteenth Century*, 1964.)

7. Martin Macpherson had succeeded his father, John Macpherson, joint author with Kenneth Macaulay of *The History of St. Kilda*. See p. 26, n. 7 above. "Mr. McPherson is minister of Slate and tacksman of Ostig" (Boswell, *Remarks*). See *Life*, v.547.

OSTIG IN SKY

At Ostig, of which Mr. Macpherson is minister, we were entertained for some days, then removed to Armidel, where we finished our observations on the island of Sky.

As this island lies in the fifty-seventh degree, the air cannot be supposed to have much warmth. The long continuance of the sun above the horizon, does indeed sometimes produce great heat in northern latitudes; but this can only happen in sheltered places, where the atmosphere is to a certain degree stagnant, and the same mass of air continues to receive for many hours the rays of the sun, and the vapours of the earth. Sky lies open on the west and north to a vast extent of ocean, and is cooled in the summer by perpetual ventilation, but by the same blasts is kept warm in winter. Their weather is not pleasing. Half the year is deluged with rain. From the autumnal to the vernal equinox, a dry day is hardly known, except when the showers are suspended by a tempest. Under such skies can be expected no great exuberance of vegetation. Their winter overtakes their summer, and their harvest lies upon the ground drenched with rain. The autumn struggles hard to produce some of our early fruits. I gathered gooseberries in September; but they were small, and the husk was thick.

Their winter is seldom such as puts a full stop to the growth of plants, or reduces the cattle to live wholly on the surplusage of the summer. In the year seventy-one they had a severe season, remembered by the name of the Black Spring, from which the island has not yet recovered. The snow lay long upon the ground, a calamity hardly known before. Part of their cattle died for want, part were unseasonably sold to buy sustenance for the owners; and, what I have not read or heard of before, the kine that survived were so emaciated and dispirited, that they did not require the male at the usual time. Many of the roebucks perished.

The soil, as in other countries, has its diversities. In some parts there is only a thin layer of earth spread upon a rock, which bears nothing but short brown heath, and perhaps is not generally capable of any better product. There are many bogs or mosses of greater or less extent, where the soil cannot be supposed to want depth, though it is too wet for the plow. But we did not observe in these any aquatick plants. The vallies and the mountains are alike darkened with heath. Some grass, however, grows here and there, and some happier spots of earth are capable of tillage.

Their agriculture is laborious, and perhaps rather feeble than unskilful. Their chief manure is sea-weed, which, when they lay it to rot upon the field, gives them a better crop than those of the Highlands. They heap sea shells upon the dunghill, which in time moulder into a fertilising substance. When they find a vein of earth where they cannot use it, they dig it up, and add it to the mould of a more commodious place.

Their corn grounds often lie in such intricacies among the craggs, that there is no room for the action of a team and plow. The soil is then turned up by manual labour, with an instrument called a crooked spade, of a form and weight which to me appeared very incommodious, and would perhaps be soon improved in a country where workmen could be easily found and easily paid. It has a narrow blade of iron fixed to a long and heavy piece of wood, which must have, about a foot and a half above the iron, a knee or flexure with the angle downwards. When the farmer encounters a stone which is the great impediment of his operations, he drives the blade under it, and bringing the knee or angle to the ground, has in the long handle a very forcible lever.

According to the different mode of tillage, farms are distinguished into "long land" and "short land." Long land is that which affords room for a plow, and short land is turned up by the spade.

The grain which they commit to the furrows thus tediously formed, is either oats or barley. They do not sow barley without very copious manure, and then they expect from it ten for one, an increase equal to that of better countries; but the culture is so operose that they content themselves commonly with oats; and who can relate without compassion, that after all their diligence they are to expect only a triple increase? It is in vain to hope for plenty, when a third part of the harvest must be reserved for seed.[o]

When their grain is arrived at the state which they must con-

o. seed *Errata*]   food *75a, b*

sider as ripeness, they do not cut, but pull the barley: to the oats they apply the sickle. Wheel carriages they have none, but make a frame of timber, which is drawn by one horse with the two points behind pressing on the ground. On this they sometimes drag home their sheaves, but often convey them home in a kind of open panier, or frame of sticks upon the horse's back.

Of that which is obtained with so much difficulty, nothing surely ought to be wasted; yet their method of clearing their oats from the husk is by parching them in the straw. Thus with the genuine improvidence of savages, they destroy that fodder for want of which their cattle may perish. From this practice they have two petty conveniencies. They dry the grain so that it is easily reduced to meal, and they escape the theft of the thresher. The taste contracted from the fire by the oats, as by every other scorched substance, use must long ago have made grateful. The oats that are not^p parched must be dried in a kiln.

The barns of Sky I never saw. That which Macleod of Raasay had erected near his house was so contrived, because the harvest is seldom brought home dry, as by perpetual perflation to prevent the mow from heating.

Of their gardens I can judge only from their tables. I did not observe that the common greens were wanting, and suppose, that by choosing an advantageous exposition, they can raise all the more hardy esculent plants. Of vegetable fragrance or beauty they are not yet studious. Few vows are made to Flora in the Hebrides.

They gather a little hay, but the grass is mown late; and is so often almost dry and again very wet, before it is housed, that it becomes a collection of withered stalks without taste or fragrance; it must be eaten by cattle that have nothing else, but by most English farmers would be thrown away.

In the Islands I have not heard that any subterraneous treasures have been discovered, though where there are mountains, there are commonly minerals. One of the rocks in Col has a black vein, imagined to consist of the ore of lead; but it was never yet opened or essayed. In Sky a black mass was accidentally picked up, and brought into the house of the owner of the

p. not *Errata*]   *omitted 75a, b*

land, who found himself strongly inclined to think it a coal, but unhappily it did not burn in the chimney. Common ores would be here of no great value; for what requires to be separated by fire, must, if it were found, be carried away in its mineral state, here being no fewel for the smelting-house or forge. Perhaps by diligent search in this world of stone, some valuable species of marble might be discovered. But neither philosophical curiosity, nor commercial industry, have yet fixed their abode here, where the importunity of immediate want supplied but for the day, and craving on the morrow, has left little room for excursive knowledge or the pleasing fancies of distant profit.

They have lately found a manufacture considerably lucrative. Their rocks abound with kelp, a sea-plant, of which the ashes are melted into glass. They burn kelp in great quantities, and then send it away in ships, which come regularly to purchase them. This new source of riches has raised the rents of many maritime farms; but the tenants pay, like all other tenants, the additional rent with great unwillingness; because they consider the profits of the kelp as the mere product of personal labour, to which the landlord contributes nothing. However, as any man may be said to give, what he gives the power of gaining, he has certainly as much right to profit from the price of kelp as of any thing else found or raised upon his ground.

This new trade has excited a long and eager litigation between Macdonald and Macleod, for a ledge of rocks, which, till the value of kelp was known, neither of them desired the reputation of possessing.

The cattle of Sky are not so small as is commonly believed. Since they have sent their beeves in great numbers to southern marts, they have probably taken more care of their breed. At stated times the annual growth of cattle is driven to a fair, by a general drover, and with the money, which he returns to the farmer, the rents are paid.

The price regularly expected, is from two to three pounds a head; there was once one sold for five pounds. They go from the Islands very lean, and are not offered to the butcher, till they have been long fatted in English pastures.

Of their black cattle, some are without horns, called by the Scots "humble" cows, as we call a bee an "humble" bee,[8] that wants a sting. Whether this difference be specifick, or accidental, though we inquired with great diligence, we could not be informed. We are not very sure that the bull is ever without horns, though we have been told, that such bulls there are. What is produced by putting a horned and unhorned male and female together, no man has ever tried, that thought the result worthy of observation.

Their horses are, like their cows, of a moderate size. I had no difficulty to mount myself commodiously by the favour of the gentlemen. I heard of very little cows in Barra, and very little horses in Rum, where perhaps no care is taken to prevent that diminution of size, which must always happen, where the greater and the less copulate promiscuously, and the young animal is restrained from growth by penury of sustenance.

The goat is the general inhabitant of the earth, complying with every difference of climate, and of soil. The goats of the Hebrides are like others: nor did I hear any thing of their sheep, to be particularly remarked.

In the penury of these malignant regions, nothing is left that can be converted to food. The goats and the sheep are milked like the cows. A single meal of a goat[9] is a quart, and of a sheep a pint. Such at least was the account, which I could extract from those of whom I am not sure that they ever had inquired.

The milk of goats is much thinner than that of cows, and that of sheep is much thicker. Sheeps milk is never eaten before it is boiled: as it is thick, it must be very liberal of curd, and the people of St. Kilda form it into small cheeses.

The stags of the mountains are less than those of our parks, or forests, perhaps not bigger than our fallow deer. Their flesh has no rankness, nor is inferiour in flavour to our common venison. The roebuck I neither saw nor tasted. These are not countries for a regular chase. The deer are not driven with horns and hounds. A sportsman, with his gun in his hand,

---

8. The *Dictionary* (4th ed.) shows that Johnson derived this dubious etymology from Beattie.

9. *meal*: the quantity of milk given at one milking.

watches the animal, and when he has wounded him, traces him by the blood.

They have a race of brinded greyhounds, larger and stronger than those with which we course hares, and those are the only dogs used by them for the chase.

Man is by the use of fire-arms made so much an overmatch for other animals, that in all countries, where they are in use, the wild part of the creation sensibly diminishes. There will probably not be long, either stags or roebucks in the Islands. All the beasts of chase would have been lost long ago in countries well inhabited, had they not been preserved by laws for the pleasure of the rich.

There are in Sky neither rats nor mice, but the weasel is so frequent, that he is heard in houses rattling behind chests or beds, as rats in England. They probably owe to his predominance that they have no other vermin; for since the great rat took possession of this part of the world,[1] scarce a ship can touch at any port, but some of his race are left behind. They have within these few years begun[2] to infest the Isle of Col, where being left by some trading vessel, they have increased for want of weasels to oppose them.

The inhabitants of Sky, and of the other Islands, which I have seen, are commonly of the middle stature, with fewer among them very tall or very short, than are seen in England, or perhaps, as their numbers are small, the chances of any deviation from the common measure are necessarily few. The tallest men that I saw are among those of higher rank. In regions of barrenness and scarcity, the human race is hindered in its growth by the same causes as other animals.

The ladies have as much beauty here as in other places, but bloom and softness are not to be expected among the lower classes, whose faces are exposed to the rudeness of the climate, and whose features are sometimes contracted by want, and sometimes hardened by the blasts. Supreme beauty is seldom

---

1. *Rattus Norvegicus* reached Britain in 1729 and became a factor in social history.

2. All editions read *began*. The *Dictionary* allows either *began* or *begun* for the preterite, but *begun* alone for the past participle. Johnson's a/u can sometimes be misread: he cannot have written *began*.

found in cottages or work-shops, even where no real hardships are suffered. To expand the human face to its full perfection, it seems necessary that the mind should co-operate by placidness of content, or consciousness of superiority.

Their strength is proportionate to their size, but they are accustomed to run upon rough ground, and therefore can with great agility skip over the bog, or clamber the mountain. For a campaign in the wastes of America, soldiers better qualified could not have been found. Having little work to do, they are not willing, nor perhaps able to endure a long continuance of manual labour, and are therefore considered as habitually idle.

Having never been supplied with these[2a] accommodations, which life extensively diversified with trades affords, they supply their wants by very insufficient shifts, and endure many inconveniences, which a little attention would easily relieve. I have seen a horse carrying home the harvest on a crate. Under his tail was a stick for a crupper, held at the two ends by twists of straw. Hemp will grow in the islands, and therefore ropes may be had. If they wanted hemp, they might make better cordage of rushes, or perhaps of nettles, than of straw.

Their method of life neither secures them perpetual health, nor exposes them to any particular diseases. There are physicians in the Islands, who, I believe, all practise chirurgery, and all compound their own medicines.

It is generally supposed, that life is longer in places where there are few opportunities of luxury; but I found no instance here of extraordinary longevity. A cottager grows old over his oaten cakes, like a citizen at a turtle feast. He is indeed seldom incommoded by corpulence. Poverty preserves him from sinking under the burden of himself, but he escapes no other injury of time. Instances of long life are often related, which those who hear them are more willing to credit than examine. To be told that any man has attained a hundred years, gives hope and comfort to him who stands trembling on the brink of his own climacterick.[3]

Length of life is distributed impartially to very different

2a. Johnson may have written *those*; in his hand, *e* and *o* are hard to distinguish.

3. Johnson cites in the *Dictionary* Browne's *Vulgar Errors* for the belief that sixty-three (which he had just passed) is the great *climacteric* (critical year) of human life.

modes of life in very different climates; and the mountains have no greater examples of age and health than the low lands, where I was introduced to two ladies of high quality;[4] one of whom, in her ninety-fourth year, presided at her table with the full exercise of all her powers; and the other has attained her eighty-fourth, without any diminution of her vivacity, and with little reason to accuse time of depredations on her beauty.

In the Islands, as in most other places, the inhabitants are of different rank, and one does not encroach here upon another. Where there is no commerce nor manufacture, he that is born poor can scarcely become rich; and if none are able to buy estates, he that is born to land cannot annihilate his family by selling it. This was once the state of these countries. Perhaps there is no example, till within a century and half, of any family whose estate was alienated otherwise than by violence or forfeiture. Since money has been brought amongst them, they have found, like others, the art of spending more than they receive; and I saw with grief the chief of a very ancient clan, whose island was condemned by law to be sold for the satisfaction of his creditors.[5]

The name of highest dignity is laird, of which there are in the extensive Isle of Sky only three, Macdonald, Macleod, and Mackinnon. The laird is the original owner of the land, whose natural power must be very great, where no man lives but by agriculture; and where the produce of the land is not conveyed through the labyrinths of traffick, but passes directly from the hand that gathers it to the mouth that eats it. The laird has all those in his power that live upon his farms. Kings can, for the most part, only exalt or degrade. The laird at pleasure can feed or starve, can give bread, or withhold[pp] it. This inherent power was yet strengthened by the kindness of consanguinity, and the reverence of patriarchal authority. The laird was the father of

pp. withhold *85*]   withold *75a, 75b*

---

4. One of these was evidently the Dowager Countess of Loudoun (see *Letters* 337), whose age Johnson exaggerated (see *Life*, v.566); the other, the Countess of Eglintoune (see *Letters* 337 and *Life*, v.567).

5. Presumably Lauchlan MacQuarrie (see p. 141 n. 7). Johnson wrote to Mrs. Thrale: "We were introduced to Mr. Macquarry, the head of a small clan, whose ancestors have reigned in Ulva beyond memory, but who has reduced himself by his negligence and folly to the necessity of selling this venerable patrimony" (*Letters* 332).

the clan, and his tenants commonly bore his name. And to these principles of original command was added, for many ages, an exclusive right of legal jurisdiction.

This multifarious, and extensive obligation operated with force scarcely credible. Every duty, moral or political, was absorbed in affection and adherence to the chief. Not many years have passed since the clans knew no law but the laird's will. He told them to whom they should be friends or enemies, what king they should obey, and what religion they should profess.

When the Scots first rose in arms against the succession of the house of Hanover, Lovat, the chief of the Frasers,[6] was in exile for a rape. The Frasers were very numerous, and very zealous against the government. A pardon was sent to Lovat. He came to the English camp, and the clan immediately deserted to him.

Next in dignity to the laird is the tacksman; a large taker or lease-holder of land, of which he keeps part, as a domain, in his own hand, and lets part to under tenants. The tacksman is necessarily a man capable of securing to the laird the whole rent, and is commonly a collateral relation. These "tacks," or subordinate possessions, were long considered as hereditary, and the occupant was distinguished by the name of the place at which he resided. He held a middle station, by which the highest and the lowest orders were connected. He paid rent and reverence to the laird, and received them from the tenants. This tenure still subsists, with its original operation, but not with the primitive stability. Since the islanders, no longer content to live, have learned the desire of growing rich, an ancient dependent is in danger of giving way to a higher bidder, at the expence of domestick dignity and hereditary power. The stranger, whose money buys him preference, considers himself as paying for all that he has, and is indifferent about the laird's honour or safety. The commodiousness of money is indeed great; but there are some advantages which money cannot buy, and which therefore no wise man will by the love of money be tempted to forego.

I have found in the hither parts of Scotland, men not defective in judgment or general experience, who consider the

---

6. The notorious Simon Fraser, twelfth Baron Lovat (1667?–1747).

tacksman[q] as a useless burden of the ground, as a drone who lives upon the product of an estate, without the right of property, or the merit of labour, and who impoverishes at once the landlord and the tenant. The land, say they, is let to the tacksman at six-pence an acre, and by him to the tenant at tenpence. Let the owner be the immediate landlord to all the tenants; if he sets[7] the ground at eight-pence, he will increase his revenue by a fourth part,[8] and the tenant's burthen will be diminished by a fifth.

Those who pursue this train of reasoning, seem not sufficiently to inquire whither it will lead them, nor to know that it will equally shew the propriety of suppressing all wholesale trade, of shutting up the shops of every man who sells what he does not make, and of extruding all whose agency and profit intervene between the manufacturer and the consumer. They may, by stretching their understandings a little wider, comprehend, that all those who by undertaking large quantities of manufacture, and affording[r] employment to many labourers, make themselves considered as benefactors to the publick, have only been robbing their workmen with one hand, and their customers with the other. If Crowley[9] had sold only what he could make, and all his smiths had wrought their own iron with their own hammers, he would have lived on less, and they would have sold their work for more. The salaries of superintendents and clerks would have been partly saved, and partly shared, and nails been sometimes cheaper by a farthing in a hundred. But then if the smith could not have found an immediate purchaser, he must have deserted his anvil; if there had

q. tacksman *85*] tacksmen *75a, b. Syntax requires the singular.*   r. affording *Errata*] afford *75a*

7. *to set*: to let on lease. This sense fell out of general use after the eighteenth century. Compare p. 127, l. 16, "if he could set his land."

8. *"fourth part* should be *third."* RWC.

9. Johnson's cousin Cornelius Ford married Judith, daughter of Ambrose Crowley, ironmaster of Stourbridge. Her half-brother, Sir Ambrose Crow-

ley (1658–1713), was "an historic figure in the development of the north-country iron industry, whose rapid accumulation of wealth made him a butt for the satire of Steele and Addison" (A. L. Reade, *Johnsonian Gleanings* Part III, 1922, pp. 147–48). Johnson had thus more than one reason for choosing Crowley as a significant name in the history of industrial progress.

by accident at any time been more sellers than buyers, the workmen must have reduced their profit to nothing, by underselling one another; and as no great stock could have been in any hand, no sudden demand of large quantities could have been answered, and the builder must have stood still till the nailer could supply him.

According to these schemes, universal plenty is to begin and end in universal misery. Hope and emulation will be utterly extinguished; and as all must obey the call of immediate necessity, nothing that requires extensive views, or provides for distant consequences, will ever be performed.

To the southern inhabitants of Scotland, the state of the mountains and the islands is equally unknown with that of Borneo or Sumatra: Of both they have only heard a little, and guess the rest. They are strangers to the language and the manners, to the advantages and wants of the people, whose life they would model, and whose evils they would remedy.

Nothing is less difficult than to procure one convenience by the forfeiture of another. A soldier may expedite his march by throwing away his arms. To banish the tacksman is easy, to make a country plentiful by diminishing the people, is an expeditious mode of husbandry; but that abundance, which there is nobody to enjoy, contributes little to human happiness.

As the mind must govern the hands, so in every society the man of intelligence must direct the man of labour. If the tacksmen be taken away, the Hebrides must in their present state be given up to grossness and ignorance; the tenant, for want of instruction, will be unskilful, and for want of admonition will be negligent. The laird in these wide estates, which often consist of islands remote from one another, cannot extend his personal influence to all his tenants; and the steward having no dignity annexed to his character, can have little authority among men taught to pay reverence only to birth, and who regard the tacksman as their hereditary superior; nor can the steward have equal zeal for the prosperity of an estate profitable only to the laird, with the tacksman, who has the laird's income involved in his own.

The only gentlemen in the Islands are the lairds, the tacksmen, and the ministers, who frequently improve their livings by becoming farmers. If the tacksmen be banished, who will be left to impart knowledge, or impress civility? The laird must always be at a distance from the greater part of his lands; and if he resides at all upon them, must drag his days in solitude, having no longer either a friend or a companion; he will therefore depart to some more comfortable residence, and leave the tenants to the wisdom and mercy of a factor.

Of tenants there are different orders, as they have greater or less stock. Land is sometimes leased to a small fellowship, who live in a cluster of huts, called a Tenants Town, and are bound jointly and separately for the payment of their rent. These, I believe, employ in the care of their cattle, and the labour of tillage, a kind of tenants yet lower; who having a hut, with grass for a certain number of cows and sheep, pay their rent by a stipulated quantity of labour.

The condition of domestick servants, or the price of occasional labour, I do not know with certainty. I was told that the maids have sheep, and are allowed to spin for their own clothing; perhaps they have no pecuniary wages, or none but in very wealthy families. The state of life, which has hitherto been purely pastoral, begins now to be a little variegated with commerce; but novelties enter by degrees, and till one mode has fully prevailed over the other, no settled notion can be formed.

Such is the system of insular subordination, which, having little variety, cannot afford much delight in the view, nor long detain the mind in contemplation. The inhabitants were for a long time perhaps not unhappy; but their content was a muddy mixture of pride and ignorance, an indifference for pleasures which they did not know, a blind veneration for their chiefs, and a strong conviction of their own importance.

Their pride has been crushed by the heavy hand of a vindictive conqueror, whose severities have been followed by laws, which, though they cannot be called cruel, have produced much discontent, because they operate upon the surface of life, and make every eye bear witness to subjection. To be compelled to a new dress has always been found painful.

Their chiefs being now deprived of their jurisdiction, have already lost much of their influence; and as they gradually degenerate from patriarchal rulers to rapacious landlords, they will divest themselves of the little that remains.

That dignity which they derived from an opinion of their military importance, the law, which disarmed them, has abated. An old gentleman, delighting himself with the recollection of better days, related, that forty years ago, a chieftain walked out attended by ten or twelve followers, with their arms rattling. That animating rabble has now ceased. The chief has lost his formidable retinue; and the Highlander walks his heath unarmed and defenceless, with the peaceable submission of a French peasant or English cottager.

Their ignorance grows every day less, but their knowledge is yet of little other use than to shew them their wants. They are now in the period of education, and feel the uneasiness of discipline, without yet perceiving the benefit of instruction.

The last law,[10] by which the Highlanders are deprived of their arms, has operated with efficacy beyond expectation. Of former statutes made with the same design, the execution had been feeble, and the effect inconsiderable. Concealment was undoubtedly practised, and perhaps often with connivance. There was tenderness, or partiality, on one side, and obstinacy on the other. But the law, which followed the victory of Culloden, found the whole nation dejected and intimidated; informations were given without danger, and without fear, and the arms were collected with such rigour, that every house was despoiled of its defence.

To disarm part of the Highlands, could give no reasonable occasion of complaint. Every government must be allowed the power of taking away the weapon[s] that is lifted against it. But the loyal clans murmured, with some appearance of justice, that after having defended the King, they were forbidden for the future to defend themselves; and that the sword should be forfeited, which had been legally employed. Their case is undoubtedly hard, but in political regulations, good cannot be complete, it can only be predominant.

Whether by disarming a people thus broken into several tribes, and thus remote from the seat of power, more good than evil has been produced, may deserve inquiry. The supreme power in every community has the right of debarring every in-

---

s. weapon *Errata*]   treason *75a*

---

10. The Disarming Act of 1746. See p. 51 n. 8.

dividual, and every subordinate society from self-defence, only because the supreme power is able to defend them; and therefore where the governor cannot act, he must trust the subject to act for himself. These islands might be wasted with fire and sword before their sovereign would know their distress. A gang of robbers, such as has been lately found confederating themselves in the Highlands, might lay a wide region under contribution. The crew of a petty privateer might land on the largest and most wealthy of the islands, and riot without control in cruelty and waste. It was observed by one of the chiefs of Sky, that fifty armed men might, without resistance, ravage the country. Laws that place the subjects in such a state, contravene the first principles of the compact of authority: they exact obedience, and yield no protection.

It affords a generous and manly pleasure to conceive a little nation gathering its fruits and tending its herds with fearless confidence, though it lies open on every side to invasion, where, in contempt of walls and trenches, every man sleeps securely with his sword beside him; where all on the first approach of hostility come[1] together at the call to battle, as at a summons to a festal show; and committing their cattle to the care of those whom age or nature has disabled, engage the enemy with that competition for hazard and for glory, which operate in men that fight under the eye of those, whose dislike or kindness they have always considered as the greatest evil or the greatest good.

This was, in the beginning of the present century, the state of the Highlands. Every man was a soldier, who partook of national confidence, and interested himself in national honour. To lose this spirit, is to lose what no small advantage will compensate.

It may likewise deserve to be inquired, whether a great nation ought to be totally commercial? whether amidst the uncertainty of human affairs, too much attention to one mode of happiness may not endanger others? whether the pride of riches must not sometimes have recourse to the protection of courage? and whether, if it be necessary to preserve in some part of the

---

1. come RWC (MS. note)] came 75a, b; 85; 87. The syntax clearly requires the present tense. Alexander Chalmers in Works (1824) attempted to mend matters by altering engage to engaged, an ineffectual measure adopted in Works (1825).

empire the military spirit, it can subsist more commodiously in
any place, than in remote and unprofitable provinces, where it
can commonly do little harm, and whence it may be called forth
at any sudden exigence?

It must however be confessed, that a man, who places honour
only in successful violence, is a very troublesome and pernicious animal in time of peace; and that the martial character
cannot prevail in a whole people, but by the diminution of all
other virtues. He that is accustomed to resolve all right into
conquest, will have very little tenderness or equity. All the
friendship in such a life can be only a confederacy of invasion,
or alliance of defence. The strong must flourish by force, and
the weak subsist by stratagem.

Till the Highlanders lost their ferocity, with their arms, they
suffered from each other all that malignity could dictate, or
precipitance could act. Every provocation was revenged with
blood, and no man that ventured into a numerous company, by
whatever occasion brought together, was sure of returning
without a wound. If they are now exposed to foreign hostilities,
they may talk of the danger, but can seldom feel it. If they are
no longer martial, they are no longer quarrelsome. Misery is
caused for the most part, not by a heavy crush of disaster, but by
the corrosion of less visible evils, which canker enjoyment, and
undermine security.[2] The visit of an invader is necessarily rare,
but domestick animosities allow no cessation.

The abolition of the local jurisdictions,[3] which had for so
many ages been exercised by the chiefs, has likewise its evil and
its good. The feudal constitution naturally diffused itself into
long ramifications of subordinate authority. To this general
temper of the government was added the peculiar form of the
country, broken by mountains into many subdivisions scarcely
accessible but to the natives, and guarded by passes, or per-
plexed with intricacies, through which national justice could
not find its way.

---

2. Birkbeck Hill noticed the resemblance between this passage and a
sentence in the *Life of Pope*: "It has
been well observed that the misery of
man proceeds not from any single
crush of overwhelming evil, but from
small vexations continually repeated"
(*Lives*, III.234 [par. 340]). He suggests

that Johnson is "quoting himself."
The sentiment may, however, have
been a commonplace.

3. Act for the Abolition of herita-
ble jurisdictions in Scotland 1747
(Douglas, *English Historical Documents*, x.622).

The power of deciding controversies, and of punishing offences, as some such power there must always be, was intrusted to the lairds of the country, to those whom the people considered as their natural judges. It cannot be supposed that a rugged proprietor of the rocks, unprincipled and unenlightened, was a nice resolver of entangled claims, or very exact in proportioning punishment to offences. But the more he indulged his own will, the more he held his vassals in dependance. Prudence and innocence, without the favour of the chief, conferred no security; and crimes involved no danger, when the judge was resolute to acquit.

When the chiefs were men of knowledge and virtue, the convenience of a domestick judicature was great. No long journies were necessary, nor artificial delays could be practised; the character, the alliances, and interests of the litigants were known to the court, and all false pretences were easily detected. The sentence, when it was past, could not be evaded; the power of the laird superseded formalities, and justice could not be defeated by interest or stratagem.

I doubt not but that since the regular judges have made their circuits through the whole country, right has been every where more wisely, and more equally distributed; the complaint is, that litigation is grown troublesome, and that the magistrates are too few, and therefore often too remote for general convenience.

Many of the smaller islands have no legal officer within them. I once asked, If a crime should be committed, by what authority the offender could be seized? and was told, that the laird would exert his right; a right which he must now usurp, but which surely necessity must vindicate, and which is therefore yet exercised in lower degrees, by some of the proprietors, when legal processes cannot be obtained.

In all greater questions, however, there is now happily an end to all fear or hope from malice or from favour. The roads are secure in those places through which, forty years ago, no traveller could pass without a convoy. All trials of right by the sword are forgotten, and the mean are in as little danger from the powerful as in other places. No scheme of policy has, in any country, yet brought the rich and poor on equal terms into courts of judicature. Perhaps experience, improving on experience, may in time effect it.

Those who have long enjoyed dignity and power, ought not to lose it without some equivalent. There was paid to the chiefs by the publick, in exchange for their privileges, perhaps a sum greater than most of them had ever possessed, which excited a thirst for riches, of which it shewed them the use. When the power of birth and station ceases, no hope remains but from the prevalence of money. Power and wealth supply the place of each other. Power confers the ability of gratifying our desire without the consent of others. Wealth enables us to obtain the consent of others to our gratification. Power, simply considered, whatever it confers on one, must take from another. Wealth enables its owner to give to others, by taking only from himself. Power pleases the violent and proud: wealth delights the placid and the timorous. Youth therefore flies at power, and age grovels after riches.

The chiefs, divested of their prerogatives, necessarily turned their thoughts to the improvement of their revenues, and expect more rent, as they have less homage. The tenant, who is far from perceiving that his condition is made better in the same proportion, as that of his landlord is made worse, does not immediately see why his industry is to be taxed more heavily than before. He refuses to pay the demand, and is ejected; the ground is then let to a stranger, who perhaps brings a larger stock, but who, taking the land at its full price, treats with the laird upon equal terms, and considers him not as a chief, but as a trafficker in land. Thus the estate perhaps is improved, but the clan is broken.

It seems to be the general opinion, that the rents have been raised with too much eagerness. Some regard must be paid to prejudice. Those who have hitherto paid but little, will not suddenly be persuaded to pay much, though they can afford it. As ground is gradually improved, and the value of money decreases, the rent may be raised without any diminution of the farmer's profits: yet it is necessary in these countries, where the ejection of a tenant is a greater evil, than in more populous places, to consider not merely what the land will produce, but with what ability the inhabitant can cultivate it. A certain stock can allow but a certain payment; for if the land be doubled, and the stock remains the same, the tenant becomes no richer. The proprietors of the Highlands might perhaps often increase their

income, by subdividing the farms, and allotting to every oc-
cupier only so many acres as he can profitably employ, but that
they want people.

There seems now, whatever be the cause, to be through a
great part of the Highlands a general discontent. That adherence, which was lately professed by every man to the chief of
his name, has now little prevalence; and he that cannot live as
he desires at home, listens to the tale of fortunate islands, and
happy regions, where every man may have land of his own, and
eat the product of his labour without a superior.

Those who have obtained grants of American lands, have, as
is well known, invited settlers from all quarters of the globe;
and among other places, where oppression might produce a
wish for new habitations, their emissaries would not fail to try
their persuasions in the Isles of Scotland, where at the time
when the clans were newly disunited from their chiefs, and
exasperated by unprecedented exactions, it is no wonder that
they prevailed.

Whether the mischiefs of emigration were immediately perceived, may be justly questioned. They who went first, were
probably such as could best be spared; but the accounts sent by
the earliest adventurers, whether true or false, inclined many
to follow them; and whole neighbourhoods formed parties for
removal; so that departure from their native country is no
longer exile. He that goes thus accompanied, carries with him
all that makes life pleasant. He sits down in a better climate,
surrounded by his kindred and his friends: they carry with
them their language, their opinions, their popular songs, and
hereditary merriment: they change nothing but the place of
their abode; and of that change they perceive the benefit.

This is the real effect of emigration, if those that go away together settle on the same spot, and preserve their ancient union.
But some relate that these adventurous visitants of unknown
regions, after a voyage passed in dreams of plenty and felicity,
are dispersed at last upon a sylvan wilderness, where their first
years must be spent in toil, to clear the ground which is afterwards to be tilled, and that the whole effect of their undertaking is only more fatigue and equal scarcity.

Both accounts may be suspected. Those who are gone will
endeavour by every art to draw others after them; for as their

numbers are greater, they will provide better for themselves. When Nova Scotia was first peopled, I remember a letter, published under the character of a New Planter, who related how much the climate put him in mind of Italy.[3a] Such intelligence the Hebridians probably receive from their transmarine correspondents. But with equal temptations of interest, and perhaps with no greater niceness of veracity, the owners of the islands spread stories of American hardships to keep their people content at home.

Some method to stop this epidemick desire of wandering, which spreads its contagion from valley to valley, deserves to be sought with great diligence. In more fruitful countries, the removal of one only makes room for the succession of another: but in the Hebrides, the loss of an inhabitant leaves a lasting vacuity; for nobody born in any other parts of the world will choose this country for his[t] residence; and an island once depopulated will remain a desert, as long as the present facility of travel gives every one, who is discontented and unsettled, the choice of his abode.

Let it be inquired, whether the first intention of those who are fluttering on the wing,[4] and collecting a flock that they may take their flight, be to attain good, or to avoid evil. If they are dissatisfied with that part of the globe, which their birth has allotted them, and resolve not to live without the pleasures of happier climates; if they long for bright suns, and calm skies, and flowery fields, and fragrant gardens, I know not by what eloquence they can be persuaded, or by what offers they can be hired to stay.

But if they are driven from their native country by positive evils, and disgusted by ill-treatment, real or imaginary, it were fit to remove their grievances, and quiet their resentment;

t. his Errata]   their 75a

3a. Johnson probably had in mind a sentence from "Extract of a letter from Chebucto harbour, Nova Scotia" in the Gentleman's Magazine for Oct. 1749 (XIX.472): "Every body arrived at present have excellent appetites, from the good temperament of the air; which puts me in mind of Italy, and I think there is a good prospect of its being altogether as fertile, and in time as enchanting to its inhabitants."

4. "Johnson, while holding out for the conglobation of swallows, accepted the migration of woodcock as proved" (RWC, with reference to Life, II.55 and 248).

since, if they have been hitherto undutiful subjects, they will not much mend their principles by American conversation.

To allure them into the army, it was thought proper to indulge them in the continuance of their national dress. If this concession could have any effect, it might easily be made. That dissimilitude of appearance, which was supposed to keep them distinct from the rest of the nation, might disincline them from coalescing with the Pensylvanians, or people of Connecticut. If the restitution of their arms will reconcile them to their country, let them have again those weapons, which will not be more mischievous at home than in the Colonies. That they may not fly from the increase of rent, I know not whether the general good does not require that the landlords be, for a time, restrained in their demands, and kept quiet by pensions proportionate to their loss.

To hinder insurrection, by driving away the people, and to govern peaceably, by having no subjects, is an expedient that argues no great profundity of politicks. To soften the obdurate, to convince the mistaken, to mollify the resentful, are worthy of a statesman; but it affords a legislator little self-applause to consider, that where there was formerly an insurrection, there is now a wilderness.

It has been a question often agitated without solution, why those northern regions are now so thinly peopled, which formerly overwhelmed with their armies the Roman empire. The question supposes what I believe is not true, that they had once more inhabitants than they could maintain, and overflowed only because they were full.

This is to estimate the manners of all countries and ages by our own. Migration, while the state of life was unsettled, and there was little communication of intelligence between distant places, was among the wilder nations of Europe, capricious and casual. An adventurous projector heard of a fertile coast unoccupied, and led out a colony; a chief of renown for bravery, called the young men together, and led them out to try what fortune would present. When Caesar was in Gaul, he found the Helvetians preparing to go they knew not whither, and put a stop to their motions. They settled again in their own country, where they were so far from wanting room, that they had accumulated three years provision for their march.

The religion of the North was military; if they could not find enemies, it was their duty to make them: they travelled in quest of danger, and willingly took the chance of empire or death. If their troops were numerous, the countries from which they were collected are of vast extent, and without much exuberance of people great armies may be raised where every man is a soldier. But their true numbers were never known. Those who were conquered by them are their historians, and shame may have excited them to say, that they were overwhelmed with multitudes. To count is a modern practice, the ancient method was to guess; and when numbers are guessed they are always magnified.

Thus England has for several years been filled with the atchievements of seventy thousand Highlanders employed in America. I have heard from an English officer, not much inclined to favour them, that their behaviour deserved a very high degree of military praise; but their number has been much exaggerated. One of the ministers told me, that seventy thousand men could not have been found in all the Highlands, and that more than twelve thousand never took the field. Those that went to the American war, went to destruction. Of the old Highland regiment,[5] consisting of twelve hundred, only seventy-six survived to see their country again.

The Gothick swarms have at least been multiplied with equal liberality. That they bore no great proportion to the inhabitants, in whose countries they settled, is plain from the paucity of northern words now found in the provincial languages.[6] Their country was not deserted for want of room, because it was covered with forests of vast extent; and the first effect of plenitude of inhabitants is the destruction of wood. As

---

5. The 42nd, or Black Watch—called "the old Highland Regiment" to distinguish it from "those raised in the Seven Years' War" (Colonel David Stewart, *Sketches of the Highlanders of Scotland* . . . , I.289, n. †)—suffered heavy losses at Ticonderoga (1758): "more than half of the men, and two-thirds of the officers, either killed or desperately wounded" (I.285). Their next service was in the West Indies, where "they suffered more by the climate than by the enemy" (I.302). Recruitment figures in Britain after these vicissitudes suggest severe depletion.

6. Languages spoken in the Roman provinces of Gaul and Spain. "In the Provinciall languages or Romances (as the French and Spanish are called) *Il Re, Roy,* & *Re* are plainly from *Rex*" (John Selden, *Titles of Honour,* 1614, p. 44). See also Temple, *Upon Poetry,* in *Miscellanea* (1690), II.iv. 36.

the Europeans spread over America, the lands are gradually laid naked.

I would not be understood to say, that necessity had never any part in their expeditions. A nation, whose agriculture is scanty or unskilful, may be driven out by famine. A nation of hunters may have exhausted their game. I only affirm that the northern regions were not, when their irruptions subdued the Romans, overpeopled with regard to their real extent of territory, and power of fertility. In a country fully inhabited, however afterward laid waste, evident marks will remain of its former populousness. But of Scandinavia and Germany, nothing is known but that as we trace their state upwards into antiquity, their woods were greater, and their cultivated ground was less.

That causes very different from want of room may produce a general disposition to seek another country is apparent from the present conduct of the Highlanders, who are in some places ready to threaten a total secession. The numbers which have already gone, though like other numbers they may be magnified, are very great, and such as if they had gone together and agreed upon any certain settlement, might have founded an independent government in the depths of the western continent. Nor are they only the lowest and most indigent; many men of considerable wealth have taken with them their train of labourers and dependants; and if they continue the feudal scheme of polity, may establish new clans in the other hemisphere.

That the immediate motives of their desertion must be imputed to their landlords, may be reasonably concluded, because some lairds of more prudence and less rapacity have kept their vassals undiminished. From Raasa only one man had been seduced, and at Col there was no wish to go away.

The traveller who comes hither from more opulent countries, to speculate upon the remains of pastoral life, will not much wonder that a common Highlander has no strong adherence to his native soil; for of animal enjoyments, or of physical good, he leaves nothing that he may not find again wheresoever he may be thrown.

The habitations of men in the Hebrides may be distinguished into huts and houses. By a "house," I mean a building with one story over another; by a "hut," a dwelling with only one floor. The laird, who formerly lived in a castle, now lives in a house; sometimes sufficiently neat, but seldom very spacious or splendid. The tacksmen and the ministers have commonly houses. Wherever there is a house, the stranger finds a welcome, and to the other evils of exterminating tacksmen may be added the unavoidable cessation of hospitality, or the devolution of too heavy a burden on the ministers.

Of the houses little can be said. They are small, and by the necessity of accumulating stores,[u] where there are so few opportunities of purchase, the rooms are very heterogeneously filled. With want of cleanliness it were ingratitude to reproach them. The servants having been bred upon the naked earth, think every floor clean, and the quick succession of guests, perhaps not always over-elegant, does not allow much time for adjusting their apartments.

Huts are of many gradations; from murky dens, to commodious dwellings.

The wall of a common hut is always built without mortar, by a skilful adaptation of loose stones. Sometimes perhaps a double wall of stones is raised, and the intermediate space filled with earth. The air is thus completely excluded. Some walls are, I think, formed of turfs, held together by a wattle, or texture of twigs. Of the meanest huts, the first room is lighted by the entrance, and the second by the smoke-hole. The fire is usually made in the middle. But there are huts, or dwellings of only one story,[7] inhabited by gentlemen, which have walls cemented with mortar, glass windows, and boarded floors. Of these all have chimneys, and some chimneys have grates.

The house and the furniture are not always nicely suited. We were driven once, by missing a passage, to the hut of a gentleman, where, after a very liberal supper, when I was conducted to my chamber, I found an elegant bed of Indian cotton, spread with fine sheets. The accommodation was flattering; I un-

u. stores *Errata*]   stoves *75a*

7. huts, or dwellings of only one story RWC] huts, or dwellings, of only one story *75a, b; 85; 87*. Dwellings of only one story, being a definition of hut, will not admit an internal comma.

dressed myself, and felt my feet in the mire. The bed stood upon the bare earth, which a long course of rain had softened to a puddle.

In pastoral countries the condition of the lowest rank of people is sufficiently wretched. Among manufacturers, men that have no property may have art and industry, which make them necessary, and therefore valuable. But where flocks and corn are the only wealth, there are always more hands than work, and of that work there is little in which skill and dexterity can be much distinguished. He therefore who is born poor never can be rich. The son merely occupies the place of the father, and life knows nothing of progression or advancement.

The petty tenants, and labouring peasants, live in miserable cabins, which afford them little more than shelter from the storms. The boor of Norway is said to make all his own utensils. In the Hebrides, whatever might be their ingenuity, the want of wood leaves them no materials. They are probably content with such accommodations as stones of different forms and sizes can afford them.

Their food is not better than their lodging. They seldom taste the flesh of land animals; for here are no markets. What each man eats is from his own stock. The great effect of money is to break property into small parts. In towns, he that has a shilling may have a piece of meat; but where there is no commerce, no man can eat mutton but by killing a sheep.

Fish in fair weather they need not want; but, I believe, man never lives long on fish, but by constraint; he will rather feed upon roots and berries.

The only fewel of the Islands is peat. Their wood is all consumed, and coal they have not yet found. Peat is dug out of the marshes, from the depth of one foot to that of six. That is accounted the best which is nearest the surface. It appears to be a mass of black earth held together by vegetable fibres. I know not whether the earth be bituminous, or whether the fibres be not the only combustible part; which, by heating the interposed earth red hot, make a burning mass. The heat is not very strong nor lasting. The ashes are yellowish, and in a large quantity. When they dig peat, they cut it into square pieces, and pile it up to dry beside the house. In some places it has an offensive smell. It is like wood charked[8] for the smith. The common method of making peat fires, is by heaping it on the hearth; but it burns well in grates, and in the best houses is so used.

The common opinion is, that peat grows again where it has been cut; which, as it seems to be chiefly a vegetable substance, is not unlikely to be true, whether known or not to those who relate it.

There are water mills in Sky and Raasa; but where they are too far distant, the house-wives grind their oats with a quern, or hand-mill, which consists of two stones, about a foot and a half in diameter, the lower is a little convex, to which the concavity of the upper must be fitted. In the middle of the upper stone is a round hole, and on one side is a long handle. The grinder sheds the corn gradually into the hole with one hand, and works the handle round with the other. The corn slides down the convexity of the lower stone, and by the motion of the upper is ground in its passage. These stones are found in Lochabar.

The Islands afford few pleasures, except to the hardy sportsman, who can tread the moor and climb the mountain. The distance of one family from another, in a country where travelling has so much difficulty, makes frequent intercourse impracticable. Visits last several days, and are commonly paid by water; yet I never saw a boat furnished with benches, or made commodious by any addition to the first fabrick. Conveniencies are not missed where they never were enjoyed.

The solace which the bagpipe can give, they have long enjoyed; but among other changes, which the last Revolution introduced, the use of the bagpipe begins to be forgotten. Some of the chief families still entertain a piper, whose office was anciently hereditary. Macrimmon was piper to Macleod, and Rankin to Maclean of Col.

The tunes of the bagpipe are traditional. There has been in Sky, beyond all time of memory, a college of pipers, under the direction of Macrimmon, which is not quite extinct. There was another in Mull, superintended by Rankin, which expired about sixteen years ago. To these colleges, while the pipe re-

---

8. *to chark*: "to burn to a black cinder, as wood is burned to make charcoal" (*Dictionary*).

tained its honour, the students of musick repaired for education. I have had my dinner exhilarated by the bagpipe, at Armidale, at Dunvegan, and in Col.

The general conversation of the Islanders has nothing particular. I did not meet with the inquisitiveness of which I have
read, and suspect the judgment to have been rashly made. A
stranger of curiosity comes into a place where a stranger is seldom seen: he importunes the people with questions, of which
they cannot guess the motive, and gazes with surprise on things
which they, having had them always before their eyes, do not
suspect of any thing wonderful. He appears to them like some
being of another world, and then thinks it peculiar that they
take their turn to inquire whence he comes, and whither he is
going.

The Islands were long unfurnished with instruction for
youth, and none but the sons of gentlemen could have any literature. There are now parochial schools, to which the lord of
every manor pays a certain stipend. Here the children are
taught to read; but by the rule of their institution, they teach
only English, so that the natives read a language which they
may never use or understand. If a parish, which often happens,
contains several islands, the school being but in one, cannot
assist the rest. This is the state of Col, which, however, is more
enlightened than some other places; for the deficiency is supplied by a young gentleman,[9] who, for his own improvement,
travels every year on foot over the Highlands to the session at
Aberdeen; and at his return, during the vacation, teaches to
read and write in his native island.

In Sky there are two grammar schools, where boarders are
taken to be regularly educated. The price of board is from three
pounds, to four pounds ten shillings a year, and that of instruction is half a crown a quarter. But the scholars are birds of
passage, who live at school only in the summer; for in winter
provisions[1] cannot be made for any considerable number in one
place. This periodical dispersion impresses strongly the scarcity
of these countries.

---

9. Another Donald Maclean, son of
Neil Maclean. See p. 130 n. 5.
1. Eighteenth-century usage allowed the plural (provisions) in
phrases where modern usage would
prefer the singular.

Having heard of no boarding-school for ladies nearer than Inverness, I suppose their education is generally domestick. The elder daughters of the higher families are sent into the world, and may contribute by their acquisitions to the improvement of the rest.

Women must here study to be either pleasing or useful. Their deficiencies are seldom supplied by very liberal fortunes. A hundred pounds is a portion beyond the hope of any but the laird's daughter. They do not indeed often give money with their daughters; the question is, How many cows a young lady will bring her husband. A rich maiden has from ten to forty; but two cows are a decent fortune for one who pretends to no distinction.

The religion of the Islands is that of the Kirk of Scotland. The gentlemen with whom I conversed are all inclined to the English liturgy; but they are obliged to maintain the established minister, and the country is too poor to afford payment to another, who must live wholly on the contribution of his audience.

They therefore all attend the worship of the Kirk, as often as a visit from their minister, or the practicability of travelling gives them opportunity; nor have they any reason to complain of insufficient pastors; for I saw not one in the Islands, whom I had reason to think either deficient in learning, or irregular in life; but found several with whom I could not converse without wishing, as my respect increased, that they had not been Presbyterians.

The ancient rigour of puritanism is now very much relaxed, though all are not yet equally enlightened. I sometimes met with prejudices sufficiently malignant, but they were prejudices of ignorance. The ministers in the Islands had attained such knowledge as may justly be admired in men, who have no motive to study, but generous curiosity, or, what is still better, desire of usefulness; with such politeness as so narrow a circle of converse could not have supplied, but to minds naturally disposed to elegance.

Reason and truth will prevail at last. The most learned of the Scottish doctors would now gladly admit a form of prayer, if the people would endure it. The zeal or rage of congregations has its different degrees. In some parishes the Lord's Prayer is suffered:[2] in others it is still rejected as a form; and he that should make it part of his supplication would be suspected of heretical pravity.

The principle upon which extemporary prayer was originally introduced, is no longer admitted. The minister formerly, in the effusion of his prayer, expected immediate, and perhaps perceptible inspiration, and therefore thought it his duty not to think before what he should say. It is now universally confessed, that men pray as they speak on other occasions, according to the general measure of their abilities and attainments. Whatever each may think of a form prescribed by another, he cannot but believe that he can himself compose by study and meditation a better prayer than will rise in his mind at a sudden call; and if he has any hope of supernatural help, why may he not as well receive it when he writes as when he speaks.

In the variety of mental powers, some must perform extemporary prayer with much imperfection; and in the eagerness and rashness of contradictory opinions, if publick liturgy be left to the private judgment of every minister, the congregation may often be offended or misled.

There is in Scotland, as among ourselves, a restless suspicion of popish machinations, and a clamour of numerous converts to the Romish religion. The report is, I believe, in both parts of the island equally false. The Romish religion is professed only in Egg and Canna, two small islands, into which the Reformation never made its way. If any missionaries are busy in the Highlands, their zeal entitles them to respect, even from those who cannot think favourably of their doctrine.

---

2. For a record of one phase of the controversy as to the use of the Lord's Prayer in Presbyterian worship, see: *A Collection of Letters, Relative to an Essay upon the Lords Prayer, which was printed, Anno 1704. And now reprinted Anno 1709. both by Sir Hugh Campbell of Calder . . . The Essay itself is printed at the end of the Collection* (1709). Sir Hugh had pleaded for the admission of the Lord's Prayer in public worship, and incurred severe censure. See also William Metcalfe, *Sir Hugh Campbell and the Lord's Prayer* (1937). Thomas Morer, in his *Short Account of Scotland* (1702)—which Boswell lent to Johnson; see *Life*, III.242—observes: "The Episcopal Minister . . . concludes his *own Prayer* with that of the Lord's (sic), which the Presbyterian refuses to do" (pp. 61–62).

The political tenets of the Islanders I was not curious to investigate,[3] and they were not eager to obtrude. Their conversation is decent and inoffensive. They disdain to drink for their principles, and there is no disaffection at their tables. I never heard a health offered by a Highlander that might not have circulated with propriety within the precincts of the King's palace.

Legal government has yet something of novelty to which they cannot perfectly conform. The ancient spirit, that appealed only to the sword, is yet among them. The tenant of Scalpa, an island belonging to Macdonald, took no care to bring his rent; when the landlord talked of exacting payment, he declared his resolution to keep his ground, and drive all intruders from the island, and continued to feed his cattle as on his own land, till it became necessary for the Sheriff to dislodge him by violence.

The various kinds of superstition which prevailed here, as in all other regions of ignorance, are by the diligence of the ministers almost extirpated.

Of Browny, mentioned by Martin,[4] nothing has been heard for many years. Browny was a sturdy fairy; who, if he was fed, and kindly treated, would, as they said, do a great deal of work. They now pay him no wages, and are content to labour for themselves.

In Troda, within these three-and-thirty years, milk was put every Saturday for *Greogach*,[5] or "the old man with the long beard." Whether *Greogach* was courted as kind, or dreaded as terrible, whether they meant, by giving him the milk, to obtain good, or avert evil, I was not informed. The minister is now living by whom the practice was abolished.

They have still among them a great number of charms for

---

3. "You have touched the tenets of the islanders with a very soft address" (Boswell, *Remarks*). Horace Walpole describes George III as startled by his first reading of the *Journey*: "I protest, Johnson seems to be a Papist and a Jacobite!" (*Correspondence*, ed. W. S. Lewis, 1965, XXXII.225; quoted in *Life*, II.290, n. 2). Johnson wrote to Hector a month later: "The King says, I must go into that country no more" (*Letters* 376.1).

4. *Description*, pp. 110, and 391–92.
5. Kenneth Macaulay, *History of St. Kilda* (1764), describes a stone "on which they formerly poured, on the Sundays, *libations of milk*, to a subordinate Divinity, whose name was *Gruagach* . . . this *Gruagach* was a good humoured, sportive and placable Deity. . . . The name of the God signifies, in the Galic tongue, one with fine hair or long tresses" (pp. 86–87).

the cure of different diseases; they are all invocations, perhaps transmitted to them from the times of popery, which increasing knowledge will bring into disuse.

They have opinions, which cannot be ranked with superstition, because they regard only natural effects. They expect better crops of grain, by sowing their seed in the moon's increase. The moon has great influence in vulgar philosophy. In my memory it was a precept annually given in one of the English Almanacks,[6] "to kill hogs when the moon was increasing, and the bacon would prove the better in boiling."

We should have had little claim to the praise of curiosity, if we had not endeavoured with particular attention to examine the question of the "second sight." Of an opinion received for centuries by a whole nation, and supposed to be confirmed through its whole descent, by a series of successive facts, it is desirable that the truth should be established, or the fallacy detected.

The "second sight" is an impression made either by the mind upon the eye, or by the eye upon the mind, by which things distant or future are perceived, and seen as if they were present. A man on a journey far from home falls from his horse, another, who is perhaps at work about the house, sees him bleeding on the ground, commonly with a landscape of the place where the accident befalls him. Another seer, driving home his cattle, or wandering in idleness, or musing in the sunshine, is suddenly surprised by the appearance of a bridal ceremony, or funeral procession, and counts the mourners or attendants, of whom, if he knows them, he relates the names, if he knows them not, he can describe the dresses. Things distant are seen at the instant when they happen. Of things future I know not that there is any rule for determining the time between the "sight" and the event.

This receptive faculty, for power it cannot be called, is neither voluntary nor constant. The appearances have no dependence upon choice: they cannot be summoned, detained, or recalled. The impression is sudden, and the effect often painful.

---

6. "A fit time to kill fat swine is in the increase, nigh the full moone, the lard will the better indure the boiling"   (John Neve's *Almanac* for 1653, B 2ᵇ). LFP.

By the term "second sight," seems to be meant a mode of seeing, superadded to that which Nature generally bestows. In the Earse it is called *taisch*;[7] which signifies likewise a spectre, or a vision. I know not, nor is it likely that the Highlanders ever examined, whether by *taisch*, used for "second sight," they mean the power of seeing, or the thing seen.

I do not find it to be true, as it is reported, that to the "second sight" nothing is presented but phantoms of evil. Good seems to have the same proportion in those visionary scenes, as it obtains in real life: almost all remarkable events have evil for their basis; and are either miseries incurred, or miseries escaped. Our sense is so much stronger of what we suffer, than of what we enjoy, that the ideas of pain predominate in almost every mind. What is recollection but a revival of vexations, or history but a record of wars, treasons, and calamities?[8] Death, which is considered as the greatest evil, happens to all. The greatest good, be it what it will, is the lot but of a part.

That they should often see death is to be expected; because death is an event frequent and important. But they see likewise more pleasing incidents. A gentleman told me, that when he had once gone far from his own island, one of his labouring servants predicted his return, and described the livery of his attendant, which he had never worn at home; and which had been, without any previous design, occasionally given him.

Our desire of information was keen, and our inquiry frequent. Mr. Boswell's frankness and gaiety made every body communicative; and we heard many tales of these airy shows, with more or less evidence[9] and distinctness.

It is the common talk of the Lowland Scots, that the notion of the "second sight" is wearing away with other superstitions; and that its reality is no longer supposed, but by the grossest people. How far its prevalence ever extended, or what ground it has lost, I know not. The Islanders of all degrees, whether of rank or understanding, universally admit it, except the ministers, who universally deny it, and are suspected to deny it, in

---

7. *taibhse*: apparition, or vision of the second sight (Dwelly).

8. Cf. *Rambler* 175: "What are all the records of history, but narratives of successive villanies, of treasons and usurpations, massacres and wars?"

9. *evidence*: "the state of being evident . . . indubitable certainty" (*Dictionary*).

consequence of a system, against conviction. One of them honestly told me, that he came to Sky with a resolution not to believe it.[1]

Strong reasons for incredulity will readily occur. This faculty of seeing things out of sight is local, and commonly useless. It is a breach of the common order of things, without any visible reason or perceptible benefit. It is ascribed only to a people very little enlightened; and among them, for the most part, to the mean and the ignorant.

To the confidence of these objections it may be replied, that by presuming to determine what is fit, and what is beneficial, they presuppose more knowledge of the universal system than man has attained; and therefore depend upon principles too complicated and extensive for our comprehension; and that there can be no security in the consequence, when the premises are not understood; that the "second sight" is only wonderful because it is rare, for, considered in itself, it involves no more difficulty than dreams, or perhaps than the regular exercise of the cogitative faculty; that a general opinion of communicative impulses, or visionary representations, has prevailed in all ages and all nations; that particular instances have been given, with such evidence, as neither Bacon nor Bayle[2] has been able to resist; that sudden impressions, which the event has verified, have been felt by more than own or publish them; that the "second sight" of the Hebrides implies only the local frequency of a power, which is nowhere totally unknown; and that where we are unable to decide by antecedent reason, we must be content to yield to the force of testimony.

By pretension to "second sight," no profit was ever sought or

---

1. Martin Macpherson of Sleat. See p. 77 n. 7. "I believe all the ministers in Sky are natives. Mr. Macpherson who told you he was *resolved* not to believe, was born at Ostig—so he did not *come* to Sky resolved—I am wrong. He was born in the island of Barra" (Boswell, *Remarks*).

2. RWC observed that an association between Bacon and *Boyle* would be more natural—"they are coupled in a famous passage of the Preface to the Dictionary"—but forbore to emend.

Professor Sherbo has shown that Boyle is by far the more probable name: Johnson frequently coupled it with Bacon's; Birch, in his edition of Boyle's *Works* (1772), had mentioned manuscript notes by Boyle on the second sight; the emendation was made in five early editions. See "The Text of Johnson's *Journey to the Western Islands of Scotland*: 'Bayle' or 'Boyle'?" *Notes and Queries*, 26 April 1952, pp. 182–84.

gained. It is an involuntary affection, in which neither hope nor fear are known to have any part. Those who profess to feel it, do not boast of it as a privilege, nor are considered by others as advantageously distinguished. They have no temptation to feign; and their hearers have no motive to encourage the imposture.[2a]

To talk with any of these seers is not easy. There is one living in Sky, with whom we would have gladly conversed; but he was very gross and ignorant, and knew no English. The proportion in these countries of the poor to the rich is such, that if we suppose the quality to be accidental, it can very rarely happen to a man of education; and yet on such men it has sometimes fallen. There is now a "second sighted" gentleman in the Highlands, who complains of the terrors to which he is exposed.

The foresight of the seers is not always prescience: they are impressed with images, of which the event only shews them the meaning. They tell what they have seen to others, who are at that time not more knowing than themselves, but may become at last very adequate witnesses, by comparing the narrative with its verification.

To collect sufficient testimonies for the satisfaction of the publick, or of ourselves, would have required more time than we could bestow. There is, against it, the seeming analogy of things confusedly seen, and little understood; and for it, the indistinct cry of national persuasion, which may be perhaps resolved at last into prejudice and tradition. I never could advance my curiosity to conviction; but came away at last only willing to believe.

As there subsists no longer in the Islands much of that peculiar and discriminative form of life, of which the idea had delighted our imagination, we were willing to listen to such accounts of past times as would be given us. But we soon found what memorials were to be expected from an illiterate people, whose whole time is a series of distress; where every morning is labouring with expedients for the evening; and where all mental pains or pleasure[3] arose from the dread of winter, the ex-

---

2a. In this paragraph Johnson's argument follows closely one in Martin's *Description*, p. 309.

3. RWC conjectured that Johnson may have written *pleasures*. But cf.

Johnson's *Cowley*: ". . . which enables us to conceive and to excite the pains and the pleasure of other minds . . ." (*Lives*, 1.20 [par. 57]).

pectation of spring, the caprices of their chiefs, and the motions
of the neighbouring clans; where there was neither shame from
ignorance, nor pride in knowledge; neither curiosity to inquire, nor vanity to communicate.

The chiefs indeed were exempt from urgent penury, and
daily difficulties; and in their houses were preserved what accounts remained of past ages. But the chiefs were sometimes
ignorant and careless, and sometimes kept busy by turbulence
and contention; and one generation of ignorance effaces the
whole series of unwritten history. Books are faithful repositories, which may be a while neglected or forgotten; but when
they are opened again, will again impart their instruction:
memory, once interrupted, is not to be recalled. Written learning is a fixed luminary, which, after the cloud that had hidden
it has past away, is again bright in its proper station. Tradition
is but a meteor, which, if once it falls, cannot be rekindled.

It seems to be universally supposed, that much of the local
history was preserved by the bards, of whom one is said to have
been retained by every great family. After these bards were
some of my first inquiries; and I received such answers as, for
a while, made me please myself with my increase of knowledge;
for I had not then learned how to estimate the narration of a
Highlander.

They said that a great family had a bard and a *senachi*,[4]
who were the poet and historian of the house; and an old gentleman told me that he remembered one of each. Here was a
dawn of intelligence. Of men that had lived within memory,
some certain knowledge might be attained. Though the office
had ceased, its effects might continue; the poems might be
found, though there was no poet.

Another conversation indeed informed me, that the same
man was both bard and *senachi*. This variation discouraged
me; but as the practice might be different in different times, or
at the same time in different families, there was yet no reason
for supposing that I must necessarily sit down in total ignorance.

Soon after I was told by a gentleman, who is generally acknowledged the greatest master of Hebridian antiquities,[5] that

---

4. *seanachaidh*: reciter of tales, keeper of records, genealogist (Dwelly).

5. Sir James Foulis, 5th baronet of Colinton (1714–91). See *Life*, v.150, 518.

there had indeed once been both bards and *senachies*; and that *senachi* signified "the man of talk," or of conversation; but that neither bard nor *senachi* had existed for some centuries. I have no reason to suppose it exactly known at what time the custom ceased, nor did it probably cease in all houses at once. But whenever the practice of recitation was disused, the works, whether poetical or historical, perished with the authors; for in those times nothing had been written in the Earse language.

Whether the "man of talk" was a historian, whose office was to tell truth, or a story-teller, like those which were in the last century, and perhaps are now among the Irish, whose trade was only to amuse, it now would be vain to inquire.

Most of the domestick offices were, I believe, hereditary; and probably the laureat of a clan was always the son of the last laureat. The history of the race could no otherwise be communicated, or retained; but what genius could be expected in a poet by inheritance?

The nation was wholly illiterate. Neither bards nor *senachies* could write or read; but if they were ignorant, there was no danger of detection; they were believed by those whose vanity they flattered.

The recital of genealogies, which has been considered as very efficacious to the preservation of a true series of ancestry, was anciently made, when the heir of the family came to manly age. This practice has never subsisted within time of memory, nor was much credit due to such rehearsers, who might obtrude fictitious pedigrees, either to please their masters, or to hide the deficiency of their own memories.

Where the chiefs of the Highlands have found the histories of their descent is difficult to tell; for no Earse genealogy was ever written. In general this only is evident, that the principal house of a clan must be very ancient, and that those must have lived long in a place, of whom it is not known when they came thither.

Thus hopeless are all attempts to find any traces of Highland learning. Nor are their primitive customs and ancient manner of life otherwise than very faintly and uncertainly remembered by the present race.

The peculiarities which strike the native of a commercial country, proceeded in a great measure from the want of money.

To the servants and dependents that were not domesticks, and if an estimate be made from the capacity of any of their old houses which I have seen, their domesticks could have been but few, were appropriated certain portions of land for their support. Macdonald has a piece of ground yet, called the bards' or *senachies'* field. When a beef was killed for the house, particular parts were claimed as fees by the several officers, or workmen. What was the right of each I have not learned. The head belonged to the smith, and the udder of a cow to the piper: the weaver had likewise his particular part; and so many pieces followed these prescriptive claims, that the laird's was at last but little.

The payment of rent in kind has been so long disused in England, that it is totally forgotten. It was practised very lately in the Hebrides, and probably still continues, not only in St. Kilda, where money is not yet known, but in others of the smaller and remoter islands. It were perhaps to be desired, that no change in this particular should have been made. When the laird could only eat the produce of his lands, he was under the necessity of residing upon them; and when the tenant could not convert his stock into more portable riches, he could never be tempted away from his farm, from the only place where he could be wealthy. Money confounds subordination, by overpowering the distinctions of rank and birth, and weakens authority by supplying power of resistance, or expedients for escape. The feudal system is formed for a nation employed in agriculture, and has never long kept its hold where gold and silver have become common.

Their arms were anciently the *glaymore*, or great two-handed sword, and afterwards the two-edged sword and target, or buckler, which was sustained on the left arm. In the midst of the target, which was made of wood, covered with leather, and studded with nails, a slender lance, about two feet long, was sometimes fixed; it was heavy and cumberous, and accordingly has for some time past been gradually laid aside. Very few targets were at Culloden. The dirk, or broad dagger, I am afraid, was of more use in private quarrels than in battles. The Lochaber-ax is only a slight alteration of the old English bill.

After all that has been said of the force and terrour of the Highland sword, I could not find that the art of defence was any part of common education. The gentlemen were perhaps sometimes skilful gladiators, but the common men had no other powers than those of violence and courage. Yet it is well known, that the onset of the Highlanders was very formidable. As an army cannot consist of philosophers, a panick is easily excited by any unwonted mode of annoyance. New dangers are naturally magnified; and men accustomed only to exchange bullets at a distance, and rather to hear their enemies than see them, are discouraged and amazed when they find themselves encountered hand to hand, and catch the gleam of steel flashing in their faces.

The Highland weapons gave opportunity for many exertions of personal courage, and sometimes for single combats in the field; like those which occur so frequently in fabulous wars. At Falkirk, a gentleman now living, was, I suppose after the retreat of the King's troops, engaged at a distance from the rest with an Irish dragoon. They were both skilful swordsmen, and the contest was not easily decided: the dragoon at last had the advantage, and the Highlander called for quarter; but quarter was refused him, and the fight continued till he was reduced to defend himself upon his knee. At that instant one of the Macleods came to his rescue; who, as it is said, offered quarter to the dragoon, but he thought himself obliged to reject what he had before refused, and, as battle gives little time to deliberate, was immediately killed.

Funerals were formerly solemnized by calling multitudes together, and entertaining them at great expence. This emulation of useless cost has been for some time discouraged, and at last in the Isle of Sky is almost suppressed.

Of the Earse language, as I understand nothing, I cannot say more than I have been told. It is the rude speech of a barbarous people, who had few thoughts to express, and were content, as they conceived grossly, to be grossly understood. After what has been lately talked of Highland bards, and Highland genius, many will startle when they are told, that the Earse never was a written language; that there is not in the world an Earse manuscript a hundred years old; and that the sounds of the Highlanders were never expressed by letters, till some little books of piety were translated, and a metrical version of the Psalms was made by the Synod of Argyle.[6] Whoever therefore now writes in this language, spells according to his own perception of the sound, and his own idea of the power of the letters. The Welsh and the Irish are cultivated tongues. The Welsh, two hundred years ago, insulted their English neighbours for the instability of their orthography;[7] while the Earse merely floated in the breath of the people, and could therefore receive little improvement.

When a language begins to teem with books, it is tending to refinement; as those who undertake to teach others must have undergone some labour in improving themselves, they set a proportionate value on their own thoughts, and wish to enforce them by efficacious expressions; speech becomes embodied and permanent; different modes and phrases are compared, and the best obtains an establishment. By degrees one age improves upon another. Exactness is first obtained, and afterwards elegance. But diction, merely vocal, is always in its childhood. As no man leaves his eloquence behind him, the new generations have all to learn. There may possibly be books without a pol-

---

6. For an account of the arrangements made by the Synod of Argyle for translation into Scots Gaelic of the Shorter Catechism and the Psalms, see *Minutes of the Synod of Argyle,* ed. Duncan C. MacTavish (Scottish History Society, 3rd series: XXXVII [1943], 1639–51; XXXVIII [1944], 1652–61). "The Synod's activities . . . eventually comprised a Gaelic translation of the Shorter Catechism (1653), a Gaelic metrical version of the Psalms (first fifty 1659, complete edition 1694) and a translation of the Old Testament, possibly of the whole Bible, which failed to secure the permanence of print and the manuscript of which has now probably disappeared" (XXXVII.xix). In 1751 the Synod approved a complete version of the Psalms made by Alexander MacFarlain, and *Sailm Dhaibhidh ann Dan Gaoidhealach* appeared (Glasgow, 1753). For Johnson's interest in these translations, see L. F. Powell, "Samuel Johnson: An Early 'Friend of the Bod-

leian'," *Bodleian Quarterly* 59, December 1928, pp. 280–81; also *Life,* II.508.

7. Johnson refers to the censure of English orthography by Sir John Price: *Historiae Brytannicae Defensio, Joanne Priseo Equestris Ordinis Brytanno Authore* (1573), pp. 5–6. His attention may have been drawn to it by Charles Butler's plea for spelling reform: *The English Grammar, or the Institution of Letters, Syllables and Words in the English Tongue* (Oxford, 1633), in which an illustrative anecdote from the *Defensio* is thus translated: the instability of English orthography "gave occasion to Sir John Price (wheither more tartly or truely I know not) taxing our orthographie to preferre his own: where he saith, that foure good secretaries, writing a sentence in English from his mouth, differed all, one from an other, in many letters: whereas so many Welch, writing the same in their tongue, varied not in any one letter" (fol. 3ʳ).

ished language, but there can be no polished language without books.

That the bards could not read more than the rest of their countrymen, it is reasonable to suppose; because, if they had read, they could probably have written; and how high their compositions may reasonably be rated, an inquirer may best judge by considering what stores of imagery, what principles of ratiocination, what comprehension of knowledge, and what delicacy of elocution he has known any man attain who cannot read. The state of the bards was yet more hopeless. He that cannot read, may now converse with those that can; but the bard was a barbarian among barbarians, who, knowing nothing himself, lived with others that knew no more.

There has lately been in the Islands one of these illiterate poets,[8] who hearing the Bible read at church, is said to have turned the sacred history into verse. I heard part of a dialogue, composed by him, translated by a young lady in Mull,[9] and thought it had more meaning that I expected from a man totally uneducated; but he had some opportunities of knowledge; he lived among a learned people. After all that has been done for the instruction of the Highlanders, the antipathy between their language and literature still continues; and no man that has learned only Earse is, at this time, able to read.

The Earse has many dialects, and the words used in some islands are not always known in others. In literate nations, though the pronunciation, and sometimes the words of common speech may differ, as now in England, compared with the south of Scotland, yet there is a written diction, which pervades all dialects, and is understood in every province. But where the whole language is colloquial, he that has only one part, never gets the rest, as he cannot get it but by change of residence.

In an unwritten speech, nothing that is not very short is transmitted from one generation to another. Few have opportunities of hearing a long composition often enough to learn it, or have inclination to repeat it so often as is necessary to retain it; and what is once forgotten is lost for ever. I believe there

---

8. John Maclean of Mull. His poems were taken down by Dr. Hector Maclean. See *Life*, v.555.

9. Mary, daughter of Dr. Hector Maclean. See p. 137.

cannot be recovered, in the whole Earse language, five hundred lines of which there is any evidence to prove them a hundred years old. Yet I hear that the father of Ossian[1] boasts of two chests more of ancient poetry, which he suppresses, because they are too good for the English.

He that goes into the Highlands with a mind naturally acquiescent, and a credulity eager for wonders, may come back with an opinion very different from mine; for the inhabitants knowing the ignorance of all strangers in their language and antiquities, perhaps are not very scrupulous adherents to truth; yet I do not say that they deliberately speak studied falsehood, or have a settled purpose to deceive. They have inquired and considered little, and do not always feel their own ignorance. They are not much accustomed to be interrogated by others; and seem never to have thought upon interrogating themselves; so that if they do not know what they tell to be true, they likewise do not distinctly perceive it to be false.

Mr. Boswell was very diligent in his inquiries; and the result of his investigations was, that the answer to the second question was commonly such as nullified the answer to the first.

We were a while told, that they had an old translation of the scriptures; and told it till it would appear obstinacy to inquire again. Yet by continued accumulation of questions we found, that the translation meant, if any meaning there were, was nothing else than the Irish Bible.[2]

---

1. James Macpherson (1736–96) claimed that his *Fingal* (1762) and *Tamora* (1763) were translations from the Gaelic of Ossian. Johnson denied their authenticity, besides thinking meanly of their poetic value. For the course taken by the quarrel between Johnson and Macpherson, so far as it can be traced, see *Life*, ii.510–14.

2. The complete translation of the Bible into Irish Gaelic, prepared "by the care and diligence of" William Bedell (1571–1642), when Bishop of Kilmore, but not published until 1685. (The New Testament, a reprint of the Elizabethan translation, has its own title-page, bearing the date 1681). Johnson may have first learned of it

from *The Life of William Bedell, D.D. . . . Bishop of Kilmore in Ireland*, by Gilbert Burnet, Bishop of Salisbury, published anonymously in 1685 —this being most probably the life of Bedell which he possessed. The reprint of the Irish text in Roman characters in 1690, under the superintendence of Robert Kirk, and with a little vocabulary, may have given rise to belief in a Scottish version, for it was popularly known as "Kirke's Bible" (Alexander Cameron, *Reliquiae Celticae*, Inverness, 1892, i.cxxxvii–viii). A copy of the Gaelic New Testament, by R. Kirk, Glasgow, 1754, inscribed "Bt. at the sale of Dr. Johnson's Library" is at Trinity College, Glasgow.

We heard of manuscripts that were, or that had been in the hands of somebody's father, or grandfather; but at last we had no reason to believe they were other than Irish. Martin mentions Irish,[3] but never any Earse manuscripts, to be found in the Islands in his time.

I suppose my opinion of the poems of Ossian is already discovered. I believe they never existed in any other form than that which we have seen. The editor, or author, never could shew the original;[4] nor can it be shewn by any other; to revenge reasonable incredulity, by refusing evidence, is a degree of insolence, with which the world is not yet acquainted; and stubborn audacity is the last refuge of guilt. It would be easy to shew it if he had it; but whence could it be had? It is too long to be remembered, and the language formerly had nothing written. He has doubtless inserted names that circulate in popular stories, and may have translated some wandering ballads, if any can be found; and the names, and some of the images being recollected, make an inaccurate auditor imagine, by the help of Caledonian bigotry, that he has formerly heard the whole.

I asked a very learned minister in Sky, who had used all arts to make me believe the genuineness of the book, whether at last he believed it himself? but he would not answer.[5] He wished me to be deceived, for the honour of his country; but would not directly and formally deceive me. Yet has this man's testimony been publickly produced, as of one that held *Fingal* to be the work of Ossian.

It is said, that some men of integrity profess to have heard parts of it, but they all heard them when they were boys; and it was never said that any of them could recite six lines. They remember names, and perhaps some proverbial sentiments; and, having no distinct ideas, coin a resemblance without an original. The persuasion of the Scots, however, is far from uni-

---

3. "Ancient Irish manuscripts in the Irish character" (Martin, *Description*, p. 89).

4. For the probability that an answer to this charge, in M'Nicol's *Remarks on Dr. Samuel Johnson's Journey to the Hebrides* (1779), was interpolated by Macpherson himself,

see Chapman, pp. 484–85.

5. A very learned Minister: Donald Macqueen. "He would not answer": Edward Topham reports, at second hand, that Macqueen denied this. See E. T., *Letters from Edinburgh* (1776), p. 143.

versal; and in a question so capable of proof, why should doubt be suffered to continue? The editor has been heard to say, that part of the poem was received by him, in the Saxon character. He has then found, by some peculiar fortune, an unwritten language, written in a character which the natives probably never beheld.

I have yet supposed no imposture but in the publisher,[6] yet I am far from certainty, that some translations have not been lately made, that may now be obtruded[7] as parts of the original work. Credulity on one part is a strong temptation to deceit on the other, especially to deceit of which no personal injury is the consequence, and which flatters the author with his own ingenuity. The Scots have something to plead for their easy reception of an improbable fiction: they are seduced by their fondness for their supposed ancestors. A Scotchman must be a very sturdy moralist, who does not love Scotland better than truth: he will always love it better than inquiry; and if falsehood flatters his vanity, will not be very diligent to detect it. Neither ought the English to be much influenced by Scotch authority; for of the past and present state of the whole Earse nation, the Lowlanders are at least as ignorant as ourselves. To be ignorant is painful; but it is dangerous to quiet our uneasiness by the delusive opiate of hasty persuasion.

But this is the age in which those who could not read, have been supposed to write; in which the giants of antiquated romance have been exhibited as realities. If we know little of the ancient Highlanders, let us not fill the vacuity with Ossian. If we have not searched the Magellanick regions, let us however forbear to people them with Patagons.

Having waited some days at Armidel, we were flattered at last with a wind that promised to convey us to Mull. We went on board a boat that was taking in kelp, and left the Isle of Sky behind us. We were doomed to experience, like others, the danger of trusting to the wind, which blew against us, in a short

---

6. *"publisher,* of course, has the same reference as *editor* above, and does not mean the *bookseller.* Johnson calls Pope and Theobald 'publishers of Shakespeare'." RWC.

7. "Johnson's uncertainty cannot concern the fact of translations lately made; it must refer to their purpose, or to their probable effects. I suspect that he is thinking of the motive, and that he wrote *that they may now be obtruded.*" RWC.

time, with such violence, that we, being no seasoned sailors, were willing to call it a tempest.[8] I was sea-sick and lay down. Mr. Boswell kept the deck. The master knew not well whither to go; and our difficulties might perhaps have filled a very pathetick page, had not Mr. Maclean of Col,[9] who, with every other qualification which insular life requires, is a very active and skilful mariner,[v] piloted us safe into his own harbour.

COL

In the morning we found ourselves under the Isle of Col, where we landed; and passed the first day and night with Captain Maclean,[1] a gentleman who has lived some time in the East Indies; but having dethroned no Nabob, is not too rich to settle in his own country.

Next day the wind was fair, and we might have had an easy passage to Mull; but having, contrarily to our own intention, landed upon a new island, we would not leave it wholly unexamined. We therefore suffered the vessel to depart without us, and trusted the skies for another wind.

v. is a very active and skilful mariner *Errata*] in a very active and skilful manner *75a*

---

8. Boswell, after correcting some details of the sea-passage, which is admirably recounted in his *Tour*, objects: "You treat the storm too lightly" (*Remarks*). Johnson's admission of the danger they were in may be inferred from his tribute to Donald Maclean: but for his seamanship, "our difficulties might perhaps have filled a very pathetic page"—an obituary notice. For a circumstantial estimate of the risk they ran, see Francis E. Skipp, "Johnson and Boswell Afloat," *The New Rambler, The Journal of the Johnson Society of London,* B.XVI, January 1965.

9. Donald Maclean (see p. 62 n. 5), usually distinguished as "young Col." Boswell characterizes him more fully

in his *Journal* than in the published *Tour,* as though concerned to explain the pleasure Johnson took in his society: "He had a constant good humour, and readiness of conversation upon common things. Then he had a clear sharp voice, and was not afraid to talk to Mr. Johnson; informed him as to many particulars, and stuck to his point when Mr. Johnson opposed what he said, until very handsomely driven off. With all this he had as much civility as could be wished, and very great attention to have everything right about Mr. Johnson" (*Journal*, p. 258).

1. Captain Lauchlan Maclean, retired from the Bengal Service. See *Journal*, p. 428.

Mr. Maclean of Col,[2] having a very numerous family, has, for some time past, resided at Aberdeen, that he may superintend their education, and leaves the young gentleman, our friend, to govern his dominions, with the full power of a Highland chief. By the absence of the Laird's family, our entertainment was made more difficult, because the house was in a great degree disfurnished; but young Col's kindness and activity supplied all defects, and procured us more than sufficient accommodation.

Here I first mounted a little Highland steed; and if there had been many spectators, should have been somewhat ashamed of my figure in the march. The horses of the Islands, as of other barren countries, are very low: they are indeed musculous and strong, beyond what their size gives reason for expecting; but a bulky man upon one of their backs makes a very disproportionate appearance.

From the habitation of Captain Maclean, we went to Grissipol, but called by the way on Mr. Hector Maclean, the Minister of Col, whom we found in a hut, that is, a house of only one floor, but with windows and chimney, and not inelegantly furnished. Mr. Maclean has the reputation of great learning: he is seventy-seven years old, but not infirm, with a look of venerable dignity, excelling what I remember in any other man.

His conversation was not unsuitable to his appearance. I lost some of his good-will, by treating a heretical writer[3] with more regard than, in his opinion, a heretick could deserve. I honoured his orthodoxy, and did not much censure his asperity. A man who has settled his opinions, does not love to have the tranquillity of his conviction disturbed; and at seventy-seven it is time to be in earnest.

Mention was made of the Earse translation of the New Testament,[4] which has been lately published, and of which the

2. Hugh Maclean, 13th Laird of Coll, father of "young Col."

3. Samuel Clarke (1675–1729). Boswell makes it clear that, while Johnson and Hector Maclean were talking at cross-purposes about Bayle, Clarke, and Leibnitz, the heretic whom Johnson defended was Clarke. See *Life*, v.288; also William Seward's *Anecdotes* (1795), II.313: "A friend of Dr. Johnson asked him one day, whose sermons were the best in the English language. 'Why, Sir, bating a little heresy those of Dr. Samuel Clarke'." For evidence of Johnson's regard for Clarke, see Maurice J. Quinlan, *Samuel Johnson: a Layman's Religion* (Madison, University of Wisconsin Press, 1964), Chapter II.

4. By James Stuart, minister of Killin (Edinburgh, 1767). See *Letters* 360 and *Life*, II.508.

learned Mr. Macqueen of Sky spoke with commendation; but Mr. Maclean said he did not use it, because he could make the text more intelligible to his auditors by an extemporary version. From this I inferred, that the language of the translation was not the language of the Isle of Col.

He has no publick edifice for the exercise of his ministry; and can officiate to no greater number, than a room can contain; and the room of a hut is not very large. This is all the opportunity of worship that is now granted to the inhabitants of the island, some of whom must travel thither perhaps ten miles. Two chapels were erected by their ancestors, of which I saw the skeletons, which now stand faithful witnesses of the triumph of Reformation.

The want of churches is not the only impediment to piety: there is likewise a want of ministers. A parish often contains more islands than one; and each island can have the minister only in its own turn. At Raasa they had, I think, a right to service only every third Sunday. All the provision made by the present ecclesiastical constitution, for the inhabitants of about a hundred square miles, is a prayer and sermon in a little room, once in three weeks: and even this parsimonious distribution is at the mercy of the weather; and in those islands where the minister does not reside, it is impossible to tell how many weeks or months may pass without any publick exercise of religion.

GRISSIPOL IN COL

After a short conversation with Mr. Maclean, we went on to Grissipol, a house and farm tenanted by Mr. Macsweyn, where I saw more of the ancient life of a Highlander, than I had yet found.[5] Mrs. Macsweyn could speak no English, and had never seen any other places than the islands of Sky, Mull, and Col: but she was hospitable and good-humoured, and spread her table with sufficient liberality. We found tea here, as in every other place, but our spoons were of horn.

The house of Grissipol stands by a brook very clear and

---

5. To Boswell, Johnson was more explicit; see *Life*, v.305. It was Mac-
Sweyn who distrusted Young Col's agricultural innovations; see p. 124.

quick; which is, I suppose, one of the most copious streams in the island. This place was the scene of an action, much celebrated in the traditional history of Col, but which probably no two relaters will tell alike.

Some time, in the obscure ages, Macneil of Barra married the Lady Maclean, who had the Isle of Col for her jointure. Whether Macneil detained Col, when the widow was dead, or whether she lived so long as to make her heirs impatient, is perhaps not now known. The younger son, called John Gerves, or "John the Giant," a man of great strength, who was then in Ireland, either for safety, or for education, dreamed of recovering his inheritance; and getting some adventurers together, which, in those unsettled times, was not hard to do, invaded Col. He was driven away, but was not discouraged, and collecting new followers, in three years came again with fifty men. In his way he stopped at Artorinish in Morvern, where his uncle was prisoner to Macleod, and was then with his enemies in a tent. Maclean took with him only one servant, whom he ordered to stay at the outside; and where he should see the tent pressed outwards, to strike with his dirk; it being the intention of Maclean, as any man provoked him, to lay hands upon him, and push him back. He entered the tent alone, with his Lochabar-axe in his hand, and struck such terror into the whole assembly, that they dismissed his uncle.

When he landed at Col, he saw the sentinel, who kept watch towards the sea, running off to Grissipol, to give Macneil, who was there with a hundred and twenty men, an account of the invasion. He told Macgill, one of his followers, that if he intercepted that dangerous intelligence, by catching the courier, he would give him certain lands in Mull. Upon this promise, Macgill pursued the messenger, and either killed, or stopped him; and his posterity, till very lately, held the lands in Mull.

The alarm being thus prevented, he came unexpectedly upon Macneil. Chiefs were in those days never wholly unprovided for an enemy. A fight ensued, in which one of their followers is said to have given an extraordinary proof of activity, by bounding backwards over the brook of Grissipol. Macneil being killed, and many of his clan destroyed, Maclean took possession of the island, which the Macneils attempted to conquer by another invasion, but were defeated and repulsed.

Maclean, in his turn, invaded the estate of the Macneils, took the castle of Brecacig, and conquered the Isle of Barra, which he held for seven years, and then restored it to the heirs.

CASTLE OF COL

From Grissipol, Mr. Maclean conducted us to his father's seat; a neat new house, erected near the old castle, I think, by the last proprietor. Here we were allowed to take our station, and lived very commodiously, while we waited for moderate weather and a fair wind, which we did not so soon obtain, but we had time to get some information of the present state of Col, partly by inquiry, and partly by occasional excursions.

Col is computed to be thirteen miles in length, and three in breadth. Both the ends are the property of the Duke of Argyle, but the middle belongs to Maclean, who is called Col, as the only laird.

Col is not properly rocky; it is rather one continued rock, of a surface much diversified with protuberances, and covered with a thin layer of earth, which is often broken, and discovers the stone. Such a soil is not for plants that strike deep roots; and perhaps in the whole island nothing has ever yet grown to the height of a table. The uncultivated parts are clothed with heath, among which industry has interspersed spots of grass and corn; but no attempt has yet been made to raise a tree. Young Col, who has a very laudable desire of improving his patrimony, purposes some time to plant an orchard; which, if it be sheltered by a wall, may perhaps succeed. He has introduced the culture of turnips, of which he has a field, where the whole work was performed by his own hand. His intention is to provide food for his cattle in the winter. This innovation was considered by Mr. Macsweyn as the idle project of a young head, heated with English fancies; but he has now found that turnips will really grow, and that hungry sheep and cows will really eat them.

By such acquisitions as these, the Hebrides may in time rise above their annual distress. Wherever heath will grow, there is reason to think something better may draw nourishment; and by trying the production of other places, plants will be found suitable to every soil.

Col has many lochs, some of which have trouts and eels, and others have never yet been stocked; another proof of the negligence of the Islanders, who might take fish in the inland waters, when they cannot go to sea.

Their quadrupeds are horses, cows, sheep, and goats. They have neither deer, hares, nor rabbits. They have no vermin, except rats, which have been lately brought thither by sea, as to other places; and are free from serpents, frogs, and toads.

The harvest in Col, and in Lewis, is ripe sooner than in Sky; and the winter in Col is never cold, but very tempestuous. I know not that I ever heard the wind so loud in any other place; and Mr. Boswell observed, that its noise was all its own, for there were no trees to increase it.

Noise is not the worst effect of the tempests; for they have thrown the sand from the shore over a considerable part of the land; and it is said still to encroach and destroy more and more pasture; but I am not of opinion, that by any surveys or landmarks, its limits have been ever fixed, or its progression ascertained. If one man has confidence enough to say, that it advances, nobody can bring any proof to support him[6] in denying it. The reason why it is not spread to a greater extent, seems to be, that the wind and rain come almost together, and that it is made close and heavy by the wet before the storms can put it in motion. So thick is the bed, and so small the particles, that if a traveller should be caught by a sudden gust in dry weather, he would find it very difficult to escape with life.

For natural curiosities, I was shown only two great masses of stone,[6a] which lie loose upon the ground; one on the top of a hill, and the other at a small distance from the bottom. They certainly were never put into their present places by human strength or skill; and though an earthquake might have broken off the lower stone, and rolled it into the valley, no account can be given of the other, which lies on the hill, unless, which I forgot to examine, there be still near it some higher rock, from

---

6. *Sc.* himself.   6a. Glacial boulders on Beinn
                                      Hogh (LFP).

which it might be torn. All nations have a tradition, that their earliest ancestors were giants, and these stones are said to have been thrown up and down by a giant and his mistress. There are so many more important things, of which human knowledge can give no account, that it may be forgiven us, if we speculate no longer on two stones in Col.

This island is very populous. About nine-and-twenty years ago,[7] the fencible[8] men of Col were reckoned one hundred and forty, which is the sixth of eight hundred and forty; and probably some contrived to be left out of the list. The minister told us, that a few years ago the inhabitants were eight hundred, between the ages of seven and of seventy. Round numbers are seldom exact. But in this case the authority is good, and the errour likely to be little. If to the eight hundred be added what the laws of computation require, they will be increased to at least a thousand; and if the dimensions of the country have been accurately related, every mile maintains more than twenty-five.

This proportion of habitation is greater than the appearance of the country seems to admit; for wherever the eye wanders, it sees[9] much waste and little cultivation. I am more inclined to extend the land, of which no measure has ever been taken, than to diminish the people, who have been really numbered. Let it be supposed, that a computed mile contains a mile and a half, as was commonly found true in the mensuration of the English roads, and we shall then allot nearly twelve to a mile, which agrees much better with ocular observation.

Here, as in Sky and other islands, are the laird, the tacksmen, and the under tenants.

Mr. Maclean, the laird, has very extensive possessions, being proprietor, not only of far the greater part of Col, but of the extensive island of Rum, and a very considerable territory in Mull.

Rum is one of the larger islands, almost square, and there-

---

7. Another of Johnson's indirect references to the '45. Cf. p. 63 n. 1.

8. *fencible*: "capable of defence" (*Dictionary*). Johnson is however using it here in the Scottish sense: fit and liable to be called on for defensive military service. He is presumably quoting his informant verbatim.

9. sees *75a*] seems *75b*. *Sees* appears the better reading; *seems*, a repetition from the first part of the sentence (dittography).

fore of great capacity in proportion to its sides. By the usual method of estimating computed extent, it may contain more than a hundred and twenty square miles.

It originally belonged to Clanronald, and was purchased by Col; who, in some dispute about the bargain, made Clanronald prisoner, and kept him nine months in confinement. Its owner represents it as mountainous, rugged, and barren. In the hills there are red deer. The horses are very small, but of a breed eminent for beauty. Col, not long ago, bought one of them from a tenant; who told him, that as he was of a shape uncommonly elegant, he could not sell him but at a high price; and that whoever had him should pay a guinea and a half.

There are said to be in Barra a race of horses yet smaller, of which the highest is not above thirty-six inches.

The rent of Rum is not great. Mr. Maclean declared, that he should be very rich, if he could set his land[9a] at two-pence halfpenny an acre. The inhabitants are fifty-eight families, who continued Papists for some time after the laird became a Protestant. Their adherence to their old religion was strengthened by the countenance of the laird's sister, a zealous Romanist, till one Sunday, as they were going to mass under the conduct of their patroness, Maclean met them on the way, gave one of them a blow on the head with a "yellow stick," I suppose a cane, for which the Earse had no name, and drove them to the kirk, from which they have never since departed. Since the use of this method of conversion, the inhabitants of Egg and Canna, who continue Papists, call the Protestantism of Rum, the religion of the Yellow Stick.

The only Popish islands are Egg and Canna. Egg is the principal island of a parish, in which, though he has no congregation, the Protestant minister resides. I have heard of nothing curious in it, but the cave in which a former generation of the Islanders were smothered by Macleod.

If we had travelled with more leisure, it had not been fit to have neglected the Popish islands. Popery is favourable to ceremony; and among ignorant nations, ceremony is the only preservative of tradition. Since Protestantism was extended to the savage parts of Scotland, it has perhaps been one of the chief

9a. See p. 87 n. 7.

labours of the ministers to abolish stated observances, because they continued the remembrance of the former religion. We therefore who came to hear old traditions, and see antiquated manners, should probably have found them amongst the Papists.[1]

Canna, the other Popish island, belongs to Clanronald. It is said not to comprise more than twelve miles of land, and yet maintains as many inhabitants as Rum.

We were at Col under the protection of the young Laird, without any of the distresses, which Mr. Pennant, in a fit of simple credulity, seems to think almost worthy of an elegy by Ossian.[2] Wherever we roved, we were pleased to see the reverence with which his subjects regarded him. He did not endeavour to dazzle them by any magnificence of dress: his only distinction was a feather in his bonnet; but as soon as he appeared, they forsook their work and clustered about him: he took them by the hand, and they seemed mutually delighted. He has the proper disposition of a chieftain, and seems desirous to continue the customs of his house. The bagpiper played regularly, when dinner was served, whose person and dress made a good appearance; and he brought no disgrace upon the family of Rankin, which has long supplied the Lairds of Col with hereditary musick.

The tacksmen of Col seem to live with less dignity and convenience than those of Sky; where they had good houses, and tables not only plentiful, but delicate. In Col only two houses pay the window tax; for only two have six windows, which, I suppose, are the Laird's and Mr. Macsweyn's.

1. This passage was substituted by Johnson for one in which he had inadvertently repeated himself. See discussion of cancels, pp. xxxiv–xxxv and illustration.

2. A retort to Pennant's quip: "To the north . . . is the isle of Col, still more celebrated for being the place where Doctor Samuel Johnson had long and woeful experience of oats being the food of men in Scotland, as they are of horses in England" (Thomas Pennant, *A Tour in Scotland, and Voyage to the Hebrides MDCCLXXII*, Chester, 1774, p. 270).

Pennant must surely have learnt of that last day's delay when, still anchored off Coll, Johnson and Boswell shared a cabin and compared their liking for oatmeal, of which Boswell had found some in a barrel. See *Life*, v.308. He had the last word: see *Of London* (1790), where he calls Johnson's rejoinder "a tender hug" (p. 200). This reference to Pennant and that on p. 149 must have been written after 17 May 1774: the *London Chronicle* for 17–19 May announces Pennant's *Tour* as "this day . . . published."

teftant. Their adherence to their old religion was ftrengthened by the countenance
of the Laird's fifter, a zealous Romanift,
till one Sunday, as they were going to mafs
under the conduct of their patronefs, *Maclean* met them on the way, gave one of
them a blow on the head with a *yellow
ftick*, I fuppofe a cane, for which the *Earfe*
had no name, and drove them to the kirk,
from which they have never fince departed.
Since the ufe of this method of converfion,
the inhabitants of *Egg* and *Canna*, who
continue Papifts, call the Proteftantifm of
Rum, the religion of the *Yellow Stick*.

The only popifh Iflands are *Egg* and
Canna. Egg is the principal Ifland of a
parifh, in which, though he has no congregation, the Proteftant Minifter refides. I
have heard of nothing curious in it, but a
cave which contains memorials of an old
tranfaction.

U 4   The

The cancelled text of leaf U4. By kind permission of Mrs. Donald F. Hyde.

The inhabitants once laid hold on a boat manned by *Macleod*, and tying the crew hand and foot, pushed them off into the ocean. Which way they escaped is not told. *Macleod* was informed how his vassals had been treated, and demanded the offenders, whom the inhabitants refused to deliver. Nothing now remained but force. The people of *Egg* had a very capacious cavern, to which they all retreated, and where they imagined themselves safe; but *Macleod* used the usual method of forcing subterraneous fortresses, and kept a fire at the mouth till they were all destroyed.

Canna, the other popish Island, belongs to *Clanronald*. It is said not to comprise more than twelve miles of land, and yet maintains as many inhabitants as *Rum*.

We were at *Col* under the protection of the young Laird, without any of the distresses, which Mr. *Pennant*, in a fit of simple

ple

The rents have, till within seven years, been paid in kind, but the tenants finding that cattle and corn varied in their price, desired for the future to give their landlord money; which, not having yet arrived at the philosophy of commerce, they consider as being every year of the same value.

We were told of a particular mode of undertenure. The tacksman admits some of his inferiour neighbours to the cultivation of his grounds, on condition that performing all the work, and giving a third part of the seed, they shall keep a certain number of cows, sheep, and goats, and reap a third part of the harvest. Thus by less than the tillage of two acres they pay the rent of one.

There are tenants below the rank of tacksmen, that have yet[3] smaller tenants under them; for in every place, where money is not the general equivalent, there must be some whose labour is immediately paid by daily food.

A country that has no money, is by no means convenient for beggars, both because such countries are commonly poor, and because charity requires some trouble and some thought. A penny is easily given upon the first impulse of compassion, or impatience of importunity; but few will deliberately search their cupboards or their granaries to find out something to give. A penny is likewise easily spent; but victuals, if they are unprepared, require houseroom, and fire, and utensils, which the beggar knows not where to find.

Yet beggars there sometimes are, who wander from island to island. We had, in our passage to Mull, the company of a woman and her child, who had exhausted the charity of Col. The arrival of a beggar on an island is accounted a sinistrous event. Every body considers that he shall have the less for what he gives away. Their alms, I believe, is generally oatmeal.

Near to Col is another island called Tireye, eminent for its fertility. Though it has but half the extent of Rum, it is so well peopled, that there have appeared, not long ago, nine hundred and fourteen at a funeral. The plenty of this island enticed beggars to it, who seemed so burdensome to the inhabitants,

---

3. yet RWC (MS. note)] got 75a, b; 85; 87. Despite the agreement of the early editions, it is incredible that Johnson should have written "have got" in a comparative construction. Moreover, yet/got is a familiar source of error in his handwriting.

that a formal compact was drawn up, by which they obliged themselves to grant no more relief to casual wanderers, because they had among them an indigent woman of high birth, whom they considered as entitled to all that they could spare. I have read the stipulation, which was indited with juridical formality, but was never made valid by regular subscription.

If the inhabitants of Col have nothing to give, it is not that they are oppressed by their landlord: their leases seem to be very profitable. One farmer,[4] who pays only seven pounds a year, has maintained seven daughters and three sons, of whom the eldest is educated at Aberdeen for the ministry; and now, at every vacation, opens a school in Col.[5]

Life is here, in some respects, improved beyond the condition of some other islands. In Sky what is wanted can only be bought, as the arrival of some wandering pedlar may afford an opportunity; but in Col there is a standing shop, and in Mull there are two. A shop in the Islands, as in other places of little frequentation, is a repository of every thing requisite for common use. Mr. Boswell's journal was filled, and he bought some paper in Col. To a man that ranges the streets of London, where he is tempted to contrive wants for the pleasure of supplying them, a shop affords no image worthy of attention; but in an island, it turns the balance of existence between good and evil. To live in perpetual want of little things, is a state not indeed of torture, but of constant vexation. I have in Sky had some difficulty to find ink for a letter; and if a woman breaks her needle, the work is at a stop.

As it is, the Islanders are obliged to content themselves with succedaneous[6] means for many common purposes. I have seen the chief man of a very wide district riding with a halter for a bridle, and governing his hobby[7] with a wooden curb.

---

4. Neil Maclean of Crocepole or Crussapoll. See *Life*, v.553.

5. Donald Maclean. See p. 103 and *Life*, v.553–54; also Boswell's narrative: "Dr. Johnson said, 'There is something noble in a young man's walking two hundred miles and back again, every year, for the sake of learning'" (*Life*, v.301). Boswell further recorded Johnson's promise to send the young man a copy of his *Dictionary* (*Journal*,

pp. 283 and 431). This copy (8°, 1770) was inscribed "To Mr Maclean, Teacher of Languages in the Island of Coll, from the Author," and remained in the Maclean family until 1929. It is now at Trinity College, Cambridge.

6. *succedaneous*: "supplying the place of something else" (*Dictionary*).

7. *hobby*: "an Irish or Scottish horse" (*Dictionary*).

The people of Col, however, do not want dexterity to supply some of their necessities. Several arts which make trades, and demand apprenticeships in great cities, are here the practices of daily economy. In every house candles are made, both moulded and dipped. Their wicks are small shreds of linen cloth. They all know how to extract from the cuddy, oil for their lamps. They all tan skins, and make brogues.

As we travelled through Sky, we saw many cottages, but they very frequently stood single on the naked ground. In Col, where the hills opened a place convenient for habitation, we found a petty village, of which every hut had a little garden adjoining; thus they made an appearance of social commerce and mutual offices, and of some attention to convenience and future supply. There is not in the Western Islands any collection of buildings that can make pretensions to be called a town, except in the Isle of Lewis, which I have not seen.

If Lewis is distinguished by a town, Col has also something peculiar. The young Laird has attempted what no Islander perhaps ever thought on. He has begun a road capable of a wheel-carriage. He has carried it about a mile, and will continue it by annual elongation from his house to the harbour.

Of taxes here is no reason for complaining; they are paid by a very easy composition. The malt-tax for Col is twenty shillings. Whisky is very plentiful: there are several stills in the island, and more is made than the inhabitants consume.

The great business of insular policy is now to keep the people in their own country. As the world has been let in upon them, they have heard of happier climates, and less arbitrary government; and if they are disgusted, have emissaries among them ready to offer them land and houses, as a reward for deserting their chief and clan. Many have departed both from the main of Scotland, and from the Islands; and all that go may be considered as subjects lost to the British crown; for a nation scattered in the boundless regions of America resembles rays diverging from a focus. All the rays remain, but the heat is gone. Their power consisted in their concentration: when they are dispersed, they have no effect.

It may be thought that they are happier by the change; but they are not happy as a nation, for they are a nation no longer. As they contribute not to the prosperity of any community, they must want that security, that dignity, that happiness, whatever it be, which a prosperous community throws back upon individuals.

The inhabitants of Col have not yet learned to be weary of their heath and rocks, but attend their agriculture and their dairies, without listening to American seducements.

There are some however who think that this emigration has raised terrour disproportionate to its real evil; and that it is only a new mode of doing what was always done. The Highlands, they say, never maintained their natural inhabitants; but the people, when they found themselves too numerous, instead of extending cultivation, provided for themselves by a more compendious method, and sought better fortune in other countries. They did not indeed go away in collective bodies, but withdrew invisibly, a few at a time; but the whole number of fugitives was not less, and the difference between other times and this, is only the same as between evaporation and effusion.

This is plausible, but I am afraid it is not true. Those who went before, if they were not sensibly missed, as the argument supposes, must have gone either in less number, or in a manner less detrimental, than at present; because formerly there was no complaint. Those who then left the country were generally the idle dependants on overburdened families, or men who had no property; and therefore carried away only themselves. In the present eagerness of emigration, families, and almost communities, go away together. Those who were considered as prosperous and wealthy sell their stock and carry away the money. Once none went away but the useless and poor; in some parts there is now reason to fear, that none will stay but those who are too poor to remove themselves, and too useless to be removed at the cost of others.

Of antiquity there is not more knowledge in Col than in other places; but every where something may be gleaned.

How ladies were portioned, when there was no money, it would be difficult for an Englishman to guess. In 1649, Maclean of Dronart[8] in Mull married his sister Fingala to Maclean of Coll, with a hundred and eighty kine; and stipulated, that if

---

8. The name is Duart. "For *Dronart* r *Dowart*" (Boswell, *Remarks*). For Boswell's correction of proper names which, though usually inaccurate, are elsewhere recognizable, see the Index (explanatory note).

she became a widow, her jointure should be three hundred and sixty. I suppose some proportionate tract of land was appropriated to their pasturage.

The disposition to pompous and expensive funerals, which has at one time or other prevailed in most parts of the civilized world, is not yet suppressed in the Islands, though some of the ancient solemnities are worn away, and singers are no longer hired to attend the procession. Nineteen years ago, at the burial of the Laird of Col, were killed thirty cows, and about fifty sheep. The number of the cows is positively told, and we must suppose other victuals in like proportion.

Mr. Maclean informed us of an odd game, of which he did not tell the original, but which may perhaps be used in other places, where the reason of it is not yet forgot. At New-year's Eve, in the hall or castle of the laird, where, at festal seasons, there may be supposed a very numerous company, one man dresses himself in a cow's hide, upon which other men beat with sticks. He runs with all this noise round the house, which all the company quits in a counterfeited fright: the door is then shut. At New-year's Eve there is no great pleasure to be had out of doors in the Hebrides. They are sure soon to recover from their terrour enough to solicit for re-admission; which, for the honour of poetry, is not to be obtained but by repeating a verse, with which those that are knowing and provident take care to be furnished.

Very near the house of Maclean stands the castle of Col, which was the mansion of the Laird, till the house was built. It is built upon a rock, as Mr. Boswell remarked, that it might not be mined. It is very strong, and having been not long uninhabited, is yet in repair. On the wall was, not long ago, a stone with an inscription, importing, that "if any man of the clan of Maclonich shall appear before this castle, though he come at midnight, with a man's head in his hand, he shall there find safety and protection against all but the King."

This is an old Highland treaty made upon a very memorable occasion. Maclean, the son of John Gerves, who recovered Col, and conquered Barra, had obtained, it is said, from James the Second, a grant of the lands of Lochiel, forfeited, I suppose, by some offence against the state.

Forfeited estates were not in those days quietly resigned;

Maclean, therefore, went with an armed force to seize his new possessions, and, I know not for what reason, took his wife with him. The Camerons rose in defence of their chief, and a battle was fought at the head of Loch Ness, near the place where Fort Augustus now stands, in which Lochiel obtained the victory, and Maclean, with his followers, was defeated and destroyed.

The lady fell into the hands of the conquerours, and being found pregnant was placed in the custody of Maclonich, one of a tribe or family branched from Cameron, with orders, if she brought a boy, to destroy him, if a girl, to spare her.

Maclonich's wife, who was with child likewise, had a girl about the same time at which lady Maclean brought a boy, and Maclonich with more generosity to his captive, than fidelity to his trust, contrived that the children should be changed.

Maclean being thus preserved from death, in time recovered his original patrimony; and in gratitude to his friend, made his castle a place of refuge to any of the clan that should think himself in danger; and, as a proof of reciprocal confidence, Maclean took upon himself and his posterity the care of educating the heir of Maclonich.

This story, like all other traditions of the Highlands, is variously related, but though some circumstances are uncertain, the principal fact is true. Maclean undoubtedly owed his preservation to Maclonich; for the treaty between the two families has been strictly observed: it did not sink into disuse and oblivion, but continued in its full force while the chieftains retained their power. I have read a demand of protection, made not more than thirty-seven years ago, for one of the Maclonichs, named Ewen Cameron, who had been accessary to the death of Macmartin, and had been banished by Lochiel, his lord, for a certain term; at the expiration of which he returned married from France, but the Macmartins, not satisfied with the punishment, when he attempted to settle, still threatened him with vengeance. He therefore asked, and obtained shelter in the Isle of Col.

The power of protection subsists no longer, but what the law permits is yet continued, and Maclean of Col now educates the heir of Maclonich.

There still remains in the Islands, though it is passing fast away, the custom of fosterage. A laird, a man of wealth and eminence, sends his child, either male or female, to a tacksman, or tenant, to be fostered. It is not always his own tenant, but some distant friend that obtains this honour; for an honour such a trust is very reasonably thought. The terms of fosterage seem to vary in different islands. In Mull the father sends with his child a certain number of cows, to which the same number is added by the fosterer. The father appropriates a proportionable extent of ground, without rent, for their pasturage. If every cow brings a calf, half belongs to the fosterer, and half to the child; but if there be only one calf between two cows, it is the child's, and when the child returns to the parents, it is accompanied by all the cows given, both by the father and by the fosterer, with half of the increase of the stock by propagation. These beasts are considered as a portion, and called *macalive* cattle,[9] of which the father has the produce, but is supposed not to have the full property, but to owe the same number to the child, as a portion to the daughter, or a stock for the son.

Children continue with the fosterer perhaps six years, and cannot, where this is the practice, be considered as burdensome. The fosterer, if he gives four cows, receives likewise four, and has, while the child continues with him, grass for eight without rent, with half the calves, and all the milk, for which he pays only four cows when he dismisses his *dalt*,[1] for that is the name for a foster child.

Fosterage is, I believe, sometimes performed upon more liberal terms. Our friend, the young Laird of Col, was fostered by Macsweyn of Grissipol.[2] Macsweyn then lived a tenant to Sir James Macdonald in the Isle of Sky; and therefore Col, whether he sent him cattle or not, could grant him no land. The *dalt*, however, at his return, brought back a considerable number of *macalive* cattle, and of the friendship so formed there have been good effects. When Macdonald raised his rents, Macsweyn

9. *macaladh*: fostering, rearing a child after weaning (Dwelly).

1. *dalta*: foster-child (Dwelly).

2. MacSweyn was foster-father to "the young Laird's" father, Hugh Maclean (See *Journal*, p. 259). Young Col, Boswell continues, was fostered by a Campbell and may therefore rank with Romulus and Remus, foster-children of a wolf (p. 260). This pleasantry is not in the *Tour*.

MULL

As we were to catch the first favourable breath, we spent the night not very elegantly, nor pleasantly in the vessel, and were landed next day at Tobor Morar, a port in Mull, which appears to an unexperienced eye formed for the security of ships; for its mouth is closed by a small island, which admits them through narrow channels into a bason sufficiently capacious. They are indeed safe from the sea, but there is a hollow between the mountains, through which the wind issues from the land with very mischievous violence.

There was no danger while we were there, and we found several other vessels at anchor; so that the port had a very commercial appearance.

The young Laird of Col, who had determined not to let us lose his company, while there was any difficulty remaining, came over with us. His influence soon appeared; for he procured us horses, and conducted us to the house of Doctor Maclean,[3a] where we found very kind entertainment, and very pleasing conversation. Miss Maclean, who was born, and had been bred at Glasgow, having removed with her father to Mull, added to other qualifications, a great knowledge of the Earse language, which she had not learned in her childhood, but gained by study, and was the only interpreter of Earse poetry that I could ever find.

The Isle of Mull is perhaps in extent the third of the Hebrides. It is not broken by waters, nor shot into promontories, but is a solid and compact mass, of breadth nearly equal to its length. Of the dimensions of the larger islands, there is no knowledge approaching to exactness. I am willing to estimate it as containing about three hundred square miles.

Mull had suffered like Sky by the black winter of seventy-one, in which, contrary to all experience, a continued frost detained the snow eight weeks upon the ground. Against a calamity never known, no provision had been made, and the people could only pine in helpless misery. One tenant was mentioned, whose cattle perished to the value of three hundred

---

3a. Dr. Hector Maclean, physician.

pounds; a loss which probably more than the life of man is necessary to repair. In countries like these, the descriptions of famine become intelligible. Where by vigorous and artful cultivation of a soil naturally fertile, there is commonly a superfluous growth both of grain and grass; where the fields are crowded with cattle; and where every hand is able to attract wealth from a distance, by making something that promotes ease, or gratifies vanity, a dear year produces only a comparative want, which is rather seen than felt, and which terminates commonly in no worse effect, than that of condemning the lower orders of the community to sacrifice a little luxury to convenience, or at most a little convenience to necessity.

But where the climate is unkind, and the ground penurious, so that the most fruitful years will produce[w] only enough to maintain themselves; where life unimproved, and unadorned, fades into something little more than naked existence, and every one is busy for himself, without any arts by which the pleasure of others may be increased; if to the daily burden of distress any additional weight be added, nothing remains but to despair and die. In Mull the disappointment of a harvest, or a murrain among the cattle, cuts off the regular provision; and they who have no manufactures can purchase no part of the superfluities of other countries. The consequence of a bad season is here not scarcity, but emptiness; and they whose plenty was barely a supply of natural and present need, when that slender stock fails, must perish with hunger.

All travel has its advantages. If the passenger visits better countries, he may learn to improve his own, and if fortune carries him to worse, he may learn to enjoy it.

Mr. Boswell's curiosity strongly impelled him to survey Iona, or Icolmkil, which was to the early ages the great school of theology, and is supposed to have been the place of sepulture for the ancient kings. I, though less eager, did not oppose him.

That we might perform this expedition, it was necessary to traverse a great part of Mull. We passed a day at Dr. Maclean's, and could have been well contented to stay longer. But Col provided us horses, and we pursued our journey. This was a day of

w. years will produce 75a]   years produce 75b. Either reading is admissible.

inconvenience, for the country is very rough, and my horse was but little. We travelled many hours through a tract, black and barren, in which, however, there were the reliques of humanity; for we found a ruined chapel in our way.

It is natural, in traversing this gloom of desolation, to inquire, whether something may not be done to give nature a more cheerful face, and whether those hills and moors that afford heath cannot with a little care and labour bear something better? The first thought that occurs is to cover them with trees, for that in many of these naked regions trees will grow,[4] is evident, because stumps and roots are yet remaining; and the speculatist hastily proceeds to censure that negligence and laziness that has omitted for so long a time so easy an improvement.

To drop seeds into the ground, and attend their growth, requires little labour and no skill. He who remembers that all the woods, by which the wants of man have been supplied from the Deluge till now, were self-sown, will not easily be persuaded to think all the art and preparation necessary, which the Georgick writers[5] prescribe to planters. Trees certainly have covered the earth with very little culture. They wave their tops among the rocks of Norway, and might thrive as well in the Highlands and Hebrides.

But there is a frightful interval between the seed and timber. He that calculates the growth of trees, has the unwelcome remembrance of the shortness of life driven hard upon him. He knows that he is doing what will never benefit himself; and when he rejoices to see the stem rise, is disposed to repine that another shall cut it down.

Plantation is naturally the employment of a mind unburdened with care, and vacant to futurity, saturated with present good, and at leisure to derive gratification from the prospect of posterity. He that pines with hunger, is in little care how others shall be fed. The poor man is seldom studious to make his grandson rich. It may be soon discovered, why in a place, which hardly supplies the cravings of necessity, there has been little

---

4. Donald Monro mentions the "maney woods" of Skye and the "birkin woods" of Raasay (*Description*, pp. 25 and 27: a record of a journey said to have been made in 1549).

5. Writers of poetical advice on husbandry.

attention to the delights of fancy, and why distant convenience is unregarded, where the thoughts are turned with incessant solicitude upon every possibility of immediate advantage.

Neither is it quite so easy to raise large woods, as may be conceived. Trees intended to produce timber must be sown where they are to grow; and ground sown with trees must be kept useless for a long time, inclosed at an expence from which many will be discouraged by the remoteness of the profit, and watched with that attention, which, in places where it is most needed, will neither be given nor bought. That it cannot be plowed is evident; and if cattle be suffered to graze upon it, they will devour the plants as fast as they rise. Even in coarser countries, where herds and flocks are not fed, not only the deer and the wild goats will browse upon them, but the hare and rabbit will nibble them. It is therefore reasonable to believe, what I do not remember any naturalist to have remarked, that there was a time when the world was very thinly inhabited by beasts, as well as men, and that the woods had leisure to rise high before animals had bred numbers sufficient to intercept them.

Sir James Macdonald, in part of the wastes of his territory, set or sowed trees, to the number, as I have been told, of several millions, expecting, doubtless, that they would grow up into future navies and cities; but for want of inclosure, and of that care which is always necessary, and will hardly ever be taken, all his cost and labour have been lost, and the ground is likely to continue an useless heath.

Having not any experience of a journey in Mull, we had no doubt of reaching the sea by day-light, and therefore had not left Dr. Maclean's very early. We travelled diligently enough, but found the country, for road there was none, very difficult to pass. We were always struggling with some obstruction or other, and our vexation was not balanced by any gratification of the eye or mind. We were now long enough acquainted with hills and heath to have lost the emotion that they once raised, whether pleasing or painful, and had our mind employed only on our own fatigue. We were however sure, under Col's protection, of escaping all real evils. There was no house in Mull to which he could not introduce us. He had intended to lodge us, for that night, with a gentleman that lived upon the coast, but discovered on the way, that he then lay in bed without hope of life.

We resolved not to embarrass a family, in a time of so much sorrow, if any other expedient could be found; and as the island of Ulva was over-against us, it was determined that we should pass the strait and have recourse to the laird, who, like the other gentlemen of the Islands, was known to Col. We expected to find a ferry-boat, but when at last we came to the water, the boat was gone.

We were now again at a stop. It was the sixteenth of October, a time when it is not convenient to sleep in the Hebrides without a cover, and there was no house within our reach, but that which we had already declined.

ULVA

While we stood deliberating, we were happily espied from an Irish ship, that lay at anchor in the strait. The master saw[6] that we wanted a passage, and with great civility sent us his boat, which quickly conveyed us to Ulva, where we were very liberally entertained by Mr. Macquarry.[7]

To Ulva we came in the dark, and left it before noon the next day. A very exact description therefore will not be expected. We were told, that it is an island of no great extent, rough and barren, inhabited by the Macquarrys; a clan not powerful nor numerous, but of antiquity, which most other families are content to reverence. The name is supposed to be a depravation of some other; for the Earse language does not afford it any etymology. Macquarry is proprietor both of Ulva and some adjacent islands, among which is Staffa, so lately raised to renown by Mr. Banks.[8]

When the Islanders were reproached with their ignorance,

6. Boswell corrects this particular in his *Remarks*, and gives his own account in the *Tour*: "We should have been in a very bad situation, had there not fortunately been lying in the little sound of Ulva an Irish vessel, the Bonnetta, of Londonderry, Captain M'Lure, master. He himself was at M'Quarrie's; but his men obligingly came with their long-boat, and ferried us over" (*Life*, v.319).

7. Lauchlan MacQuarrie, 16th chief. See *Life*, v.556.

8. Banks contributed the Account of Staffa to Pennant's *Tour and Voyage* (1774), pp. 261–69.

or insensibility of the wonders of Staffa, they had not much to reply. They had indeed considered it little, because they had always seen it; and none but philosophers, nor they always, are struck with wonder, otherwise than by novelty. How would it surprise an unenlightened ploughman, to hear a company of sober men, inquiring by what power the hand tosses a stone, or why the stone, when it is tossed, falls to the ground!

Of the ancestors of Macquarry, who thus lies hid in his unfrequented island, I have found memorials in all places where they could be expected.

Inquiring after the reliques of former manners, I found that in Ulva, and, I think, no where else, is continued the payment of the *mercheta mulierum*; a fine in old times due to the laird at the marriage of a virgin. The original of this claim, as of our tenure of "Borough English,"[9] is variously delivered. It is pleasant to find ancient customs in old families. This payment, like others, was, for want of money, made anciently in the produce of the land. Macquarry was used to demand a sheep, for which he now takes a crown, by that inattention to the uncertain proportion between the value and the denomination of money, which has brought much disorder into Europe. A sheep has always the same power of supplying human wants, but a crown will bring at one time more, at another less.

Ulva was not neglected by the piety of ancient times: it has still to show what was once a church.

INCH KENNETH

In the morning we went again into the boat, and were landed on Inch Kenneth, an island about a mile long, and perhaps half a mile broad, remarkable for pleasantness and fertility. It is verdant and grassy, and fit both for pasture and tillage; but it has no trees. Its only inhabitants were Sir Allan Maclean, and two young ladies, his daughters, with their servants.

Romance does not often exhibit a scene that strikes the imagination more than this little desert in these depths of western

---

9. Johnson probably recalls here Robert Plot's *Natural History of Staffordshire* (Oxford, 1686), in which "Borow English" and "Marcheta mulierum" are (mistakenly) associated (p. 278).

obscurity, occupied not by a gross herdsman, or amphibious fisherman, but by a gentleman and two ladies, of high birth, polished manners, and elegant conversation, who, in a habitation raised not very far above the ground, but furnished with unexpected neatness and convenience, practised all the kindness of hospitality, and refinement of courtesy.

Sir Allan is the chieftain of the great clan of Maclean, which is said to claim the second place among the Highland families, yielding only to Macdonald. Though by the misconduct of his ancestors, most of the extensive territory, which would have descended to him, has been alienated,[1] he still retains much of the dignity and authority of his birth. When soldiers were lately wanting for the American war, application was made to Sir Allan, and he nominated a hundred men for the service, who obeyed the summons, and bore arms under his command.

He had then, for some time, resided with the young ladies in Inch Kenneth, where he lives not only with plenty, but with elegance, having conveyed to his cottage a collection of books, and what else is necessary to make his hours pleasant.

When we landed, we were met by Sir Allan and the ladies, accompanied by Miss Macquarry, who had passed some time with them, and now returned to Ulva with her father.

We all walked together to the mansion, where we found one cottage for Sir Allan, and I think two more for the domesticks and the offices. We entered, and wanted little that palaces afford. Our room was neatly floored, and well lighted; and our dinner, which was dressed in one of the other huts, was plentiful and delicate.

In the afternoon Sir Allan reminded us, that the day was Sunday, which he never suffered to pass without some religious distinction, and invited us to partake in his acts of domestick worship; which I hope neither Mr. Boswell nor myself will be suspected of a disposition to refuse. The elder of the ladies read the English service.[2]

1. For Sir Allan's circumstances, see Carruthers, p. 259. Such of the Maclean estates as had not already "passed to younger branches of the house" were "forfeited in 1715 and 1745, and came into the hands of the Argyle family."

2. Boswell's *Journal*, though not his *Tour*, discloses that the prayer for the royal family was omitted. See *Journal*, p. 317.

Inch Kenneth was once a seminary of ecclesiasticks, subordinate, I suppose, to Icolmkill. Sir Allan had a mind to trace the foundation[3] of the college, but neither I nor Mr. Boswell, who "bends" a keener "eye on vacancy,"[4] were able to perceive them.

Our attention, however, was sufficiently engaged by a venerable chapel, which stands yet entire, except that the roof is gone. It is about sixty feet in length, and thirty in breadth. On one side of the altar is a bas relief of the blessed Virgin, and by it lies a little bell; which, though cracked, and without a clapper, has remained there for ages, guarded only by the venerableness of the place. The ground round the chapel is covered with grave-stones of chiefs and ladies; and still continues to be a place of sepulture.

Inch Kenneth is a proper prelude to Icolmkill. It was not without some mournful emotion that we contemplated the ruins of religious structures, and the monuments of the dead.

On the next day we took a more distinct view of the place, and went with the boat to see oysters in the bed, out of which the boat-men forced up as many as were wanted. Even Inch Kenneth has a subordinate island, named Sandiland, I suppose, in contempt, where we landed, and found a rock, with a surface of perhaps four acres, of which one is naked stone, another spread with sand and shells, some of which I picked up for their glossy beauty, and two covered with a little earth and grass, on which Sir Allan has a few sheep. I doubt not but when there was a college at Inch Kenneth, there was a hermitage upon Sandiland.

Having wandered over those extensive plains, we committed ourselves again to the winds and waters; and after a voyage of about ten minutes, in which we met with nothing very observable, were again safe upon dry ground.

We told Sir Allan our desire of visiting Icolmkill, and entreated him to give us his protection, and his company. He thought proper to hesitate a little, but the ladies hinted, that as they knew he would not finally refuse, he would do better if

---

3. Johnson, in his *Dictionary*, shows himself equally ready to accept singular or plural for the base of a building.
4. Alas, how is't with you,

That you do bend your eye on vacancy,
And with th'incorporal air do hold discourse?

(*Hamlet*, III.iv.117–19)

he preserved the grace of ready compliance. He took their advice, and promised to carry us on the morrow in his boat.

We passed the remaining part of the day in such amusements as were in our power. Sir Allan related the American campaign, and at evening one of the ladies played on her harpsichord, while Col and Mr. Boswell danced a Scottish reel with the other.

We could have been easily persuaded to a longer stay upon Inch Kenneth, but life will not be all passed in delight. The session at Edinburgh was approaching,[5] from which Mr. Boswell could not be absent.

In the morning our boat was ready: it was high and strong. Sir Allan victualled it for the day, and provided able rowers. We now parted from the young Laird of Col, who had treated us with so much kindness, and concluded his favours by consigning us to Sir Allan. Here we had the last embrace of this amiable man, who, while these pages were preparing to attest his virtues, perished in the passage between Ulva and Inch Kenneth.[6]

Sir Allan, to whom the whole region was well known, told us of a very remarkable cave, to which he would show us the way. We had been disappointed already by one cave, and were not much elevated by the expectation of another.

It was yet better to see it, and we stopped at some rocks on the coast of Mull. The mouth is fortified by vast fragments of stone, over which we made our way, neither very nimbly, nor very securely. The place, however, well repaid our trouble. The bottom, as far as the flood rushes in, was encumbered with large pebbles, but as we advanced was spread over with smooth sand. The breadth is about forty-five feet: the roof rises in an arch, almost regular, to a height which we could not measure; but I think it about thirty feet.

This part of our curiosity was nearly frustrated; for though

5. The Court of Session of Scotland observed two terms, of which the second began on 12 November.

6. On 25 September; recorded in *Scots Magazine* for September 1774, xxxvi, p. 503. See *Life*, v.557. On 27 October Johnson wrote, asking Boswell whether he could deny the report "in the papers" of Donald Maclean's death (*Letters* 362); but his letter crossed one from Boswell, carrying the news (*Life*, II.288). Johnson must have taken prompt action to secure the insertion of this passage in the proofs. See the Introduction: The Text, p. xxxi.

we went to see a cave, and knew that caves are dark, we forgot to carry tapers, and did not discover our omission till we were wakened by our wants. Sir Allan then sent one of the boatmen into the country, who soon returned with one little candle. We were thus enabled to go forward, but could not venture far. Having passed inward from the sea to a great depth,[7] we found on the right hand a narrow passage, perhaps not more than six feet wide, obstructed by great stones, over which we climbed and came into a second cave, in breadth twenty-five feet. The air in this apartment was very warm, but not oppressive, nor loaded with vapours. Our light showed no tokens of a feculent or corrupted atmosphere. Here was a square stone, called, as we are told, Fingal's Table.

If we had been provided with torches, we should have proceeded in our search, though we had already gone as far as any former adventurer, except some who are reported never to have returned; and, measuring our way back, we found it more than a hundred and sixty yards, the eleventh part of a mile.

Our measures were not critically exact, having been made with a walking pole, such as it is convenient to carry in these rocky countries, of which I guessed the length by standing against it. In this there could be no great errour, nor do I much doubt but the Highlander, whom we employed, reported the number right. More nicety however is better, and no man should travel unprovided with instruments for taking heights and distances.

There is yet another cause of errour not always easily surmounted, though more dangerous to the veracity of itinerary narratives, than imperfect mensuration. An observer deeply impressed by any remarkable spectacle, does not suppose, that the traces will soon vanish from his mind, and having commonly no great convenience for writing, defers the description to a time of more leisure, and better accommodation.

He who has not made the experiment, or who is not accustomed to require rigorous accuracy from himself, will scarcely believe how much a few hours take from certainty of knowl-

7. "Could not venture far . . . having passed inward . . . to a great depth." Johnson may appear to contradict himself; but the travellers began to *venture* only when they relied on "one little candle"; the depth of penetration was the 160 yards traversed from the mouth of the cave.

edge, and distinctness of imagery; how the succession of objects will be broken, how separate parts will be confused, and how many particular features and discriminations will be compressed and conglobated into one gross and general idea.

To this dilatory notation must be imputed the false relations of travellers, where there is no imaginable motive to deceive. They trusted to memory, what cannot be trusted safely but to the eye, and told by guess what a few hours before they had known with certainty. Thus it was that Wheeler and Spen described with irreconcilable contrariety[8] things which they surveyed together, and which both undoubtedly designed to show as they saw them.

When we had satisfied our curiosity in the cave, so far as our penury of light permitted us, we clambered again to our boats,[9] and proceeded along the coast of Mull to a headland, called Atun, remarkable for the columnar form of the rocks, which rise in a series of pilasters, with a degree of regularity, which Sir Allan thinks not less worthy of curiosity than the shore of Staffa.

Not long after we came to another range of black rocks, which had the appearance of broken pilasters, set one behind another to a great depth. This place was chosen by Sir Allan for our dinner. We were easily accommodated with seats, for the stones were of all heights, and refreshed ourselves and our boatmen, who could have no other rest till we were at Icolmkill.

The evening was now approaching, and we were yet at a considerable distance from the end of our expedition. We could therefore stop no more to make remarks in the way, but set forward with some degree of eagerness. The day soon failed us, and the moon presented a very solemn and pleasing scene. The

---

8. Wheler and Spon. Johnson may have written Wheeler, but the e/o difficulty with his handwriting allows the supposition that the compositor read *Spen* for *Spon*. In 1678, Spon published his *Voyage d'Italie, de Dalmatie, de Grece, et du Levant . . . par Jacob Spon . . . & George Wheler* (Lyon). This was received "with great satisfaction" by Wheler, but, when he heard of an impending English translation, he resolved to issue his own account and set right the many discrepancies in their recollections of what they had seen together in 1675–76. His *Journey into Greece, by George Wheler Esq: in company of Dr. Spon of Lyons* (1682) is accordingly punctuated with such interjections as: "Three gates, and with Mr. Spon (sic) favour no more" (p. 16); "I know not why my comrade seemeth of the contrary opinion" (p. 242).

9. There was only one boat. See p. 145 and p. 148. *Letters* 332, and *Life*, v.331. Perhaps a misprint.

sky was clear, so that the eye commanded a wide circle: the sea was neither still nor turbulent: the wind neither silent nor loud. We were never far from one coast or another, on which, if the weather had become violent, we could have found shelter, and therefore contemplated at ease the region through which we glided in the tranquillity of the night, and saw now a rock and now an island grow gradually conspicuous and gradually obscure. I committed the fault which I have just been censuring, in neglecting, as we passed, to note the series of this placid navigation.

We were very near an island, called Nun's Island, perhaps from an ancient convent. Here is said to have been dug the stone that was used in the buildings of Icolmkill. Whether it is now inhabited we could not stay to inquire.

At last we came to Icolmkill, but found no convenience for landing. Our boat could not be forced very near the dry ground, and our Highlanders carried us over the water.

We were now treading that illustrious island, which was once the luminary of the Caledonian regions, whence savage clans and roving barbarians derived the benefits of knowledge, and the blessings of religion. To abstract the mind from all local emotion would be impossible, if it were endeavoured, and would be foolish, if it were possible. Whatever withdraws us from the power of our senses; whatever makes the past, the distant, or the future predominate over the present, advances us in the dignity of thinking beings. Far from me and from my friends, be such frigid philosophy as may conduct us indifferent and unmoved over any ground which has been dignified by wisdom, bravery, or virtue. That man is little to be envied, whose patriotism would not gain force upon the plain of Marathon, or whose piety would not grow warmer among the ruins of Iona?[1]

We came too late to visit monuments: some care was necessary for ourselves. Whatever was in the island, Sir Allan could command, for the inhabitants were Macleans; but having little they could not give us much. He went to the headman of the island, whom Fame, but Fame delights in amplifying, represents as worth no less than fifty pounds. He was perhaps proud

---

1. "The mark of interrogation was still (and later) often used where we now use the mark of exclamation" (RWC).

General View of Iona. From Thomas Pennant's *Tour in Scotland and Voyage to the Hebrides MDCCXXII*, Part I. 1774. Plate XXI.

enough of his guests, but ill prepared for our entertainment;
however, he soon produced more provision than men not lux-
urious require. Our lodging was next to be provided. We found
a barn well stocked with hay, and made our beds as soft as we
could.

In the morning we rose and surveyed the place. The churches
of the two convents are both standing, though unroofed. They
were built of unhewn stone, but solid, and not inelegant. I
brought away rude measures of the buildings, such as I cannot
much trust myself, inaccurately taken, and obscurely noted.
Mr. Pennant's delineations,[2] which are doubtless exact, have
made my unskilful description less necessary.

The episcopal church[3] consists of two parts, separated by the
belfry, and built at different times. The original church had,
like others, the altar at one end, and tower at the other; but as it
grew too small, another building of equal dimension was
added, and the tower then was necessarily in the middle.

That these edifices are of different ages seems evident.[4] The
arch of the first church is Roman, being part of a circle; that of
the additional building is pointed, and therefore Gothick, or
Saracenical;[5] the tower is firm, and wants only to be floored and
covered.

Of the chambers or cells belonging to the monks, there are
some walls remaining, but nothing approaching to a complete
apartment.

The bottom of the church is so incumbered with mud and
rubbish, that we could make no discoveries of curious inscriptions, and what there are have been already published. The
place is said to be known where the black stones[6] lie concealed,

2. For Pennant's delineations of the
nunnery church, see *A Tour in Scotland, and Voyage to the Hebrides
MDCCLXXII* (Chester, 1774), p. 246.
The monastery was too ruinous for
measurement. Bailey, who likewise
acknowledges Pennant's fidelity, himself gives a full and circumstantial account of the ruins, noting their present
state (II.381–87). See p. 128 n. 2.

3. The cathedral is a "cruciform
building, with a massive central tower"
(E. C. Trenholme, *The Story of Iona,*
Edinburgh, 1909, p. 113).

4. For an examination of the singu-

lar mixture of styles in this building,
see David MacGibbon and Thomas
Ross, *The Ecclesiastical Architecture of
Scotland* (Edinburgh, 1896–97), III.49–
75.

5. "Saracenic: by Sir C. Wren erro-
neously applied to Pointed or 'Gothic'
architecture" (OED).

6. Boswell objects that this should
be *stone (Remarks).* Martin, however,
supports Johnson: "A little further to
the west lie the black stones" (*Description,* p. 259). Likewise Pennant, pp.
254–55.

on which the old Highland Chiefs, when they made contracts and alliances, used to take the oath, which was considered as more sacred than any other obligation, and which could not be violated without the blackest infamy. In those days of violence and rapine, it was of great importance to impress upon savage minds the sanctity of an oath, by some particular and extraordinary circumstances. They would not have recourse to the black stones, upon small or common occasions, and when they had established their faith by this tremendous sanction, inconstancy and treachery were no longer feared.

The chapel of the nunnery is now used by the inhabitants as a kind of general cow-house, and the bottom is consequently too miry for examination. Some of the stones which covered the later abbesses have inscriptions, which might yet be read, if the chapel were cleansed. The roof of this, as of all the other buildings, is totally destroyed, not only because timber quickly decays when it is neglected, but because in an island utterly destitute of wood, it was wanted for use, and was consequently the first plunder of needy rapacity.

The chancel of the nuns' chapel[7] is covered with an arch of stone, to which time has done no injury; and a small apartment communicating with the choir, on the north side, like the chapter-house in cathedrals, roofed with stone in the same manner, is likewise entire.[8]

In one of the churches[9] was a marble altar, which the superstition of the inhabitants has destroyed. Their opinion was, that a fragment of this stone was a defence against shipwrecks, fire, and miscarriages. In one corner of the church the bason for holy water is yet unbroken.

The cemetery of the nunnery was, till very lately, regarded with such reverence, that only women were buried in it. These reliques of veneration always produce some mournful pleasure. I could have forgiven a great injury more easily than the violation of this imaginary sanctity.

South of the chapel stand the walls of a large room, which was probably the hall, or refectory of the nunnery. This apart-

---

7. "The nunnery, like the Benedictine abbey, was founded by Reginald of the Isles" (Trenholme, p. 128).

8. Bailey, however, found it roofless in 1787 (II.384).

9. The "episcopal church"—i.e., the cathedral.

ment is capable of repair. Of the rest of the convent there are only fragments.

Besides the two principal churches, there are, I think, five chapels yet standing, and three more remembered. There are also crosses, of which two bear the names of St. John and St. Matthew.

A large space of ground about these consecrated edifices is covered with grave-stones, few of which have any inscription. He that surveys it, attended by an insular antiquary, may be told where the kings of many nations are buried, and if he loves to sooth his imagination with the thoughts that naturally rise in places where the great and the powerful lie mingled with the dust, let him listen in submissive silence; for if he asks any questions, his delight is at an end.

Iona has long enjoyed, without any very credible attestation, the honour of being reputed the cemetery of the Scottish kings. It is not unlikely, that, when the opinion of local sanctity was prevalent, the chieftains of the isles, and perhaps some of the Norwegian or Irish princes were reposited in this venerable enclosure. But by whom the subterraneous vaults are peopled is now utterly unknown. The graves are very numerous,[1] and some of them undoubtedly contain the remains of men, who did not expect to be so soon forgotten.[2]

Not far from this awful ground, may be traced the garden of the monastery: the fishponds are yet discernible, and the aqueduct, which supplied them, is still in use.

There remains a broken building, which is called the Bishop's house,[3] I know not by what authority. It was once the residence of some man above the common rank, for it has two

---

1. "As was natural for soil so sacred, Iona became a great place of sepulture, and the sites and names of some nine ancient burial-grounds survive, though, with the exception of Reilig Odhraim, they are small and little is known about them" (Trenholme, p. 123).

2. Sacheverell himself found few inscriptions, "tho the Dean of the Isles Mr. John Frazer (an honest Episcopal Minister) who since made me a visit, told me his father, who had been Dean of the Isles, left him a book with above 300 inscriptions, which he had lent to the late Earl of Argile, a man of incomparable sence, and great curiosity, and doubts they are all lost by that great man's afflictions" (*An Account of the Isle of Man . . . with a Voyage to I-Columb-kill* by William Sacheverell Esq; Late Governour of Man, 1702, p. 132).

3. Pre-Reformation Bishops of the Isles may have lived in Iona, but no records remain. See Trenholme, p. 118.

stories and a chimney. We were shewn a chimney at the other end, which was only a nich, without perforation, but so much does antiquarian credulity, or patriotick vanity prevail, that it was not much more safe to trust the eye of our instructor than the memory.

There is in the island one house more, and only one, that has a chimney: we entered it, and found it neither wanting repair nor inhabitants; but to the farmers, who now possess it, the chimney is of no great value; for their fire was made on the floor, in the middle of the room, and notwithstanding the dignity of their mansion, they rejoiced, like their neighbours, in the comforts of smoke.

It is observed, that ecclesiastical colleges are always in the most pleasant and fruitful places. While the world allowed the monks their choice, it is surely no dishonour that they chose well. This island is remarkably fruitful. The village near the churches is said to contain seventy families, which, at five in a family, is more than a hundred inhabitants to a mile. There are perhaps other villages; yet both corn and cattle are annually exported.

But the fruitfulness of Iona is now its whole prosperity. The inhabitants are remarkably gross, and remarkably neglected: I know not if they are visited by any minister. The island, which was once the metropolis of learning and piety, has now no school for education, nor temple for worship, only two inhabitants that can speak English, and not one that can write or read.

The people are of the clan of Maclean; and though Sir Allan had not been in the place for many years, he was received with all the reverence due to their chieftain. One of them being sharply reprehended by him, for not sending him some rum, declared after his departure, in Mr. Boswell's presence, that he had no design of disappointing him, "for," said he, "I would cut my bones for him; and if he had sent his dog for it, he should have had it."

When we were to depart, our boat was left by the ebb at a great distance from the water, but no sooner did we wish it afloat, than the islanders gathered round it, and, by the union of many hands, pushed it down the beach; every man who could contribute his help seemed to think himself happy in the opportunity of being, for a moment, useful to his chief.

We now left those illustrious ruins, by which Mr. Boswell was much affected, nor would I willingly be thought to have looked upon them without some emotion. Perhaps, in the revolutions of the world, Iona may be sometime again the instructress of the Western Regions.

It was no long voyage to Mull, where, under Sir Allan's protection, we landed in the evening, and were entertained for the night by Mr. Maclean,[4] a minister that lives upon the coast, whose elegance of conversation, and strength of judgment, would make him conspicuous in places of greater celebrity. Next day we dined with Dr. Maclean, another physician, and then travelled on to the house of a very powerful laird, Maclean of Lochbuy,[5] for in this country every man's name is Maclean.

Where races are thus numerous, and thus combined, none but the chief of a clan is addressed by his name. The Laird of Dunvegan is called Macleod, but other gentlemen of the same family are denominated by the places where they reside, as Raasa, or Talisker. The distinction of the meaner people is made by their Christian names. In consequence of this practice, the late Laird of Macfarlane, an eminent genealogist,[6] considered himself as disrespectfully treated, if the common addition was applied to him. Mr. Macfarlane, said he, may with equal propriety be said to many; but I, and I only, am *Macfarlane*.

Our afternoon journey was through a country of such gloomy desolation, that Mr. Boswell thought no part of the Highlands equally terrifick, yet we came without any difficulty, at evening, to Lochbuy, where we found a true Highland Laird, rough and haughty, and tenacious of his dignity; who, hearing my name, inquired whether I was of the Johnstons of Glencoe,[7] or of Ardnamurchan.

Lochbuy has, like the other insular chieftains, quitted the castle that sheltered his ancestors, and lives near it, in a man-

---

4. Boswell pointed out to Johnson that the minister was a Macleod. For his letter, see *Life*, II.291. For the Rev. Neil Macleod, see *Life*, v.338, and *Journal*, p. 339.

5. John Maclean, 17th laird of Loch Buie. See *Life*, v.558. Johnson dined with Dr. Maclean at Kilfinichen (Bailey, II.357 and 368).

6. For Boswell's note on the custom and for the dispute about it, see *Life*, v.156, n. 3. For Walter Macfarlane and his *Genealogical Collections concerning families in Scotland*, see *ibid.*, v.554.

7. See *TLS*, 2 Oct. 1970, p. 1137.

sion not very spacious or splendid. I have seen no houses in the Islands much to be envied for convenience or magnificence, yet they bear testimony to the progress of arts and civility, as they shew that rapine and surprise are no longer dreaded, and are much more commodious than the ancient fortresses.

The castles of the Hebrides, many of which are standing, and many ruined, were always built upon points of land, on the margin of the sea. For the choice of this situation there must have been some general reason, which the change of manners has left in obscurity. They were of no use in the days of piracy, as defences of the coast; for it was equally accessible in other places. Had they been sea-marks or light-houses, they would have been of more use to the invader than the natives, who could want no such directions on their own waters: for a watch-tower, a cottage on a hill would have been better, as it would have commanded a wider view.

If they be considered merely as places of retreat, the situation seems not well chosen; for the laird of an island is safest from foreign enemies in the center: on the coast he might be more suddenly surprised than in the inland parts; and the invaders, if their enterprise miscarried, might more easily retreat. Some convenience, however, whatever it was, their position on the shore afforded; for uniformity of practice seldom continues long without good reason.

A castle in the Islands is only a single tower of three or four stories, of which the walls are sometimes eight or nine feet thick, with narrow windows, and close winding stairs of stone. The top rises in a cone, or pyramid of stone, encompassed by battlements. The intermediate floors are sometimes frames of timber, as in common houses, and sometimes arches of stone, or alternately stone and timber; so that there was very little danger from fire. In the center of every floor, from top to bottom, is the chief room, of no great extent, round which there are narrow cavities, or recesses, formed by small vacuities, or by a double wall. I know not whether there be ever more than one fire-place. They had not capacity to contain many people, or much provision; but their enemies could seldom stay to blockade them; for if they failed in the first attack, their next care was to escape.

The walls were always too strong to be shaken by such desultory hostilities; the windows were too narrow to be entered, and the battlements too high to be scaled. The only danger was at the gates, over which the wall was built with a square cavity, not unlike a chimney, continued to the top. Through this hollow the defendants let fall stones upon those who attempted to break the gate, and poured down water, perhaps scalding water, if the attack was made with fire. The castle of Lochbuy was secured by double doors, of which the outer was an iron grate.

In every castle is a well and a dungeon. The use of the well is evident. The dungeon is a deep subterraneous cavity, walled on the sides, and arched on the top, into which the descent is through a narrow door, by a ladder or a rope, so that it seems impossible to escape, when the rope or ladder is drawn up. The dungeon was, I suppose, in war, a prison for such captives as were treated with severity, and, in peace, for such delinquents as had committed crimes within the laird's jurisdiction; for the mansions of many lairds were, till the late privation of their privileges, the halls of justice to their own tenants.

As these fortifications were the productions of mere necessity, they are built only for safety, with little regard to convenience, and with none to elegance or pleasure. It was sufficient for a laird of the Hebrides, if he had a strong house, in which he could hide his wife and children from the next clan. That they are not large nor splendid is no wonder. It is not easy to find how they were raised, such as they are, by men who had no money, in countries where the labourers and artificers could scarcely be fed. The buildings in different parts of the Islands[8] shew their degrees of wealth and power. I believe that for all the castles which I have seen beyond the Tweed, the ruins yet remaining of some one of those[x] which the English built in Wales, would supply materials.

These castles afford another evidence that the fictions of romantick chivalry had for their basis the real manners of the feudal times, when every lord of a seignory lived in his hold lawless and unaccountable, with all the licentiousness and insolence of uncontested superiority and unprincipled power. The traveller, whoever he might be, coming to the fortified

x. those *87; RWC*] these *75a, b; 85*

---

8. If Johnson meant—as the tenor of his sentence suggests—Great Britain and adjacent islands, he forgot that, in the context of his narrative, "the Islands" had come to signify the Hebrides.

habitation of a chieftain, would, probably, have been interrogated from the battlements, admitted with caution at the
gate, introduced to a petty monarch, fierce with habitual hostility, and vigilant with ignorant suspicion; who, according to
his general temper, or accidental humour, would have seated a
stranger as his guest at the table, or as a spy confined him in the
dungeon.

Lochbuy means the "Yellow Lake," which is the name given
to an inlet of the sea, upon which the castle of Mr. Maclean
stands. The reason of the appellation we did not learn.[9]

We were now to leave the Hebrides, where we had spent
some weeks with sufficient amusement, and where we had am-
plified our thoughts with new scenes of nature, and new modes
of life. More time would have given us a more distinct view, but
it was necessary that Mr. Boswell should return before the
courts of justice were opened; and it was not proper to live too
long upon hospitality, however liberally imparted.

Of these islands it must be confessed, that they have not
many allurements, but to the mere lover of naked nature. The
inhabitants are thin, provisions are scarce, and desolation and
penury give little pleasure.

The people collectively considered are not few, though their
numbers are small in proportion to the space which they occupy. Mull is said to contain six thousand, and Sky fifteen
thousand. Of the computation respecting Mull, I can give no
account; but when I doubted the truth of the numbers attributed to Sky, one of the ministers exhibited such facts as conquered my incredulity.

Of the proportion, which the product of any region bears to
the people, an estimate is commonly made according to the
pecuniary price of the necessaries of life; a principle of judgment which is never certain, because it supposes what is far
from truth, that the value of money is always the same, and so
measures an unknown quantity by an uncertain standard. It
is competent enough when the markets of the same country, at
different times, and those times not too distant, are to be com-

---

9. "Sir Allan told me that a hill
above the plain in which the house
stands is called [Ben] Buy from its being of a yellowish hue, and from it the
loch has been named" (*Journal*, p. 342;
the word *Ben* was supplied by the editors).

pared; but of very little use for the purpose of making one nation acquainted with the state of another. Provisions, though
plentiful, are sold in places of great pecuniary opulence for
nominal prices, to which, however scarce, where gold and silver
are yet scarcer, they can never be raised.

In the Western Islands there is so little internal commerce,
that hardly any thing has a known or settled rate. The price of
things brought in, or carried out, is to be considered as that of
a foreign market; and even this there is some difficulty in dis-
covering, because their denominations of quantity are different
from ours; and when there is ignorance on both sides, no appeal
can be made to a common measure.

This, however, is not the only impediment. The Scots, with
a vigilance of jealousy which never goes to sleep, always suspect
that an Englishman despises them for their poverty, and to convince him that they are not less rich than their neighbours, are
sure to tell him a price higher than the true. When Lesley,[1]
two hundred years ago, related so punctiliously, that a hundred
hen eggs, new laid, were sold in the Islands for a peny, he supposed that no inference could possibly follow, but that eggs
were in great abundance. Posterity has since grown wiser; and
having learned, that nominal and real value may differ, they
now tell no such stories, lest the foreigner should happen to
collect, not that eggs are many, but that pence are few.

Money and wealth have by the use of commercial language
been so long confounded, that they are commonly supposed to
be the same; and this prejudice has spread so widely in Scotland, that I know not whether I found man or woman, whom
I interrogated concerning payments of money, that could sur-
mount the illiberal desire of deceiving me, by representing
every thing as dearer than it is.

From Lochbuy we rode a very few miles to the side of Mull,
which faces Scotland, where, having taken leave of our kind
protector, Sir Allan, we embarked in a boat, in which the seat
provided for our accommodation was a heap of rough brush-

---

1. John Leslie or Lesley (1527–96),   *Moribus et Rebus Gestis Scotorum*
Bishop of Ross. Johnson wrote to   (1578). The story of the eggs is told by
George Steevens on 7 February 1774,   Lesley of the Orkneys (Dalrymple's
asking him for "Lesley's history of   translation 1596, Scottish Text Society,
Scotland" (*Letters* 345—i.e., *De Origine*   1.63).

wood; and on the twenty-second of October reposed at a tolerable inn on the main land.[1a]

On the next day we began our journey southwards. The weather was tempestuous. For half the day the ground was rough, and our horses were still small. Had they required much restraint, we might have been reduced to difficulties; for I think we had amongst us but one bridle. We fed the poor animals liberally, and they performed their journey well. In the latter part of the day, we came to a firm and smooth road, made by the soldiers, on which we travelled with great security, busied with contemplating the scene about us. The night came on while we had yet a great part of the way to go, though not so dark, but that we could discern the cataracts which poured down the hills, on one side, and fell into one general channel that ran with great violence on the other. The wind was loud, the rain was heavy, and the whistling of the blast, the fall of the shower, the rush of the cataracts, and the roar of the torrent, made a nobler chorus of the rough musick of nature than it had ever been my chance to hear before. The streams, which ran cross the way from the hills to the main current, were so frequent, that after a while I began to count them; and, in ten miles, reckoned fifty-five, probably missing some, and having let some pass before they forced themselves upon my notice. At last we came to Inverary, where we found an inn, not only commodious, but magnificent.

The difficulties of peregrination were now at an end. Mr. Boswell had the honour of being known to the Duke of Argyle, by whom we were very kindly entertained at his splendid seat, and supplied with conveniences for surveying his spacious park and rising forests.

After two days stay at Inverary we proceeded southward over Glencroe, a black and dreary region, now made easily passable by a military road, which rises from either end of the glen by an acclivity not dangerously steep, but sufficiently laborious. In the middle, at the top of the hill, is a seat with this inscription, "Rest, and be thankful." Stones were placed to mark the distances, which the inhabitants have taken away, resolved, they said, "to have no new miles."

1a. at Oban.

In this rainy season the hills streamed with waterfalls, which, crossing the way, formed currents on the other side, that ran in contrary directions as they fell to the north or south of the summit. Being, by the favour of the Duke, well mounted, I went up and down the hill with great convenience.

From Glencroe we passed through a pleasant country to the banks of Loch Lomond, and were received at the house of Sir James Colquhoun,[2] who is owner of almost all the thirty islands of the Loch, which we went in a boat next morning to survey. The heaviness of the rain shortened our voyage, but we landed on one island planted with yew, and stocked with deer, and on another containing perhaps not more than half an acre, remarkable for the ruins of an old castle, on which the osprey builds her annual nest. Had Loch Lomond been in a happier climate, it would have been the boast of wealth and vanity to own one of the little spots which it incloses, and to have employed upon it all the arts of embellishment. But as it is, the islets, which court the gazer at a distance, disgust him at his approach, when he finds, instead of soft lawns and shady thickets, nothing more than uncultivated ruggedness.

Where the Loch discharges itself into a river, called the Leven, we passed a night with Mr. Smollet, a relation of Doctor Smollet, to whose memory he has raised an obelisk on the bank near the house in which he was born.[3] The civility and respect which we found at every place, it is ungrateful to omit, and tedious to repeat. Here we were met by a post-chaise, that conveyed us to Glasgow.

To describe a city so much frequented as Glasgow, is unnecessary. The prosperity of its commerce appears by the greatness of many private houses, and a general appearance of wealth. It is the only episcopal city whose cathedral was left standing in the rage of Reformation. It is now divided into many separate places of worship, which, taken all together,

---

2. 25th chief of Colquhoun. See *Life*, v.563.

3. *The Weekly Magazine* (Edinburgh), under the date 9 September 1773 (see *Life*, v.564), and the *London Chronicle*, under 14 September 1773, report the erection of the monument.

Johnson, however, told Mrs. Thrale: "I was desired to revise the inscription" (*Letters* 336), which evidently had still to be cut. For altercation as to the form it should take, see *Life*, v.564.

compose a great pile, that had been some centuries in building, but was never finished; for the change of religion intercepted its progress, before the cross isle was added,[4] which seems essential to a Gothick cathedral.

The college has not had a sufficient share of the increasing magnificence of the place. The session was begun; for it commences on the tenth of October, and continues to the tenth of June, but the students appeared not numerous, being, I suppose, not yet returned from their several homes. The division of the academical year into one session, and one recess, seems to me better accommodated to the present state of life, than that variegation of time by terms and vacations derived from distant centuries, in which it was probably convenient, and still continued in the English universities. So many solid months as the Scotch scheme of education joins together, allow and encourage a plan for each part of the year; but with us, he that has settled himself to study in the college is soon tempted into the country, and he that has adjusted his life in the country, is summoned back to his college.[5]

Yet when I have allowed to the universities of Scotland a more rational distribution of time, I have given them, so far as my inquiries have informed me, all that they can claim. The students, for the most part, go thither boys, and depart before they are men; they carry with them little fundamental knowledge, and therefore the superstructure cannot be lofty. The grammar schools are not generally well supplied; for the character of a school-master being there less honourable than in England, is seldom accepted by men who are capable to adorn it, and where the school has been deficient, the college can effect little.

Men bred in the universities of Scotland cannot be expected to be often decorated with the splendours of ornamental erudition, but they obtain a mediocrity of knowledge, between learning and ignorance, not inadequate to the purposes of common life, which is, I believe, very widely diffused among them, and which countenanced in general by a national combination so

---

4. "The church is cruciform in design, but the shallow transepts do not project beyond the aisles" (RWC).

5. Despite Boswell's testimony (*Life*, 1.70), Johnson never went home

for a vacation and therefore had not to make this adjustment (see J. L. Clifford, *Young Samuel Johnson*, 1955, p. 128).

invidious, that their friends cannot defend it, and actuated in particulars by a spirit of enterprise, so vigorous, that their enemies are constrained to praise it, enables them to find, or to make their way to employment, riches, and distinction.

From Glasgow we directed our course to Auchinleck, an estate devolved, through a long series of ancestors, to Mr. Boswell's father, the present possessor. In our way we found several places remarkable enough in themselves, but already described by those who viewed them at more leisure, or with much more skill; and stopped two days at Mr. Campbell's, a gentleman married to Mr. Boswell's sister.[6]

Auchinleck,[7] which signifies a "stony field," seems not now to have any particular claim to its denomination. It is a district generally level, and sufficiently fertile, but like all the western side of Scotland, incommoded by very frequent rain. It was, with the rest of the country, generally naked, till the present possessor finding, by the growth of some stately trees near his old castle, that the ground was favourable enough to timber, adorned it very diligently with annual plantations.

Lord Auchinleck, who is one of the Judges of Scotland, and therefore not wholly at leisure for domestick business or pleasure, has yet found time to make improvements in his patrimony. He has built a house of hewn stone, very stately, and durable, and has advanced the value of his lands with great tenderness to his tenants.

I was, however, less delighted with the elegance of the modern mansion, than with the sullen dignity of the old castle.[8] I clambered with Mr. Boswell among the ruins, which afford striking images of ancient life. It is, like other castles, built

---

6. "For sister r sisterinlaw. Mr. Campbell and I are married to two sisters" (Boswell, *Remarks*). Writing to Mrs. Thrale, Johnson mentions Campbell as married to *Mrs.* Boswell's sister (*Letters* 337), and a misprint seems probable. He was James Campbell of Treesbank; see *Life*, v.566.

7. "You have done Auchinleck much honour and I hope have overcome my father who has never forgiven your warmth for monarchy & Episcopacy [any more than he has forgiven my marriage.] I am curious to see how your pages will operate upon

him" (Boswell, *Remarks*; "any . . . marriage" erased, but deciphered by Dr. J. D. Fleeman).

8. Johnson had delighted to hear from Boswell of "the romantick seat of my ancestors. 'I must be there, Sir (said he) and we will live in the old castle' " (*Life*, 1.462). For an account of the *three* houses at Auchinleck—the medieval castle, of which the keep remained, the 16th-century house, still standing, and the new house completed in 1762—see *Journal*, pp. 485–86.

upon a point of rock, and was, I believe, anciently surrounded with a moat. There is another rock near it, to which the drawbridge, when it was let down, is said to have reached. Here, in the ages of tumult and rapine, the laird was surprised and killed by the neighbouring chief, who perhaps might have extinguished the family, had he not in a few days been seized and hanged, together with his sons, by Douglas, who came with his forces to the relief of Auchinleck.

At no great distance from the house runs a pleasing brook, by a red rock, out of which has been hewn a very agreeable and commodious summer-house, at less expence, as Lord Auchinleck told me, than would have been required to build a room of the same dimensions. The rock seems to have no more dampness than any other wall. Such opportunities of variety it is judicious not to neglect.

We now returned to Edinburgh, where I passed some days with men of learning,[9] whose names want no advancement from my commemoration, or with women of elegance, which perhaps disclaims[1] a pedant's praise.

The conversation of the Scots grows every day less unpleasing to the English; their peculiarities wear fast away; their dialect is likely to become in half a century provincial and rustick, even to themselves. The great, the learned, the ambitious, and the vain, all cultivate the English phrase, and the English pronunciation, and in splendid companies Scotch is not much heard, except now and then from an old lady.[2]

There is one subject of philosophical curiosity to be found in Edinburgh, which no other city has to shew; a college of the deaf and dumb, who are taught to speak, to read, to write, and to practice arithmetick, by a gentleman, whose name is Braidwood.[3] The number which attends him is, I think, about twelve, which he brings together into a little school, and instructs according to their several degrees of proficiency.

---

9. The *London Chronicle* for 23–25 November 1773 contains this announcement: "Edinburgh, Nov. 20. Dr. Samuel Johnson has since his arrival here been elegantly entertained by Principal Robertson, Lord Hailes, Lord Elibank, Gen. Oughton, Sir Alex. Dick, Mr. M'Laurin, Dr. Blair, &c. This day Dr. Johnson set out on his return to London."

1. So in all early editions; but RWC thought it more probable that Johnson wrote *disdains* (MS. note).

2. Probably the Duchess of Douglas. See *Letters* 320.

3. Thomas Braidwood (1715–1806).

I do not mean to mention the instruction of the deaf as new. Having been first practised upon the son of a Constable of Spain, it was afterwards cultivated with much emulation in England, by Wallis and Holder,[4] and was lately professed by Mr. Baker,[5] who once flattered me with hopes of seeing his method published. How far any former teachers have succeeded, it is not easy to know; the improvement of Mr. Braidwood's pupils is wonderful. They not only speak, write, and understand what is written, but if he that speaks looks towards them, and modifies his organs by distinct and full utterance, they know so well what is spoken, that it is an expression scarcely figurative to say, they hear with the eye. That any have attained to the power mentioned by Burnet,[6] of feeling sounds, by laying a hand on the speaker's mouth, I know not; but I have seen so much, that I can believe more; a single word, or a short sentence, I think, may possibly be so distinguished.

It will readily be supposed by those that consider this sub-

---

4. John Wallis (1616–1703), one of the original members of the Royal Society, published, besides major works on mathematics and divinity, *Grammatica Linguae Anglicanae* (1653), containing a treatise on speech. William Holder (1616–98), likewise a member of the Royal Society, included in his *Elements of Speech* (1669) an *Appendix concerning Persons Deaf and Dumb*, in which he claimed to have taught a deaf-mute to speak. He attacked Wallis in 1678, alleging that, in his report to the Royal Society (1670) of his success with Alexander Popham and another deaf-mute, he was guilty of plagiarism, Popham being the youth he had himself taught. Wallis retorted that *his* published work on speech had preceded Holder's and that he had known nothing of the other's dealings with Popham or of his methods, which had evidently failed. Why, then, should he mention Holder, or relate "what others had said of the Constable of Castile's son?" Since this *Defence of the Royal Society and the Philosophical Transactions, Particularly those of July, 1670. In Answer to the Cavils of Dr. William Holder* (1678) is sufficient to account for Johnson's allusions, we cannot tell whether he knew more of the controversy than it contains; but, being already familiar with one of the earlier editions of the *Grammatica* (see p. 44 n. 8), he may have taken note of the sixth (1765), with an appendix in which the dispute still reverberates.

5. Henry Baker (1698–1774), son-in-law of Daniel Defoe and associated with him in journalism, developed a method of teaching the deaf, but kept it a secret.

6. Gilbert Burnet (1643–1715), in *Some Letters. containing, An account of what seemed most remarkable in Switzerland, Italy, etc.* (Rotterdam, 1686), tells of a girl in Geneva who, despite loss of hearing in her infancy, taught herself by "natural sagacity" lip-reading and the rudiments of speech. He was moreover informed that with her sister she could communicate even in the dark, by laying a hand on her mouth; but, in the absence of the sister, he was not able to verify this.

ject, that Mr. Braidwood's scholars spell accurately. Orthography is vitiated among such as learn first to speak, and then to write, by imperfect notions of the relation between letters and vocal utterance; but to those students every character is of equal importance; for letters are to them not symbols of names, but of things; when they write they do not represent a sound, but delineate a form.

This school I visited, and found some of the scholars waiting for their master, whom they are said to receive at his entrance with smiling countenances and sparkling eyes, delighted with the hope of new ideas. One of the young ladies had her slate before her, on which I wrote a question consisting of three figures, to be multiplied by two figures. She looked upon it, and quivering her fingers in a manner which I thought very pretty, but of which I know not whether it was art or play, multiplied the sum regularly in two lines, observing the decimal place; but did not add the two lines together, probably disdaining so easy an operation. I pointed at the place where the sum total should stand, and she noted it with such expedition as seemed to shew that she had it only to write.

It was pleasing to see one of the most desperate of human calamities capable of so much help: whatever enlarges hope, will exalt courage; after having seen the deaf taught arithmetick, who would be afraid to cultivate the Hebrides?

Such are the things which this journey has given me an opportunity of seeing, and such are the reflections which that sight has raised. Having passed my time almost wholly in cities, I may have been surprised by modes of life and appearances of nature, that are familiar to men of wider survey and more varied conversation. Novelty and ignorance must always be reciprocal, and I cannot but be conscious that my thoughts on national manners, are the thoughts of one who has seen but little.

FINIS

APPENDIX I[1]

THE MIDDLESEX JOURNAL AND EVENING ADVERTISER. Vol. XII. 1775–76.

From Saturday February 18 to Tuesday February 21, 1775 (No. 921).

Monday February 20.
To Dr. Johnson.
Dear Doctor,
A Copy of your journey to the Western Islands of Scotland, now lying before me, differing in almost a whole paragraph from another belonging to a friend, be pleased to inform me by what means this has happened, and which of the two readings is the true one, as my friend and I are at a loss to know which to adopt. In page 47 and 48, having told your readers of an order of Council, still extant, directing that the lead which covered the two cathedrals of Elgin and Aberdeen should be taken away and converted into money for the support of the army, but intended, as you think, for some private purse: that the churches were accordingly stripped, and that the lead was shipped to be sold in Holland; and after *piously* hoping that every reader will rejoice that this cargo of sacrilege was lost at sea,* there immediately follow in the two copies the different

*If the sacrilegious cargo was lost in the manner mentioned, does it not follow that the ship and every other part of her cargo went to the bottom also? And might not the ship's crew too share the same fate? if so ought we then to rejoice, good Doctor? A man of ordinary talents, and unendowed with a competent share of zeal for sacred things, might be apt, at the time he received the information, to feel a contrary emotion to that of joy. Such is the difference between enlightened and unenlightened reason!

1. See pp. [xxxiv]–xxxv, 24 n.

paragraphs abovementioned. In one copy the words are, 'Let us not however make too much haste to despise our neighbours; our own cathedrals are mouldering by unregarded dilapidations. It seems to be part of the despicable philosophy of the time to despise monuments of sacred magnificence, and we are in danger of doing that deliberately, which the Scots did not do but in the unsettled state of an imperfect constitution." —In the other copy the paragraph runs thus: "Let us not, however, make too much haste to despise our neighbours. There is now, I have heard, a body of men, not less decent or virtuous than the Scottish council, longing to melt the lead of an English cathedral. What they shall melt, it were just that they should swallow."

Now, Sir, if the last cited paragraph should be your favourite one, and it should be your wish to have the other degraded, as not being sufficiently expressive of that just indignation which you would willingly shew towards those robbers of heaven, as you elsewhere emphatically call them, who so impiously long to melt the sacred lead, my friend, mentioned in the beginning of this address, whose zeal for the Church, and veneration for all that belong to it, are nothing short of your own, most earnestly prays, if ever those ungracious longings are attempted to be gratified, that the act of justice you mentioned may be executed on the delinquents, and that another hundred may be added to your present pension, for performing the blessed service of pouring the melted metal down their ungodly throats.

Feb. 17 1775.   W.H.

APPENDIX II[1]

In the 1785 edition of Johnson's *Journey* p.iii[r] (the leaf following the title page) carries this notice:

Strand, Oct. 26, 1785.

☞ SINCE this Work was printed off, the Publisher having been informed that the Author, some years ago, had promised the Laird of Rasay, to correct, in a future edition, a passage concerning him, p. 133, thinks it a justice due to that Gentleman to insert here the Advertisement relative to this matter, which was published, by Dr. Johnson's desire, in the Edinburgh Newspapers in the year 1775, and which has been lately reprinted in Mr. Boswell's *Tour to the Hebrides*:

"*The Authour of the* Journey *to the Western Islands, having related that the Macleods of Rasay acknowledge the chieftainship, or superiority, of the Macleods of Sky, finds that he has been misinformed or mistaken. He means in a future edition to correct his errour, and wishes to be told of more, if more have been discovered.*"

"He has been misinformed or mistaken": Johnson had originally written: "he has misrepresented a question which in the Hebrides is of great importance." (See *Journal*, p. 451.)

---

1. See p. 59 n. 2 above, and illustration.

INDEX

Place names used by Johnson as chapter headings are given in small capitals. These are followed by the name (lc), with page references which show (as Johnson's do not) which part of the text is occupied by the account or contains references to it.

Johnson's spelling seldom corresponds with that of the present Ordnance Survey. (Boswell often gives yet a third spelling which R. W. Chapman preferred.) In the index the Ordnance Survey version is given, followed in inverted commas by Johnson's version. Where the difference between the two might trouble a reader, there is a cross reference, unless the two words are adjacent.

INDEX

Auchnashiel, "Auknasheals," Ross, 42, 48

Bacon, Francis (*1561–1626*), 1st Baron Verulam, Viscount St. Albans, 109
Bagpipe, *See* Pipers
Baker, Henry (*1698–1774*), journalist and teacher, 163
Bailey, Rev. James, Rector of Otley, Yorkshire, xiv, xix n., xxvi n., 153 n.; confirms SJ's cordial relations with all but one of his hosts, xv n.; describes nunnery church at Iona, 149 n., 150 n.; on tacksmen, xxii n.
BANFF, "BAMFF," 21f.
Banff, 21–23
Banks, Sir Joseph (*1743–1820*), "Mr. Banks," traveller and naturalist, xix, 63, 141
Bards, 111f., 113, 114, 116
Barra, Isle of, 109 n., 123f., 133; small cows in, 82; small horses in, 127
Bayle, Pierre (*1647–1706*), philosopher, 109 (*sc.* Boyle), 121 n.
Beaton (or Bethune), David (*1494–1548*), Cardinal Archbishop of St. Andrews, "Cardinal Beatoun," 6
Beattie, James (*1735–1803*), author, 18 n., 82 n.
Bedell, William (*1571–1642*), Bishop of Kilmore, translator of the Bible into Irish Gaelic, 117 n.
Beggars, 12, 129f.
Beinn Hogh, glacial boulders on, 125 n.
Benedictine Abbey, 150 n.
Bentley, Richard (*1662–1742*), classical scholar, 69 n.
Bible: in Irish Gaelic, 117; in Scots Gaelic, 57f., 114f., 116f., 121f.
Birds. *See* Wild life
Biscay (*sc.* region in northern Spain), 44
Black stones, on Iona, 149f.
Black Watch, "the old Highland regiment," in America, 98 n.
Blair, Dr. Hugh (*1718–1800*), divine and critic, 162 n.
Boece, Hector, "or Boethius," (*1465?–1536*), historian and Principal of Aberdeen University, 14f., 30f.
Bonnetta, an Irish vessel, 141 n.
Borneo, 88
Borough English, a system of inherit-

Borough English (*cont.*)
ance, 142
Boswell, Alexander (*1708–82*), Lord Auchinleck, Scottish judge and father of James Boswell, 161f.
Boswell, James (*1740–95*): mentioned in the text, 3, 8, 10, 11, 12, 13, 34, 42, 49, 71, 75, 108, 117, 120, 125, 130, 133, 138, 143, 144, 145, 152, 153, 156, 161

quoted or cited in the introduction and notes: *Journal*, 12, 17, 29, 36, 59, 120, 130, 135, 143, 153, 156, 161; *Life*, xiv, xix, xxvi, xxvii, 3, 48, 96, 145, 153, 161; *Private Papers*, xvii, xxvii, 60 n.; *Remarks*, 10, 13, 20, 26, 30, 34, 49, 66, 67, 77, 106, 109, 120, 132, 141, 149, 161; *Tour* (i.e., *Life*, v. 13–420, ed. Hill/Powell), xv, xviii, xix, xx, xxiv, 3, 10, 14, 15, 26, 27, 34, 38, 59f., 64, 67, 69, 76, 111, 120, 121, 122, 128, 130, 141, 143, 147, 153
Boswell, Margaret (d. *1789*), JB's wife, 48 n., 64 n.
Boswells of Auchinleck, the, 162
Boyd, Hon. Charles (*1728–82*), 19
Boyd, James (*1726–78*), 15th Earl of Errol, 18; his wife, Isabella (*1742–1808*), 19
Boyle, Hon. Robert (*1627–91*), natural philosopher, 109 n.
Braidwood, Thomas (*1715–1806*), and his college for the deaf and dumb, xxvi, 162–64
Breacacha, "Brecacig," castle of, 124
Britain, 44
Brooke, Henry (*1703?–83*), author, *Gustavus Vasa*, 44 n.
Browne, Sir Thomas (*1605–82*), physician and author, *Vulgar Errors*, 84 n.
Browny, "a sturdy fairy," 106
Bruce, Mrs., "an old woman," 8f.
Buchanan, George (*1506–82*), humanist, historian, and writer of Latin poetry, 5, 15
Buildings: collegiate, 6–7; *dun*, an ancient building, 71f. See Castles, Cathedrals, Chapels and churches, Forts, Houses, Huts, Monastic buildings
Bullers of Buchan, 19–21
Burleigh, J. H. S., *A Church History of Scotland*, 17 n.